A HISTORY OF
HEDNESFORD
AND SURROUNDING VILLAGES

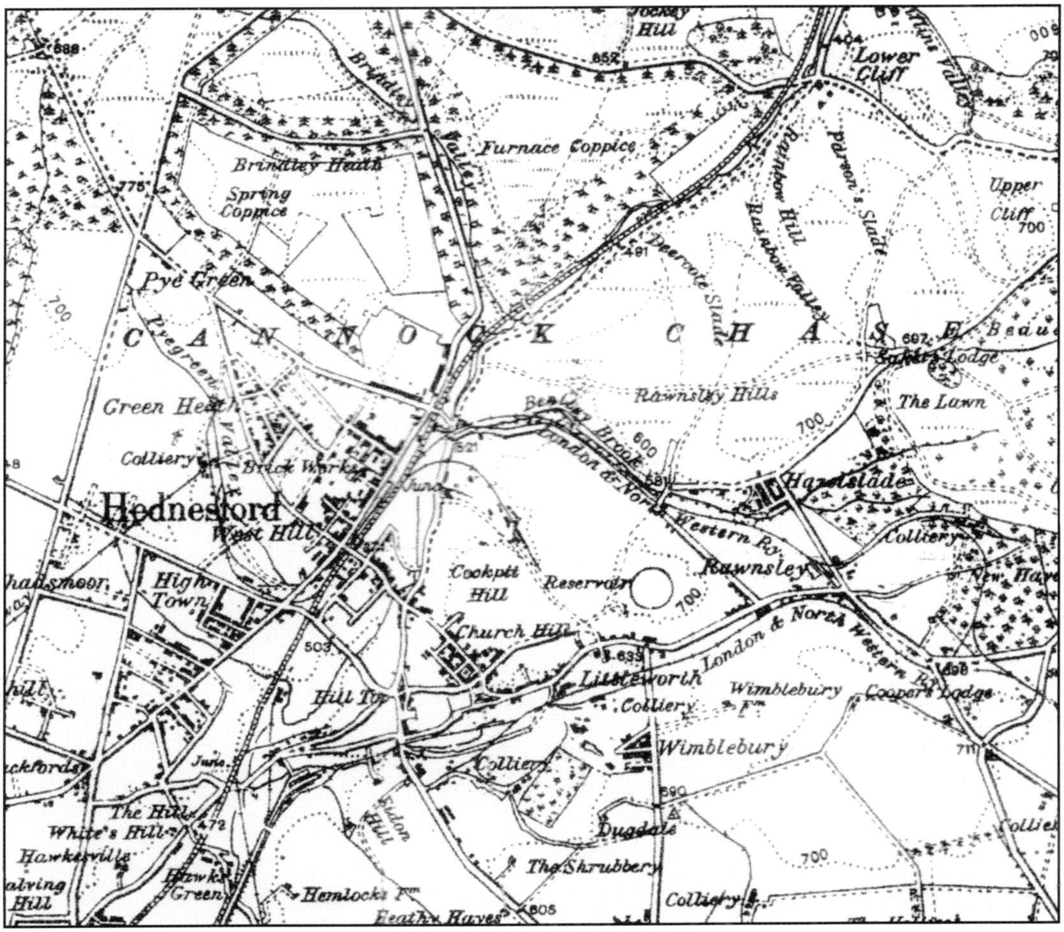

Anthony Hunt

Published by
Mount Chase Press
109 Mount Street, Hednesford, Cannock, Staffs. WS12 4DB
01543 422891

ISBN 0-9551382-0-5

Designed and produced by John Griffiths, printed by Spectrum Print Direct

Contents

List of maps

List of photographs

Acknowledgements

Many thanks to all those library staff whom I have pestered over the last few years, particularly those at Cannock Library. Also many thanks to those people who lent photographs for the book. They are as follows:-

C. Baggott for photos 39, 44; Joseph Baker for 43, 45, 72, 73, 92, 94, 95 and 116; W. Bennett for 64, 65, 75, 77 and 93; Birmingham Post for 16, 19, 32, 51, 54, 56&113; K. Brown for 76 and 101; D. Davis for 10, 13, 41, 102 and 104; W. Drinkwater for 6, 7 and 81; Mrs. Foster for 37; T. Fowler for 99; J. Griffiths for 87, 88 and 118; J. Harper for 63; Mrs. Jacks for 62, 62a, 67 and 68; Mrs. M. Jones for 28, 31, 105, 106, 107, 108, 108 and 120; B. Matthews for 21and 30; M. Metcalfe for 8, 9, 47, 61, 66, 69, 70 and 71; Museum of Cannock Chase for 1, 2, 3, 4, 17, 18, 20, 23, 29, 33, 40, 50, 52, 53, 55, 57, 58, 82, 89, 91, 100 and 119; J. Oakley for 34, 35 and 49; Our Lady of Lourdes for 46 and 48; Mrs. J. Pickerill for 79 and 79a; Mr. Pointon for 90 and 98; Mr. Poole for 36, 96 and 97; Mr and Mrs Reaney for 24, 25, 26, 27, 59 and 74; M. Rogers for 103; St. Peter's School for 12, 78, and 80; Stafford Record Office for 60; West Hill School for 83, 84, 85 and 86; Mr. Whitehead for 114 and 115.

For those photographs loaned by the Museum of Cannock Chase and the Birmingham Post, the copyright is unknown.

All photographs were lent in good faith, but apologies to anyone whose copyright may have been unintentionally infringed.

INTRODUCTION

"Why a history of Hednesford and its surrounding villages? Surely one has been written already?" was the statement by one of our local reporters when I announced that I had almost completed the book. That question somewhat annoyed me. It had injured my pride in the place where I was born and it was that pride which gave me the initiative to begin the history.

I was born in Mount Street, Hednesford in 1943, living at my grandmother's house for a few months until we managed to get our own house on the common above Heath Street, overlooking the West Cannock No. 1 Pit. Notice that I clearly state Hednesford and not Hednesford, Cannock as the Royal Mail would like us to believe. In fact, like so many others, I was deeply annoyed when the Royal Mail in their supposed wisdom decided to wipe Hednesford from the map. It was that attempt which really was the catalyst for writing the book which would prove that Hednesford and its villages do have their own history and their own separate identity.

It is certainly true to say that even each small village in the area has its own identity - ask anyone in Wimblebury or Green Heath where they live and they will be quick to tell you. That was and still is the delight of living in an area which was once dominated by the mining industry. It united people and gave them their unique position in the community. Each miner was proud to announce that he worked for West Cannock No. 2 Pit or East Cannock rather than just say that he was a coal miner for some rather nebulous industry. Likewise I will readily inform people that I live in Hednesford and nowhere else.

The second reason for writing the book is the historian's natural curiosity. What exactly was the Hednesford area like many years ago and who were the people who created the place? Just how far does our history go back and do we have any claim to fame? Hopefully those questions can be answered along with many others until an almost complete picture of the area is painted.

Here I must declare a very personal interest which helped to fire my imagination even further. My family were relative newcomers to the area having arrived here around 1914 and settling in Heath Street before they eventually moved into Mount Street. With them they brought a mystery. My father was not born here, but in Dordon, Warwickshire. Strangely though he was christened Chase, not Charles or any variation of the name. Did his mother and father know they were about to move over here and so name him after the place they were going to? If so, what was the attraction of the place which would make them want to name their first born after it. Was it a new beginning which held so much promise? That must have been the feeling of so many who arrived here from all over the country during the nineteen and early twentieth centuries. It was a further spur to my curiosity about the area.

Perhaps the most overpowering reason for the book was the idea that once complete our history would not be forgotten. Unfortunately memories eventually expire with those who experienced them unless they are recorded. For instance, how many of us know that Hednesford once rivalled Newmarket as an area for training race horses, those stables are long gone; or how many of us can remember the tank manoeuvres on Cannock Chase not long after the Second World War; or perhaps worse how many of us have forgotten exactly where Brindley Village once stood.

It was during the research that I became

increasingly aware of the amount that I had forgotten from my childhood and just how much the place has changed. Some places bear no resemblance to their original appearance. Places like Wimblebury were totally demolished and replaced with the modern facilities we see today, but unfortunately along with that demolition went the inevitable loss of memories and local stories. The hope is that some of those memories will be revived for those who once lived in those places and also help give the newcomers an experience of what the area was like before the modernisation.

Demolition also saw the eventual disappearance of the very reason for expansion – the coal mines which once festooned the area. Look today and a newcomer would be hard-pressed to find any signs of the industry. What once brought great wealth and employment to the area has long since disappeared. Only the nickname of our football team, "The Pitmen", keeps that tradition alive.

The final reason for the book is the hope that it may be able to save what is left of our heritage. So often in the past the "historical vandals" have seen fit to destroy our old buildings in the name of progress. One travel book I read recently claimed that there was little point in visiting our area as the local council years ago had demolished most of the old buildings. That fate almost befell the Cross Keys and Prospect House in the 1950's and 1960's, but thankfully they were saved after public outcry. The same nearly happened recently when the plaque above the chemist's in Market Street was in danger as developers saw fit to destroy the archway below.

It was only when the public objected to that vandalism that I learned that we have only one Grade One listed building in Hednesford, the Anglesey Hotel. As that is by no means the oldest building in the town surely the older ones deserve the same status before developers once again set their sights on them. The same applies to Hednesford Hills. It was bequeathed to the people of the area for their enjoyment and so we must continue to safeguard that legacy lest it too falls prey to progress.

A word about the book itself. You may wonder why places like Heath Hayes and Hazel Slade are not mentioned, except very briefly, as they border the area quite naturally and their mining history is closely linked with ours. As a guideline for the book I decided to concentrate only on those villages which made up the Hednesford Parish which began in 1870. Heath Hayes has always belonged to Cannock Parish, while Hazel Slade was in the Brereton Parish, despite the fact that most survey maps of the area included Hazel Slade as a matter of course. Unfortunately parishes do not always follow geographical lines as one might expect, but frequently follow historical lines.

Strangely the builders of the Hednesford War Memorial had the same difficulty when it came to whose names should appear. Their decision was to include Hazel Slade, but not Heath Hayes. Why was never made clear, except that the villagers of Heath Hayes were planning a memorial of their own.

On the same problem of what to include and what to leave out it will become evident to the reader that many chapters are far shorter than they might have been. Regretfully both time and space played their part otherwise the book would have never been completed. An apology, therefore, to anyone or any organisation who may feel that they have been neglected.

Also during the compilation of the book I was very conscious of what I call the historian's nightmare and yet strangely the historian's bread and butter - that which keeps him or her going with avid interest - that is not being able to arrive at any definitive answer to every question. Hence the chapter on "mysteries" where an inordinate amount of time was spent trying to solve the problems with very little success. Please feel free to come up with your solution should you know the answer. My only plea is that you let me know for my own peace of mind.

At times you may want to question the actual spelling of certain names, in particular High Town. Today it is all one word, but for historical accuracy I decided to leave it as it originally appeared in the nineteenth century censuses. Why changes to spelling come about often have no historical basis and sometimes they were simply a mistake on a map which was not challenged at the time. Remember the recent case of Bridgtown and BT's misspelling of Walsall?

My final comment brings to mind my old history lecturer who always maintained that it was people who made places. Therefore, with his advice in mind the book mentions as any people as possible who helped to create Hednesford and its surrounding villages. With a bit of luck you may be sufficiently intrigued to want to know more about your ancestors and your own family tree. The final chapter was researched with that in mind to give you some sort of starting point.

Good luck!

BIRTH OF A SETTLEMENT
900 -1570

Amongst those elements which identify us as individuals and create our links to the past are our families and their particular history - where they originated, what they did in their community and how they eventually arrived at their own names. Much the same applies to cities, towns and villages throughout their history and Hednesford is no exception. So where precisely does Hednesford fit into this pattern?

Most historians believe that our town began its story back in Saxon times when a man called Heddin, or perhaps Hedda, built a ford across a stream which used to flow close to where the Cross Keys is today and then proceeded to charge people for using his crossing. To all travellers it became known as Heddin's Ford, but how true might that story be?

Our only evidence lies in Dugdale's book, the *Cartularium Saxonicum*, in which he simply records all the boundary lines of the various monasteries and other properties which had been disputed in Saxon England. The only reference to someone resembling Heddin (a very unusual Saxon name) appears in the short phrase "onon ut on hedenes dene" which roughly translates as "and along Heddin's valley". Surprisingly that reference does not refer to anywhere in Staffordshire, but to land near the River Test in Hampshire. Another reference to an Heddin comes from the village of Henshaw near Haltwhistle in Northumberland which was anciently written as Hednes-halgh and which translates as "Heddin's meadow land".

The very fact that the name is so unusual in Saxon England could actually prove that the story of how Hednesford arrived at its name is correct. There is nothing stranger than truth.

However, Heddin and his descendants must have led a very lonely existence because by the time of the Domesday Book our village was not large enough to even get a mention. It must have still been a one hut place. The first mention of it appears in the *Monasticum Anglicanum* in 1153 when King Stephen II grants Hedenedford freedom from pannage dues to the local Cistercian Abbey at Radmore (now Redmoor). After that the spelling of the name varies slightly from Hedenesford in the thirteenth century, Edenesford around the same time, Heddenesford in 1307 and then to Hednesford(e) in 1362. By the time of the first maps in 1577 it had become Heddensford and on the 1665 map (the map most often sold today) it was Haddensford.

Curiously our local dialect seems to have played a part in later maps as the spelling Hedgeford or Hedgford begins to appear. In 1681 the probate will of Thomas Arnett states "An inventory or true value of the goods, land and cattle belonging to Thomas Arnett the Elder late of Hednesford, alias Hedgford, in the County of Stafford" and in 1686 Robert Plot in his *History of Staffordshire* prints it as Hedgeford. He wrote his book after interviewing local people about their town or village and no doubt recorded the name as it was pronounced.

That spelling remained on maps of Staffordshire right up to the nineteenth century (Smith's 1804 map has it) and even writers of the literary calibre of Stebbings Shaw, a most meticulous historian, used the spelling. It was not until the arrival of the dictionary and the standardisation of spelling that Hednesford finally appeared as we know it today. Also the advent of the Royal Mail meant that spellings had to be standardised for ease of delivery.

It must be made clear that when we talk of early Hednesford we are only referring to that area around today's Cross Keys Inn. The remainder only came into existence in the Victorian Era.

I. Staffordshire 1577 *(By kind permission of the William Salt Library and County Records Office)*

So much for the name, but what of the people? Throughout the remainder of this chapter there has to be some conjecture as to the size of the village and its population, not made easy as our early history is often linked with that of its larger neighbour, Cannock.

As previously mentioned the first reference to Hednesford was in 1153 when the inhabitants were granted freedom from pannage, a tax placed on those who wished to feed their animals in the nearby forest or at least have a right to do so. To take the trouble to grant such a liberty by royal proclamation must tell us that a reasonable number were living in the area trying to gain an existence from the Forest of Cank, but precisely how many would be merely guesswork.

However, by the late twelfth century the area had attracted the Trumwyne family, knights who probably came over with William the Conqueror, and they were interested enough to try and obtain land from the Bishopric of Lichfield. Interestingly in 1318 in William Trumwyne's will his possessions include "one messuage in Kannockbury" which he held from the King "by service of Keeping the Haye of Chystelyn" (now Cheslyn Hay) as bailiff. That land was considered "worth nothing beyond reprises, because it was ruinous". In the same will it lists lands "around Cannock" separately and therefore it is not beyond belief to argue that the Kannockbury land could indeed be referring to Hednesford, that is the village outside Cannock.

Staying with the Trumwynes, Roger Trumwyne, son of William, held a freehold of land in Edenesford called "le Plash" from the Bishops of Lichfield before 1350 and it was part of the dispute with his ex-wife in 1352/53 when she tried to claim it as some of the dowry granted to her on her wedding day. How the verdict went is not known, but it must be presumed that Roger won as on his death in 1361 he left the land to his sister, Katherine. That land must have been considered valuable to have warranted so much interest.

The Trumwyne legal disputes were not over then. In the Plea Rolls (legal documents written on rolls of paper) of 1361/62 "Richard de Wirleye, the executor of Roger's will, sued Hugh de Northbergh, chivalier, for taking by force eight mares and four colts belonging to Roger and worth £20 which were in the custody of the said executor at Hedenesford". Roger must have had quite a large farm to be rearing so many horses; and, of course, all those animals needed people to look after them - labourers and farriers.

Obviously other people had moved into the area around the same time as the Trumwynes as can be seen from their mention in the Plea Rolls. In 1324 "the jury of the Foreign Liberty of the Bishops of Chester presented that John de Wenforde, together with Henry and John de Boys, had, on the Feast of St. Michael, broken into the house of Adam Baker at Edenesford and taken goods to the value of 10s and had afterwards feloniously burnt the house". In 1339 Thomas de Hedenusford owned enough land to have to go to court to make sure that his boundaries were protected from exploitation in a will of a close neighbour. Also in 1343 William de Hedenesford took his wife to court concerning land that he owned in Lichfield.

The region was obviously good for farming and farms need labourers, but just how many? Perhaps the lack of a large number of farms can be seen from one rather innocuous entry in the Poll Tax Returns of Richard 11 (around 1390). A house in Lichfield mentions one Alice of Hednesford and her daughter, Joan, who were either servants or possible relatives. Had they to go to Lichfield for work as there was so little available in Hednesford? Travel in those days, especially by women, was rare and only done of necessity.

So what numbers of people were there in Hednesford? A clue to the relative small population probably lies in the fact that, apart from the Trumwyne family, only one other had a full name that we would recognise today – Adam Baker; the remainder have only been credited with a Christian name. It was common in the Middle Ages when villages were small and everyone knew everyone else to just use the first name followed by the name of the village. Hence, William de Hedenesford simply meant William of Hednesford. Everyone would know who was meant, including the courts.

If we follow that rule then after 1400 there does seem to be a fair bit of growth because villagers started to have surnames. In the 1415 Plea Rolls a John Chapman of Hedenesford was indicted for knowingly receiving and hiding one John Myers and others who had "feloniously killed Roger Kyng of Wolverhampton" in 1412. In the 1462 Plea Rolls John Reynold sued John Sutton of Heddesford, a carpenter, and John Trumwyne of Canke, a labourer, for breaking into his close (field or garden) and depasturising or feeding their cattle on his grass. While in the following year (1463) William Chapman, late of Heddesford, husbandman, was sued for depasturising his cattle on the grass belonging to William Byrches and John Atkyns, both of Heddesford. In 1472/73 one William Colmore

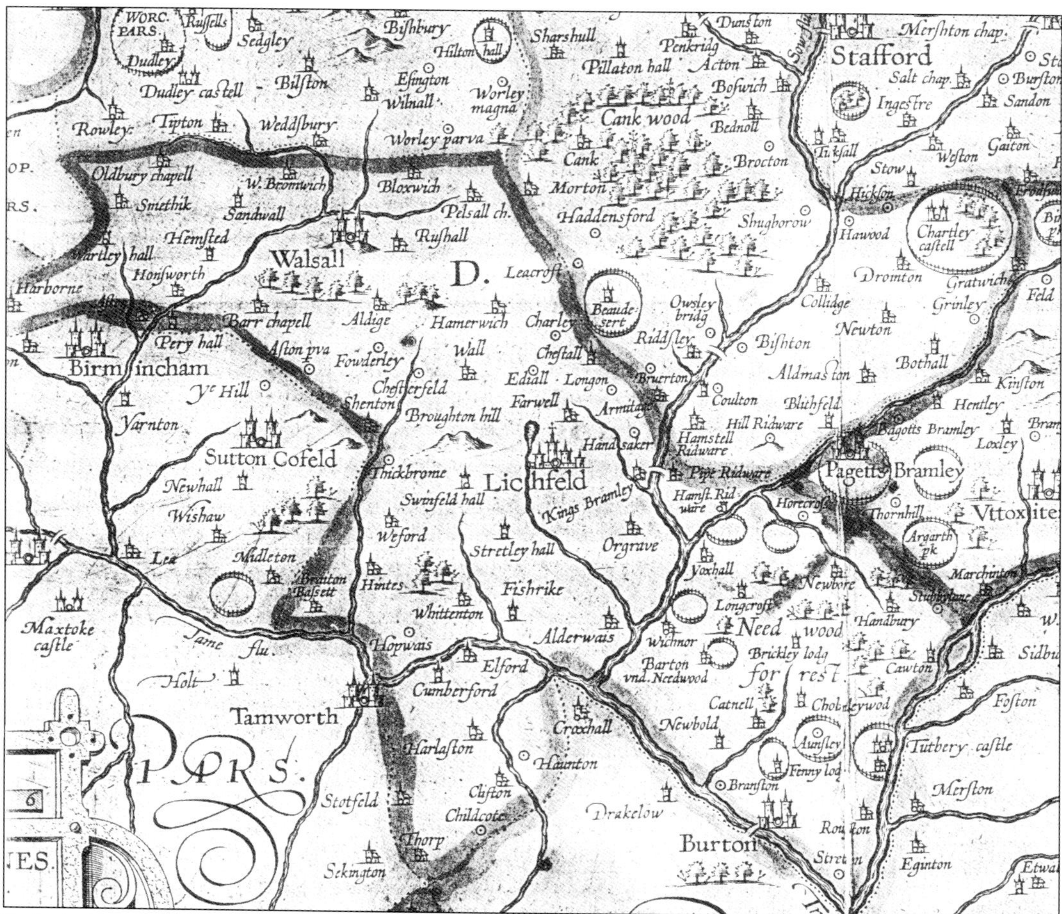

II. Ecclesiastical Map of Staffordshire Parishes under the Diocese of Lichfield 1665
(By kind permission of the William Salt Library and County Records Office)

paid 2d rent for a small plot of waste land at Hedenesford on which a forge was built in 1473.

Where exactly William Colmore had his forge is unknown, though it was possibly along today`s Rugeley Road, opposite the fishing pools.

The first attempted lists of people in the country appeared in 1532/33 when the Church, in our case the Archdiocese of Lichfield, wanted to know how many people lived in each parish. Unfortunately it was clearly not a census as Lichfield included dead wives and dead children and failed to visit lots of houses. In fact in some villages the percentage of houses visited was as low as 11%. As Hednesford had no church it was possibly missed altogether. I could only find one family name on the list, the Chapmans, and they had moved to Cannock by that time.

In 1539 Henry VIII wanted to know how many armed men he might be able to call upon to defend his realm and so he commanded that each county draw up a list of men who owned arms. Those lists were known as Muster Rolls, but once again the information for Hednesford is sketchy as it was not registered separately, but as part of Cannock. However, certain names do appear who have been mentioned before as living in Hednesford or are mentioned later. These include:-

> Roger Byrch a bowe and xxiiij arrows.
>
> John Salte a sallett.
>
> Richard Parker a gestern
>
> Richard Salte a gestern.
>
> John Jacson (weapon not named).
>
> John Smyth a bill. (possible)

During the Middle Ages the feudal system had kept people in order and each year they were supposed to report to the court to discuss the progress of law and order within their village or town or report any misdoings. That system of frankpledge, whereby every member of a tithing (a group of ten houses or so) was answerable for the good conduct or damage done by any of its members, can give a reasonable estimation of the size of a town or village. Cannock originally had 5 frankpledges, but from at least 1529 it only had 3 with Leacroft having 1 and Hednesford 1. It is safe then to say that Hednesford had at least 10 separate properties within its boundaries and probable population of around 50.

Small you might think, but England was still recovering from the Black Death. In fact one member of the Trumwyne family, William from the Cannock branch, was recorded as having died from the plague and so it most certainly reached our area, though exact numbers of how many and the names of those who succumbed have disappeared with time.

STILL A SLEEPY HAMLET
1570 - 1800

So far Hednesford's growth had been slow, accounted for by the natural birth and death rates. If it was to flourish what was desperately needed was industry or it would remain forever an agricultural village - not that there is anything wrong in that.

The first signs of industry might have happened with the arrival in the area of the Paget family. A minister during the reigns of Henry VIII, Edward VI and Mary I, William Paget was awarded many lands throughout England, including the Manor of Beaudesert. A shrewd businessman, he soon realised that Beaudesert contained coal and with the Forest of Cank on his doorstep he had the possibility of smelting iron. In 1561 he opened the first blast furnace on the Chase and by 1570/71 he had opened a second, the New Furnace. One of those furnaces was probably situated on what is now the west side of the road to Rugeley, near to where Hednesford Pool used to be.

However, William's heir, Thomas Paget, fell foul of Elizabeth I because he was suspected of being involved in the Babbington Plot to put Mary Queen of Scots on the English throne. His estates were forfeit for a while, but at his death his son, William, was granted the lands back. During the period of Thomas' ill-fortune one Fulk Grevill, a businessman from Warwickshire, was granted a lease on certain mineral rights in the Chase area. He developed the Paget furnaces and was not going to let them go without a fight. Our interest lies in where those furnaces lay and from the legal settlement we get a good idea.

"By letters patent of February 8th, 1588 Queen Elizabeth leased to Fulk Grevill two furnaces and two iron forges in the Forest of Canck with their waters, pools, vivaries and water courses: together with the woods, great trees and other trees growing in the said forest... save for the woods and underwoods of Bewdeserte Park and of certain wood or grove called Gentleshave and 3000 timber trees in the forest of Cannocke.

For his side Fulk Grevill covenanted to keep working the two forges and one onlie forge at one and the same time and to expend the timber granted only in the working and forging of iron, though he might sell the remnants of timber called malles and butt ends.

By the present denture William Paget confirms the premises to Fulk Grevill with the trees, the said five cottages and the said lands enclosed out of the said forest and the said mines of iron and ironstone."

The fact that the document expressly forbids Grevill to trespass within the boundary of Beaudesert leaves only one other place with sufficient water where those furnaces might have stood - along today's Rugeley Road and close to Hednesford. In fact the one pool became known as Furnace Pool.

A description of the Chase in the year 1588 shows how much timber was being taken for those furnaces. "Olde oakes" had been "all lopped and shred for the mayntenance of the iron works there." Also "most of them will neyther be good timber nor good firewoode, for they are all very olde and decaying and not increasing, the rather for they have lately been topped as aforesaid and being at last topping verie olde trees and never topped before, by that occasion doe nowe wax druxy at the harte and dye yerely in great numbers."

It continues, "The myne there is so base that it is not to be accounted on. The woodes in truth is all the matter of any value." Fulk Grevill had already realised that and had leased out the mines to Sir Gilbert Wakeringe along with the lease to the two pools. He had, however, kept the furnaces and iron works. A document of 1595 relates that Wakeringe held the lease on "one myne of black coales and another of Cannill coales within Cank Wood." Again those mines must have been outside Beaudesert and closer to Hednesford otherwise the lease would have been useless to Wakeringe.

That same document goes on to describe Wakeringe's tenure of the area. "Also the jurors say upon their oath that there are two pooles called Hedne Ford Poole and one poole called the Newe Poole within the said manor (Manor of Cank) nowe in the tenure of the said Wakeringe, but what rent he payeth yearly to the lord (Paget) for the same they know nott."

Further proof that the works were on the Rugeley Road, close to Hednesford and Newe Poole must be Furnace Pool created from the workings. The rent was not paid directly to Paget, but to Grevill who then paid Paget the sum of £211. 10s per year, though that included rent for furnaces in Heywood Park as well.

Also the document gave certain rights to the people living within the manor. "Freeholders and coppie holders in the said manor are not to be impeached of any waste within any of the lands or tenements there, but that they may at their pleasure fell their woods to their uses upon their "sevralls" (homesteads).

So just how many people were helping to work those furnaces and mines and where did they live? Unfortunately evidence is scant, but there are two references to miners from Hednesford, both from the court rolls or Quarter Rolls as they were then called.

"Before Edward Littleton, knight, and Walter Chetwynd and Roger Fowke, esquires, Justices on June 17th, 1603, John Hamlett of Cannocke and John Salte of Hednesford, surety for Christopher Cliffe of Hednesford, collier, licensed by the justices to keep an alehouse and to victual at Hednesford. Also John Salte and Christopher Cliffe surety for John Ady, collier, all of Hednesford, licensed to keep an alehouse and to victual for one year."

But two miners hardly make an industry and even if they were accompanied by a few others at Wakeringe's mines it would not mean that Hednesford's population was growing at any great rate. However, more alehouses in the village must mean there were more people about, though it must be remembered that those alehouses were not inns, but merely homesteads where ale could be brewed and possibly sold.

Further proof of growth came with further licenses. In 1604 John Ward was granted a license and in the same year Austen Watson and Robert Dackinton, both yeomen of Hednesforde, stood surety for John Grateley of Cannocke, while in 1606 Ward who had by then moved to Hatherton, stood surety for Thomas Hande, husbandman, and Austen Watson, yeoman, both of Edgeford.

Other court records establish further occupants of the village.

In Matthew Cradock's *Book of Remembrance* (a diary kept by one of Stafford's mayors) comes this entry:- "A bay colt, seller Richard Ranfries of Cannock, buyer Robert Hymlie of Shefield, price 24s 5d. Vouchers, William Lander and John Salte of Hednesforde, tool 4d." Also "Between Thomas Browne, gentleman, complainant, and Walter Abberley and Anne, his wife, deforciants of 6 acres of furze and heath and common pasture in Hednesford, otherwise Hedgford" all rights were given to Thomas Browne and his heirs.

*Anne Abberley is the first woman mentioned by name in Hednesford's history! Any relation?

But why was growth so slow if there were mines and forges in Hednesford? With both the trouble was the lack in advancement in technology, especially with coal mining. To get any quantities of coal in our area you have to go deep and they simply could not. The system used was the "bell pit", "Jacky pit" or "gin pit". These were dug into the ground to a depth of around twenty foot; any more and there was danger of collapse. Once that depth had been reached and excavated for a safe distance, possibly only a few yards sideways, the pit had to be abandoned and another dug close by. Though manually very hard it was not labour intensive, probably only needing two or three men at the most. Worse, it was not very economical.

As to the smelting of iron and forging when the furnace owners of South Staffordshire developed methods of smelting with coal rather than charcoal our small industry was doomed as it could not compete economically.

For the time being Hednesford would remain predominantly agricultural and growth was slow but steady. Fortunately it was that "backwater" status which allowed the people to remain apart from the political upheavals of the period. With no church the Reformation almost passed us by; in fact an 1586 survey proclaimed that Cannock had around 400 citizens "almost all papists"(Catholics). That must have included Hednesford. Similarly the Civil War barely affected the village save that we know of some of the people's political leanings. Thomas Lightwood, for example, favoured the Parliamentarians as did John Booth; while Charles Coleman and Mariery Stiche, wife of Francis, favoured the King and were labelled as Recusants. Strangely both Coleman and the Stiche family had moved out of Hednesford by the time of Charles II, moving to Cannock. Did their political allegiance drive them from the village?

Staying with Charles II it is in his time that we get the first real clue as to the actual size of Hednesford. In 1666 he introduced the much hated Hearth Tax whereby every person in the country paid a tax (2 shillings per hearth per year) according to the number of hearths in their home. Very poor people were deemed not chargeable or they may simply have had no fireplace (one deliberately constructed), but they were still listed. From the list we learn that Hednesford had 53 homes and it is safe to estimate the population at around 120 to 140, taking into account people who lived alone. Unlike a modern census wives and children were not included, merely the home owner.

By way of an interesting anecdote Charles Coleman appears to have somewhat of a family oddball. He lived apart from the remainder of his family who were in Cannock and built a large house in Hednesford. A man of considerable wealth he was wildly interested in anything mechanical and spent his fortune trying to invent a wagon which would go without horse power. Sir Simon Degg, a historian of the time, writes, "There was in my time one Charles Coleman who wasted his estate in fitting out a wagon to go by itself and I heard him tell the first Lord Aston that he had brought it to pass in some measure, but with these defects – that when it had strength it wanted speed, and when it had speed it wanted strength."

Unfortunately his fanaticism ruined him financially and so the house was demolished and

HEDGFORD'S HEARTH TAX RECORDS

Hearths Chargeable (38 homes)

Thomas Lightwood	5	Robert Baylies	2	Anne Barler	2
Thomas Yeavaston	4	Robert Burrowes, Sen.	3	William Elsmore	2
Francis Austens	3	James Chaddocke	1	William Elsmore, Jun.	2
Joanne Watson	3	Thomas Chaddocke	1	Thomas Taylor	1
Walter Standley	2	John Tymminges	1	Francis Kendricke	1
William Drakeford	3	Daniell Lane	1	Henry Rowley	1
Widdow Byshopp	2	John Cottrell	1	John Taylor/	
Edward Smythiman	1	Roger Kynnersley	1	Thomas Beech	2
John Salte	2	Edward Stringer	2		
Thomas Austen, Sen.	1	Thomas Coape	2	*A Mr. Charles Coleman had*	
Edward Huddle	1	Thomas Welch	2	*been included in the list, but his*	
Widdow Coape	1	Thomas Devenall	1	*house with 9 hearths had been*	
Anthony Brymill	1	James Brindley	1	*demolished and the land sold.*	
Edward Hopkins	3	Robert Bowers	1	*He had moved to Cannock to*	
John Smith	3	Thomas Quinton	1	*join his relatives.*	

HEDGFORD'S HEARTH TAX RECORDS

Not Chargeable (15 homes)

Thomas Tyrer	Thomas Woolaston	John Brockhurst
Widdow Tingle	Richard Smith	Thomas Watson
Thomas Salt	Thomas Stringer	Robert Richardes
Widdow Amery	Ralph Pattricke	William Edwardes
William Podmore	Widdow Uppadine	Thomas Arnold

★ *For any reader trying to trace their ancestors do some of your family names appear here?*
Some will appear again in the Trace Your Ancestors chapter.

the land auctioned. If only his invention had worked Hednesford might have been the home of the first ever steam-driven engine.

Things had not changed much towards the end of the seventeenth century. Robert Plot, in the agricultural section of his *History of Staffordshire* (1686), makes a special mention of "the neighbourhood of Hedgford" which rears "rams and ewes, grey-faced without horns". He adds that their distinguishing characteristics are "grey faces, light or dark legs with fine wool, closely compact and covering the carcass". Those sheep are of "moderate size" and "have a good disposition to fatten and produce mutton at the table to equal that of any breed in the Kingdom". If they had a fault it was that "they want thickness in proportion to length".

Despite a lengthy description of the iron and coal industry in Staffordshire he does not mention anything of those industries in our area and so they must have been so small that they were not worth a mention. Production was probably only at the level of producing enough for local consumption. Iron smelting may have almost died out, but coal mining does have the occasional mention in the following century.

In 1742, after the Borough of Stafford had set up a workhouse in the grounds of St. Mary's Church in Stafford in 1735, it was decided after a meeting that the "master of the workhouse be allowed 12 tons of coal per annum from the pits in Hedgford" to heat the building in winter. In 1747 an item in the same workhouse accounts tells that the cost of "a wagon load of coal from Hedgford was 10s 6d" which was costly due to the difficulties of hauling it by horse-drawn cart along poor public roads.

Then in a letter, dated January 11th, 1788, to the Earl of Uxbridge (the Pagets had been granted that title) by John Bennett, an Abbotts Bromley lawyer, on behalf of John Startin, he complains of the behaviour of John and William Craddock who worked one of the Earl's pits under contract. The letter reads:-

Dear Sir, Farme, servant to John Startin, went to Fiddler's Pit by 4 o'clock in the morning, where his cart had been set down eleven days earlier, As the coals came up Farme had loaded the wagon with 6 or 7 horse loads, towards the compliment of a full cart load. John Craddock, the banksman and bailiffe was not attending, but William Craddock was in the pit and came up. He told Farme that he should not be loaded there that day and immediately took the coals which Farme had loaded in the cart out again. Whereupon Farme went to Hedgeford, but meeting with none there, returned that day to some of my Lord's pits."

Our interest lies in the fact that Farme thought that he might be loaded at Hednesford and so there must have been pits there which could produce enough coal in a few days to load his cart. Unfortunately who ran those pits and exactly where they were situated was not recorded, but Parish Records of Marriage Banns at St. Luke's in Cannock dating from 1754 do tell of Hednesford families involved in mining. Among them were Thomas and William Clewley, John Bradbury and Robert, Moses and Job Benton. Matthew Brindley had married into the Benton family, having wed Elizabeth Benton in 1768, and recorded his trade as a collier. (He was probably an ancestor of the Brindley who was Lord Paget's forest keeper in the sixteenth century.)

Thomas, Joseph, Abraham, Robert, Isaac and Samuel Craddock also lived in Hednesford in the latter part of the eighteenth century and like

III. Robert Plot's Map of Staffordshire 1686 *(By kind permission of the Staffordshire County Records Office)*

their Cannock Wood namesakes mentioned in the letter they too worked as colliers. By the turn of the century they had been joined by the Hitchens and Brockhouse families.

But still Hednesford was predominantly agricultural and the eighteenth century seems to have passed by with little growth and development. The major problem, as with so many villages in England at the time, was lack of transport and a good road system. Had there been considerable industry then by necessity it would have been catered for. Our only major road was Blake Street, often called Black Street because on either side of the road was gorse and heath, known locally as black or wild land.

That road ran from Birmingham through Perry Barr, over Barr Beacon, through Aldridge and over Druid's Heath and Walsall Wood where it crossed the Chester Road near Brownhills. Then it went by Knaves Castle and through what is now the middle of Norton Pool, a little to the north of Five Ways and down to

1 Greetings card from the Chase

Hednesford. Leaving Hednesford it went by Deakin's Grave to Huntington Belt and on to Brocton Gate, finally arriving at Stafford. Although a major route through the area it was still really only a dirt track and other roads using the Cannock route were more popular.

However, it was along the Blake Road that one John Wesley travelled in 1738 delivering his religious message to village people. From his diary he records that he passed through Hednesford in March.

"The next day (March 18th) we dined at Birmingham and soon after were prepared for our negligence (he gave no sermon) by a severe shower of hail. At Hednesford about five we endeavoured to be more faithful and all who heard seemed serious and affected."

He must have returned some days later as he continues, " Tuesday, March 21st, 1738. Between nine and ten in the morning we came down to Hednesford, Just then one was given an account of a young woman who had dropped down dead there the day before. This gave us fair occasion to exhort all that were present so to number their own days that they might apply their hearts to wisdom."

Wesley was back in the area in 1746 and once again must have travelled through Hednesford, though that time there is no record of him staying there or preaching. The Cross Keys Inn was under construction at the time, but probably not habitable and anyway he was only too keen to arrive in Stafford as his journey over the heath had been terrible.

He writes, "February 20th, 1746. We set out (from Birmingham presumably) as soon as it was light. Before we came to Aldridge Heath the rain changed to snow which northerly winds drove full in our faces and encrusted us over from head to foot in less than an hour. We enquired of one who lived close to the moors which was our best way to Stafford. "Sir," said he, "tis a thousand pounds to a penny that you do not come there today. Why tis four long miles to the far side of this common, and in a clear day I am not sure to go right across it; and now the roads are covered in snow and it snows so that you cannot see before you."

Wesley did continue and added in his diary "we did not get ten yards out of the way before we came to Stafford."

Another glimpse we get of the rural nature of Hednesford in the eighteenth century lies in the Fox Hunting Diaries of Sir Edward Littleton (1777-1789) when his hunt frequently roamed all over the area and those diaries describe hunting over large tracts of agricultural land.

"February 6th, 1777. Killed at Hednesford Coal Pit Field 1 fox.
January 31st, 1781. Found in Brocton Copy Killed at Hednesford 1 fox.
October 26th, 1782. Chance fox killed three quarters of an hour on Hednesford Hills.
February 7th, 1783. This morning we draw from Hednesford X to the Kennel Pitts. Eventually killed a dogfox at the Sycamores.
November 4th, 1783. Killed in Shirebrook, run to ground in Heywood Park and near Hednesford 1 fox.
November 11th, 1788. Found in Cook's Gorse at Hilton and killed at Hednesford 1fox.
February 6th, 1789. Frost. Found in Horsemoor, lost in Hednesford Road 1 fox."

What little can be gleaned from those entries is that because the hunt seemed to roam at will over the whole of the Hednesford area it must have been almost completely rural. No huntsman would take the risk of injuring himself or his horse by riding through industrial landscape. However, mining was there and the "Hednesford Coal Pit Field" referred to was certainly outlined on the Yates Map of the area in 1775. It probably stood within close proximity to today's Splash Lane and the roundabout leading to the factory units. In fact when the old Hednesford Brickworks were extending their property in the 1960's some of the old "bell pits" were exposed.

The final word on the area in the late eighteenth century comes from Stebbings Shaw who wrote:- "The wood from Rugeley to Cannock winds along the vallies of the forest and at about four miles and a half is a small pool, at the head of which is a large heap of the refuse of a furnace, formerly there and on the opposite hill on the right hand side is a full wood of full grown oaks, well-known to the sportsmen as good for fox cover, by the name of Furnace Coppice.

Hedgeford Pool is a large sheet of water of several acres. Opposite on the right they get coal with an engine and there is also a brick kiln nearby. Beyond this, a mile, is Hedgeford Hamlet, in Cank Parish, belonging to the Earl of Uxbridge. The place is famous for a fine extensive plain upon a hill on the forest where, with the advantages of good turf and excellent air, racehorses from various parts are brought to exercise, about a dozen being there breathing when I passed over in June, 1792."

In 1794 he writes:- "the best land on Cannock Chase for sheep and crops, especially barley and turnips, lay on the west and north sides and around Hedgeford, the soil being light."

The coal workings and brick kiln are shown on the Yates Map as just north of Hednesford Pool and may have been owned or run by the Wallbank family who certainly had a farm there in the 1840's. Some of the Clewley family, already mentioned as colliers, also had a home there.

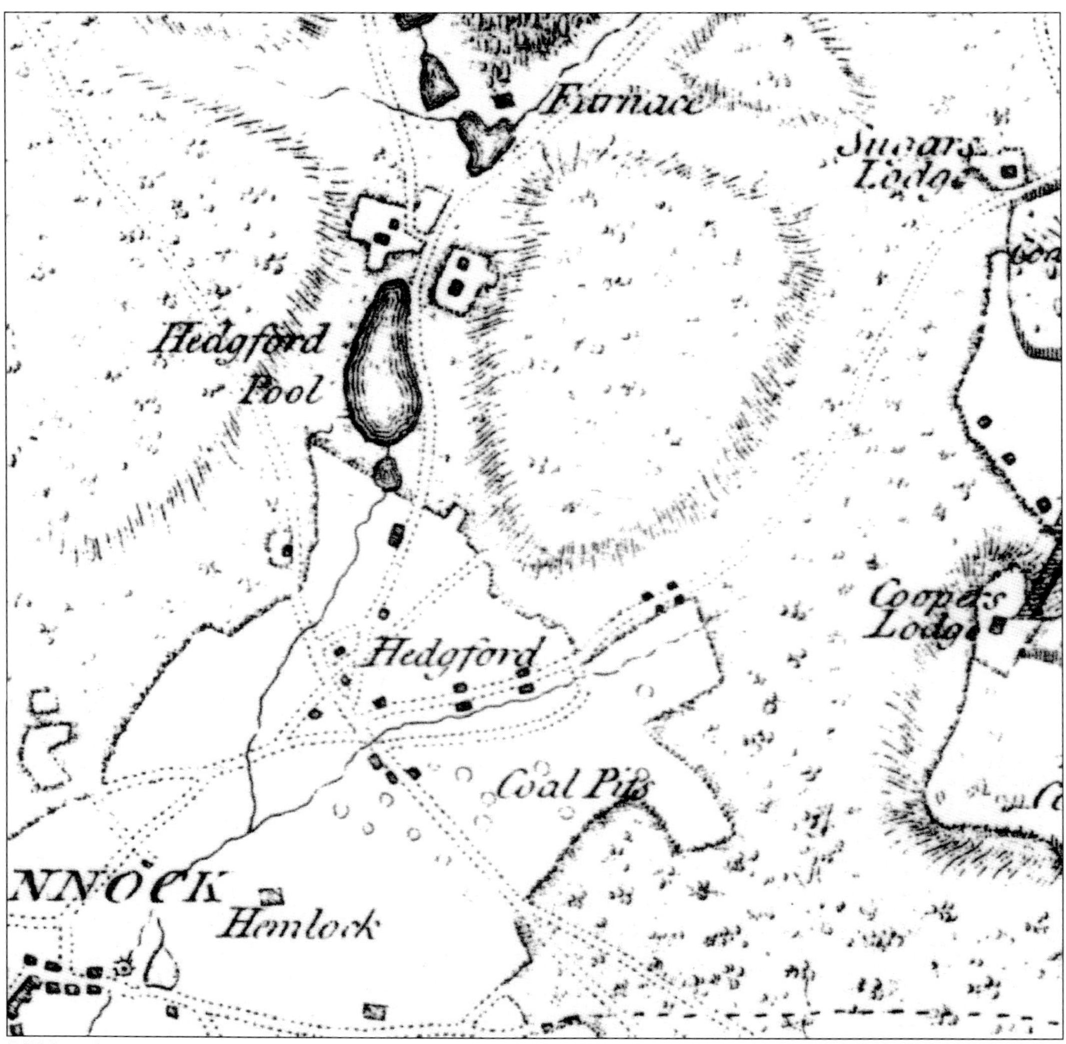

IV. Taken from the Yates Map of Staffordshire 1775, showing main roads, large buildings and geographical features. *(By kind permission of the William Salt Library)*

THE VILLAGE AWAKES
1800 - 1870

By the beginning of the nineteenth century Hednesford was still very much a village whose main source of income was farming. However, because of the Hills which dominate the area and their excellent turf, Hednesford was gaining a reputation for the training of racehorses. Such was its reputation that White's *Directory for Staffordshire* for 1834 contained the following description of the village:-

"Hedgeford is an enclosed hamlet on Cannock Chase containing a number of scattered houses, a large lake called Hedgeford Pool covering about 27 acres and abounding in pike, perch and roach. Here also is a good inn and extensive stabling of blood horses of which about 100 are generally trained here in the season and exercised on the excellent turf of Hedgeford Hills. Edmund Peel, Esquire of Fazeley, has built a mansion, Hedgeford Lodge, with stabling for his race horses. He occasionally rides here in the summer."

That Directory mentions no less than seven people who were training horses. Apart from Sir Edmund Peel (who incidentally did not train himself, but employed a trainer), there was Henry Arthur, Thomas Flintoff, Samuel Lord, Saul Sanders, and Richard Spencer, while John Massey, who kept the Cross Keys, also had horses. With so many stables in the village there were two men who acted as farriers whilst farming as well. They were Robert Benton and Thomas Grimley. Unfortunately the Directory gives no details of stable lads or jockeys, but there must have been a considerable number to keep the stables going.

By the time of the 1841 Census (the first real attempt to count the population of England, though it had plenty of omissions and errors) the number of trainers had increased to eight with over thirty other people directly involved with the training of horses. In total 87 villagers were involved in one way or another. (More detail will be given in the chapter on Sport and Leisure).

But what of those "scattered houses" which White mentions? The village had grown from being just centred around Splash Lane and the Cross Keys to include several houses near the Pool, along the Rugeley Road, as well as houses in Littleworth (so named because the land was considered to be of no real value).

2 Splash Lane c.1920

There were also homes at Hill Top and a farm at Wimblebury owned by the Dean family. How Wimblebury got its name is still the subject of some debate. Some historians believe that it came from the Anglo-Saxon for "Winebald's fortified place" though that is difficult to substantiate; others believe that it came from the "wimbel", a device for boring holes into the ground to dig for coal and "bury" was the place; while I prefer the idea that "wimbleberries" were the local name for bilberries, hence the farm where those berries grew profusely.

At the top of the hill, beyond Littleworth, was Heathy Leasows, a farm owned by the Clewley family. Later between 1861 and 1871 that area was to be known as Rawnsley. Again there is debate as to how exactly that name came about. Some believe that it took its name from the Rawnpike Oak, an old tree which was situated a few feet outside Beaudesert Park at the foot of Castle Ring by the side of the path which led from Cannock Wood to the Wood Pit. (The tree was over 800 years old and survived until 1932 when it was hit by lightning and after set fire to by vandals.) Other historians think that Rawnsley came from the Saxon meaning "woodland glade of the raven" or "conical hill frequented by ravens". I prefer the Rawnpike version, though who can tell.

The total number of occupied dwellings in the Hednesford area in 1841 was only 56 with 2 unoccupied and the population a mere 297 or thereabouts. Unlike today's census, which in itself is not totally accurate because of people "hiding" their existence, the 1841 Census definitely missed out some villagers who were certainly living in

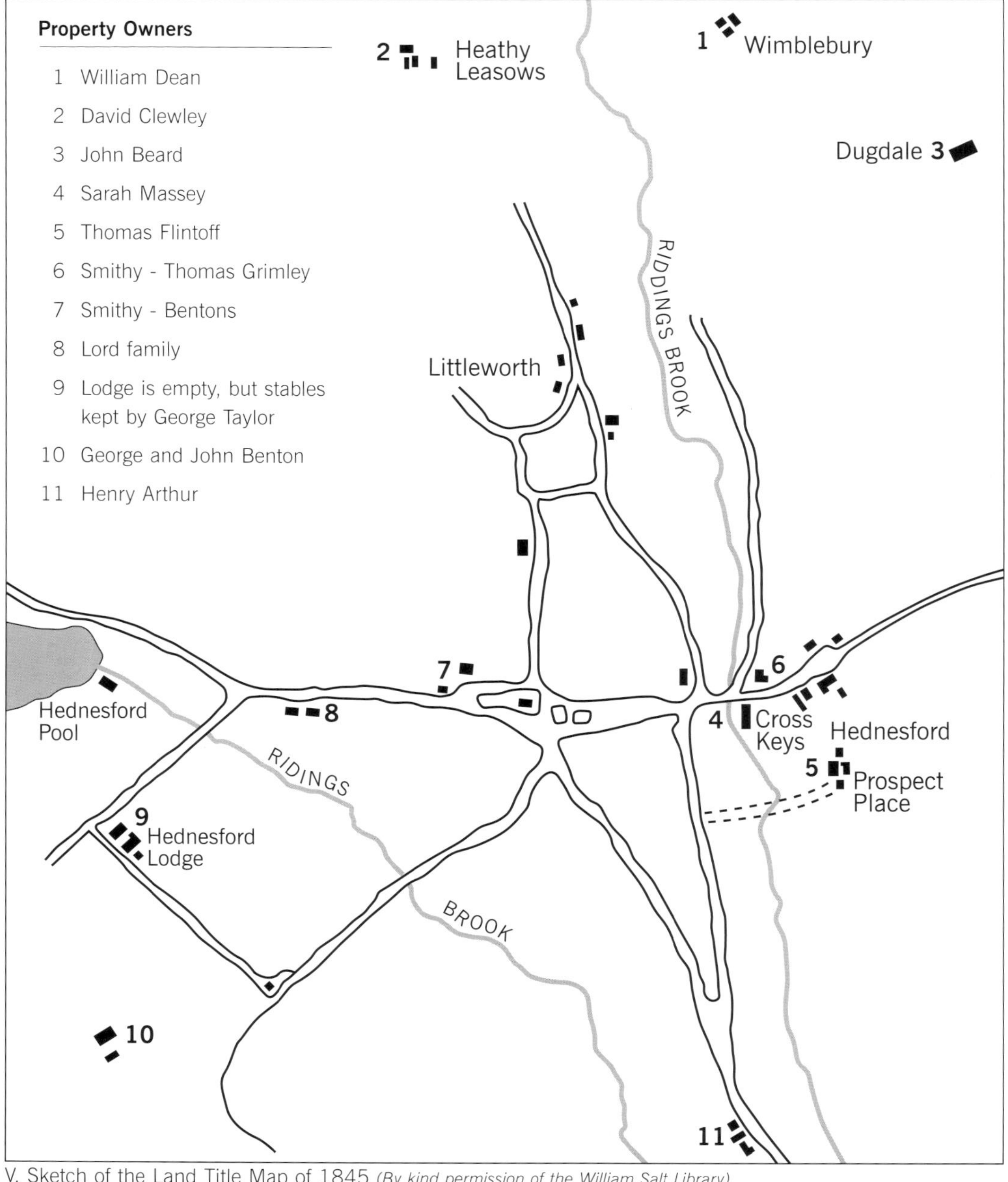

V. Sketch of the Land Title Map of 1845 *(By kind permission of the William Salt Library)*

3 Stafford Lane c.1920

the area at the time. For example, there was no mention of the Martin or Hitchens families who appear in the Baptismal Records of St. Luke's quite prominently. In fact Edward and Elizabeth Martin kept a beerhouse in the village as well as a sawyer's business and had five children; while Joseph and Elizabeth Hitchens also kept a beerhouse to suppliment his work as a collier and they had six girls. Joseph had died in 1840, but his family were still in the area.

What the census does tell us is that the majority of people were still involved in farming. In 1819 some 38 freeholders from Hednesford and Leacroft were pasturing 1782 sheep, 28 cows, 1 ass and 6 horses. There were nine separate farms in Hednesford, employing 35 agricultural labourers, which of course did not include their wives and children. In total 128 villagers depended on farming for their livelihoods. (There was also one Benjamin Witchston who was employed as a shepherd and lived near the Cross Keys with his wife, Mary, and two children.)

Strangely White fails to mention anything to do with coal mining in his Directory, probably because he thought it of no great wealth, but it was certainly still taking place. The 1841 Census shows that 6 families gained their living from the small pits between Hednesford and the Wimblebury Farm and out towards Leacroft. These included the Greens (Thomas and

William), James and Job Saunders, William Bradbury and John Harvey.

A court case between Lord Hatherton and the Pagets in 1842 held at Worcester over mining rights around Hednesford clearly shows that there were several active pits at the time. Fortunately for historians Sir Thomas Noon Talfourd, the judge, kept private notes on the trial which he fancifully wrote in poetic form.

When John Harvey (mentioned above) was questioned he said:-

Hedgeford is a country village
Very near to Cannock Wood
Round the country is in tillage
But the coal is thick and good.

And Jane Holcroft another witness said:-
I recollect the Riddock's Field
When I was a tiny child
Where poor Benton's fate was seal'd
And the slack and cinders pil'd.

Then my name was Benton
To poor Robert Benton niece
And he took a field to rent
Which we knew was Levitt's Piece.

Robert Benton had an engine
Which was work'd by Levitt's Hole
And the people each paid sixpence
When they purchased Benton's coal.

Robert Benton (that same Benton mentioned in St. Luke's Marriage banns in 1757) had died in an accident in one of the pits when he fell from a plank across the pit mouth into the hole. From the Land Title Map of 1845 Riddock's Field, which Benton rented from Richard Levett, lies near today's Levitts Hollow.

John Holcroft, another witness, said:-
My name is John Holcroft, my age is eighty three
My father an engineer was before me;
I recollect Benton who occupied land
Where my father and Benton an engine pit plann'd;
In a border enclosure I think was plac'd
And a second was sunk at the edge of the waste,
All the coal Francis Benton obtain'd from the spot
From mines 'neath the Common I fancy we got,
I think Francis began after Robert had ceas'd
And that coal 'neath the Common to Francis was leas'd.

*Francis Benton was born in 1753 and died in 1814. He must have taken over the pit after the death of Robert Benton.

The land that John Holcroft refers to was clearly in the Hednesford area and close to the same spot as Riddock's Field. Although the case refers to land at Rumer Hill, where Hatherton had opened up a mine, our interest lies in the fact that to try and prove that land owners did not own mineral rights below the ground level, he used the mining of coal at Hednesford, which had clearly taken place for many years, to prove his case. His argument was that copyholders who leased the land from the Pagets had rights to mine coal on that leased land. He even went as far back as Elizabethan documents by which copyholders were given the mining rights. He lost his case.

For us it shows that mining was still a viable industry in Hednesford, if on a very small scale.

Hednesford was beginning to grow in other ways. Because of its size there had never been a church in the village. Those people who practised their religion went to St. Luke's in Cannock. That brings to mind a rather morbid thought - no church, no cemetery - so where on earth were people buried? Some funerals and burials did take place at St. Luke's as can be seen from the Burial Registers, but not all. Where the remainder were buried is a mystery.

However, at the turn of the nineteenth century various houses began to hold services for the local people whose beliefs did not coincide with those of the Church of England and whose numbers were such that they needed somewhere to worship as a group. In 1817 a house at Littleworth, occupied by John Beard, the same man who farmed Dugdale at the top of the hill above today's football ground, was registered for Protestant Dissenters. In the same year John Bradbury, also of Littleworth, had his home registered for services by Dissenters. By 1824 a third house, occupied by William Noakes, was also registered. Not a mass move away from the Church of England, but a steady rise in the numbers who were of a new faith. The 1841 Tithe Map shows a chapel and school run by Edward Selman, but does not say what denomination it is.

Another sign of semi-independence in Hednesford was the growth of trades in the village. The 1841 Census mentions:-
Thomas Wallbank, a tailor
Samuel Lawrence, a shoemaker
William Beachstone, assistant tailor
Sarah Jenkinson, a grocer
Joseph Littler, a sawyer
Jacob Spenser, a butcher
Not forgetting Edward Martin, a sawyer.

Others, like Daniel Bird, a tile maker, and Robert Cope and William Wooley, both brickmakers, show that new housing was in need. There was by the late 1840's the Blue Yard Brickworks at Littleworth owned by Mr. Thomas Cotton who incidentally lent out his cottage for religious services before the Littleworth Primitive Chapel was built in 1852. Those small works were the continuation of a trade which had started in the eighteenth century and were to continue at Hednesford well into the twentieth century, the last closing in the early 1970's.

By the 1850's Hednesford also had a Post Office, though it was merely an extension of Mr. Wolverton's chemist shop near the Cross Keys. Letters were displayed in the shop window and people scanned them to see if they had any mail.

Finally in the 1840's there were those whose trade centred around the horse trainers, namely blacksmiths and nailers, though nailers were obviously in demand for other work. The

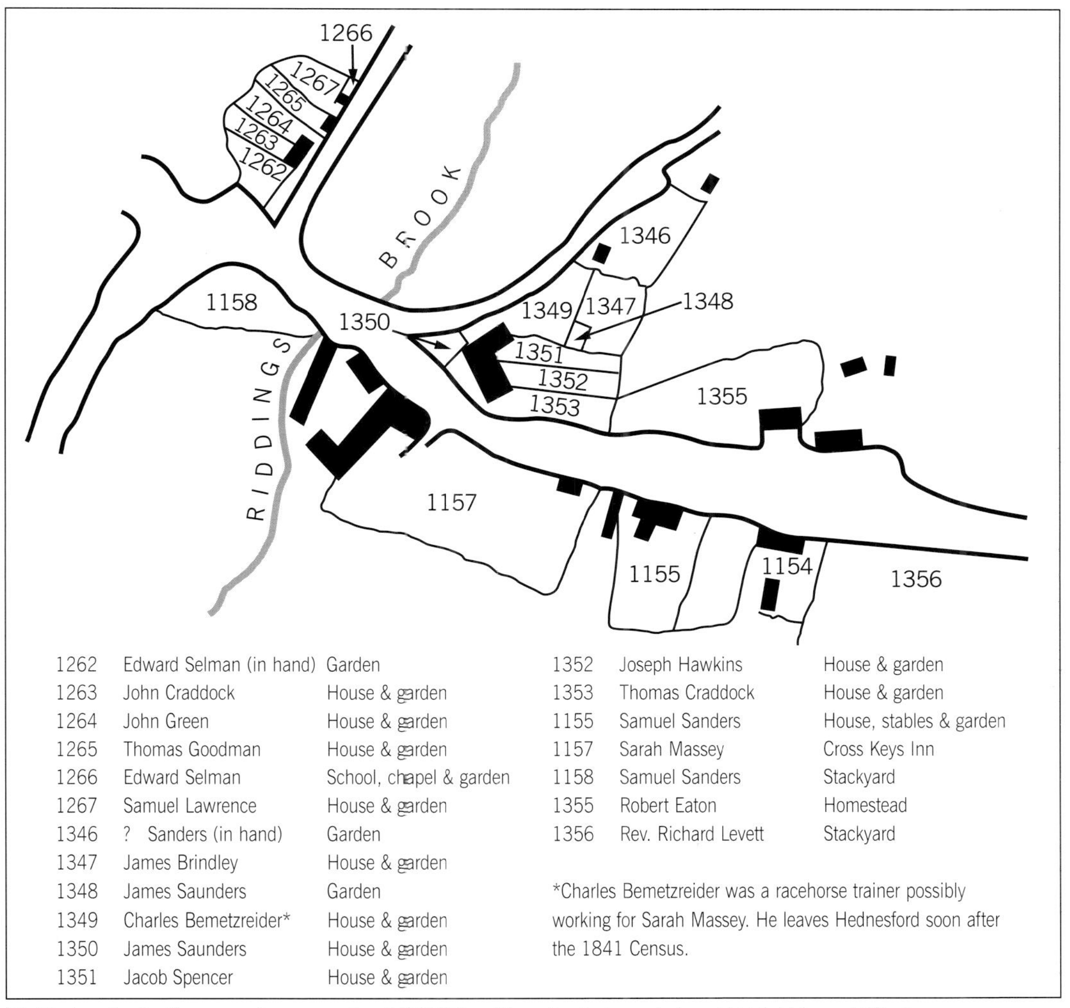

1262	Edward Selman (in hand)	Garden	1352	Joseph Hawkins	House & garden
1263	John Craddock	House & garden	1353	Thomas Craddock	House & garden
1264	John Green	House & garden	1155	Samuel Sanders	House, stables & garden
1265	Thomas Goodman	House & garden	1157	Sarah Massey	Cross Keys Inn
1266	Edward Selman	School, chapel & garden	1158	Samuel Sanders	Stackyard
1267	Samuel Lawrence	House & garden	1355	Robert Eaton	Homestead
1346	? Sanders (in hand)	Garden	1356	Rev. Richard Levett	Stackyard
1347	James Brindley	House & garden			
1348	James Saunders	Garden			
1349	Charles Bemetzreider*	House & garden			
1350	James Saunders	House & garden			
1351	Jacob Spencer	House & garden			

*Charles Bemetzreider was a racehorse trainer possibly working for Sarah Massey. He leaves Hednesford soon after the 1841 Census.

VI. Hednesford village as shown on the 1841 Tithe Map *(By kind permission of Lichfield Record Office)*

Benton family, George and John, ran a blacksmith's forge at Hill Top and rented the land around which by 1845 was owned by John Massey, owner of the Cross Keys, hence Forge Street today. It was taken over by one John Wright a few years later. Littleworth was the centre for the nailers, namely the Jenkinson family of William and his two sons, also William and Robert, and Henry Saunders and his assistant, Thomas Cotton (the same who was to own the brickworks). Another Jenkinson, also William, had a nailers works near the Cross Keys Inn, while yet another member of the family, Thomas Jenkinson, opened up a nailer's forge at Hill Top in the 1840's.

It was not much of an expansion, but Hednesford's problem still lay in the poor road network. The introduction of turnpike roads between Birmingham and Stafford via Wolverhampton and Walsall and through Cannock meant that the Blake Road running through Hednesford had fallen into a bad state of repair in the late 1760's and although it was still used by some Chester traffic it was gradually getting worse. Also, despite the eighteenth century being the age of canal building, it was thought uneconomical to pay for a canal into the Chase area. A lack of any worthwhile industry had meant it was not viable. Railways, the revolutionary new transport, also saw little monetary benefit in investing in a line through the area.

The 1851 Census then barely shows any difference in Hednesford's population. There were 311 people in the village (186 men and 125 women) and still only 56 occupied houses with 3 unoccupied. But things were about to change. By the time of the 1861 Census numbers had dramatically increased. There were 95 occupied dwellings and the population had risen to 572 (333 men and 239 women). Such had been the sudden rise that there were not enough houses for all the people and many dwellings had more than one family living in them.

But what had caused such a sudden rise? Obviously the locals had not suddenly decided to reproduce at a fantastic rate, so where had all the new people come from and why?

Sometime during the late 1850's an entrepreneur named Francis Piggott had arrived in the Hednesford area and had started the Hednesford Colliery Company. (Scott Street in Wimblebury used to be called Piggott Street.) He had leased land between Hednesford and Wimblebury Farm from Lieutenant Colonel Levett and had begun mining operations. His first mine was only about twenty yards deep and after only six months working a "gob" fire damaged the pit. Later that mine was closed and two other were sunk in the vicinity, namely the "Brooch" and the "Five Feet", both much deeper mines.

Those mines attracted young men from around the country who settled in Hednesford and Wimblebury. The population soon increased rapidly, borne out by a study of the 1861 Census. In 1851 there were only 4 miners in the village, but by 1861 that figure had grown to 36, most of them settling in the area around the new mines, that is Hill Street and out towards what would

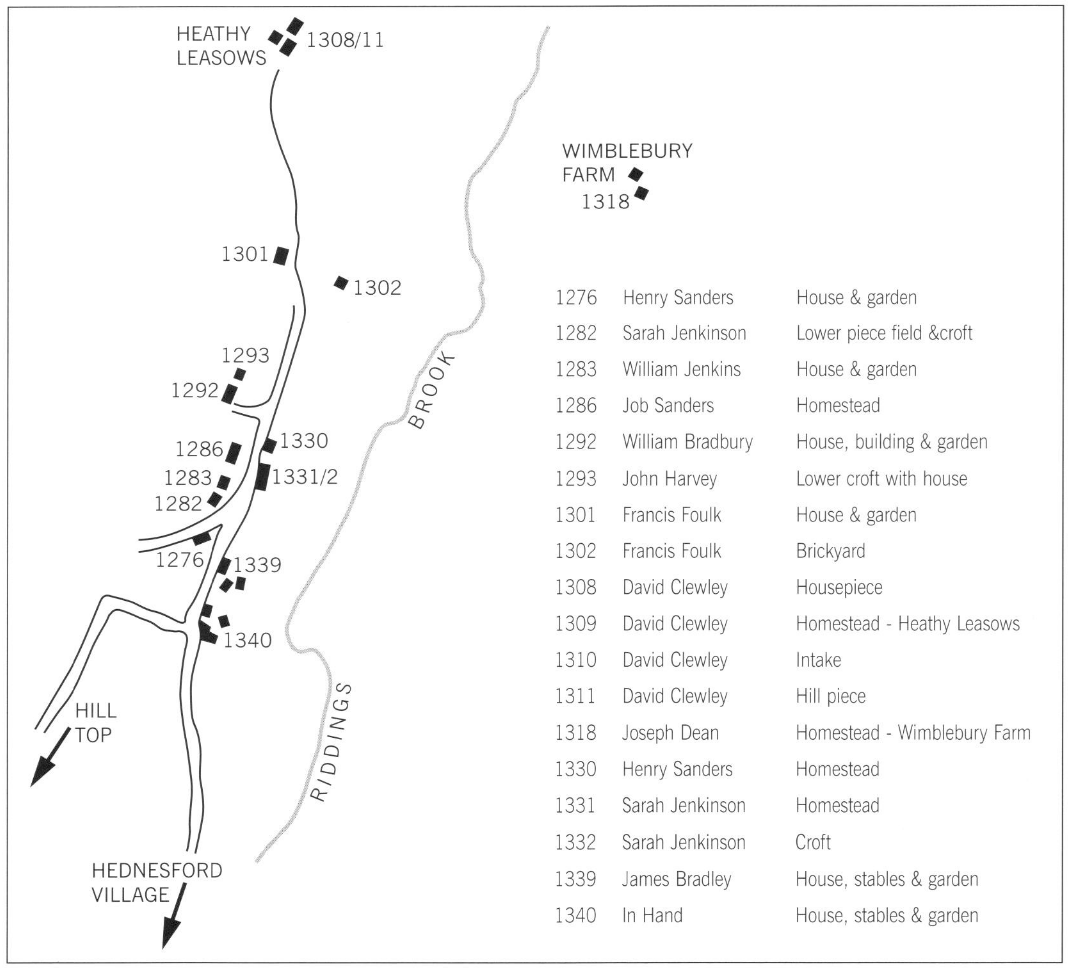

1276	Henry Sanders	House & garden
1282	Sarah Jenkinson	Lower piece field &croft
1283	William Jenkins	House & garden
1286	Job Sanders	Homestead
1292	William Bradbury	House, building & garden
1293	John Harvey	Lower croft with house
1301	Francis Foulk	House & garden
1302	Francis Foulk	Brickyard
1308	David Clewley	Housepiece
1309	David Clewley	Homestead - Heathy Leasows
1310	David Clewley	Intake
1311	David Clewley	Hill piece
1318	Joseph Dean	Homestead - Wimblebury Farm
1330	Henry Sanders	Homestead
1331	Sarah Jenkinson	Homestead
1332	Sarah Jenkinson	Croft
1339	James Bradley	House, stables & garden
1340	In Hand	House, stables & garden

VII. Littleworth as shown on the 1841 Tithe Map *(By kind permission of Lichfield Record Office)*

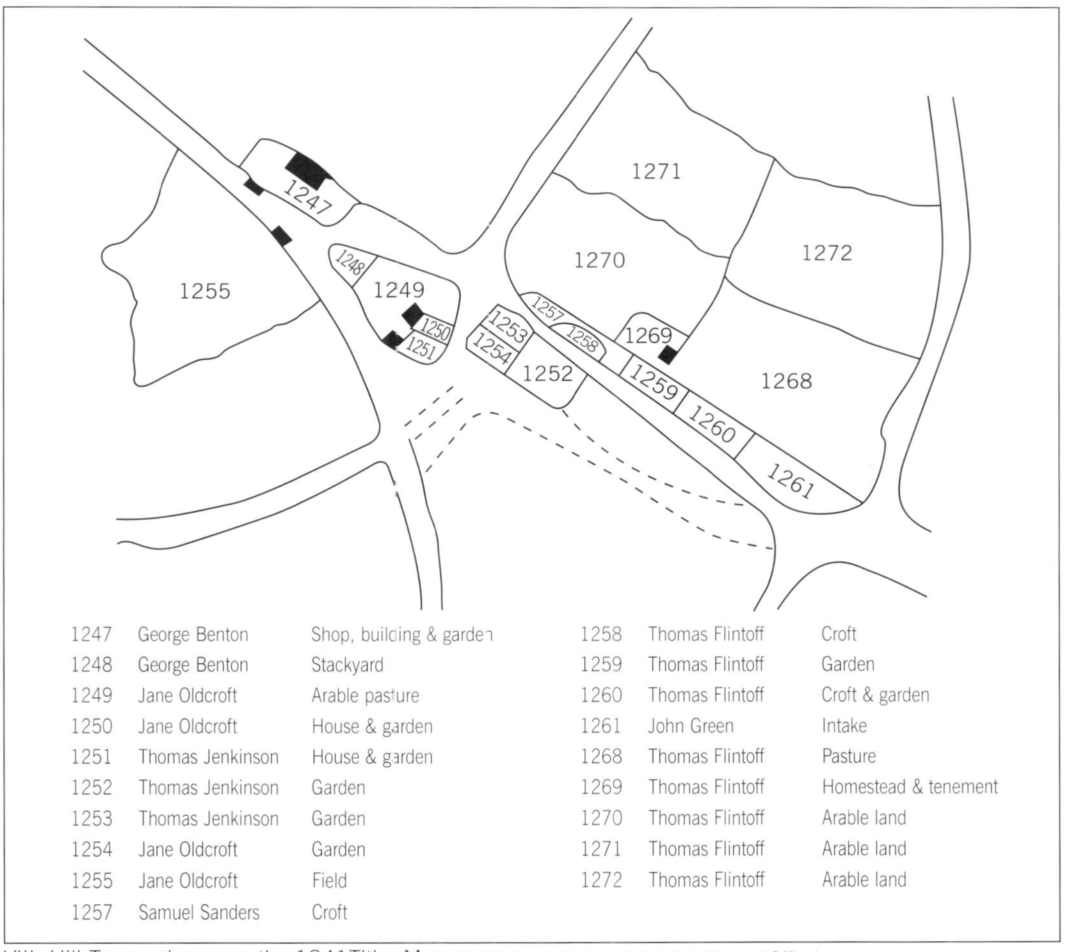

1247	George Benton	Shop, building & garden		1258	Thomas Flintoff	Croft
1248	George Benton	Stackyard		1259	Thomas Flintoff	Garden
1249	Jane Oldcroft	Arable pasture		1260	Thomas Flintoff	Croft & garden
1250	Jane Oldcroft	House & garden		1261	John Green	Intake
1251	Thomas Jenkinson	House & garden		1268	Thomas Flintoff	Pasture
1252	Thomas Jenkinson	Garden		1269	Thomas Flintoff	Homestead & tenement
1253	Thomas Jenkinson	Garden		1270	Thomas Flintoff	Arable land
1254	Jane Oldcroft	Garden		1271	Thomas Flintoff	Arable land
1255	Jane Oldcroft	Field		1272	Thomas Flintoff	Arable land
1257	Samuel Sanders	Croft				

VIII. Hill Top as shown on the 1841 Tithe Map *(By kind permission of Lichfield Record Office)*

later be Wimblebury village. To help his new workforce Piggott built houses for his workers and himself in the Hill Street area, just over twenty in total. Closer study of the Census shows that his workforce came from all over the Midlands and even further afield.

Hednesford itself	10	Warwickshire	2
Surrounding area	8	Shropshire	1
South Staffs.	7	Yorkshire	1
Leicestershire	4	Essex	1
Derbyshire	2		

★Were your ancestors part of that influx? Samuel Parking was from Essex, George Bould from Shropshire and James Beeley from Yorkshire.

Hednesford's own figures in the mines rose from 4 to 10 because some local men left agriculture for the pits.

But why had Piggott chosen Hednesford? In 1853 the Birmingham Navigation Company, to meet the threat of the railways, had proposed an extension of the Wyrley and Essington Canal to Hednesford and Brereton and an extension from the Lord Hay's Branch to Wyrley Bank with tramways to Littleworth. The first was started, but by the late 1850's it had only reached Hednesford where it was decided to halt operations and go no further, probably because it was proving very expensive and the railways had already started to move into the area. On September 1st, 1860 Piggott signed a contract with the Birmingham Canal Navigation Company to construct a tramway linking the canal basin at East Cannock with his new mines at Littleworth. That tramway was completed by 1862.

By 1855 all the railroads north of the South

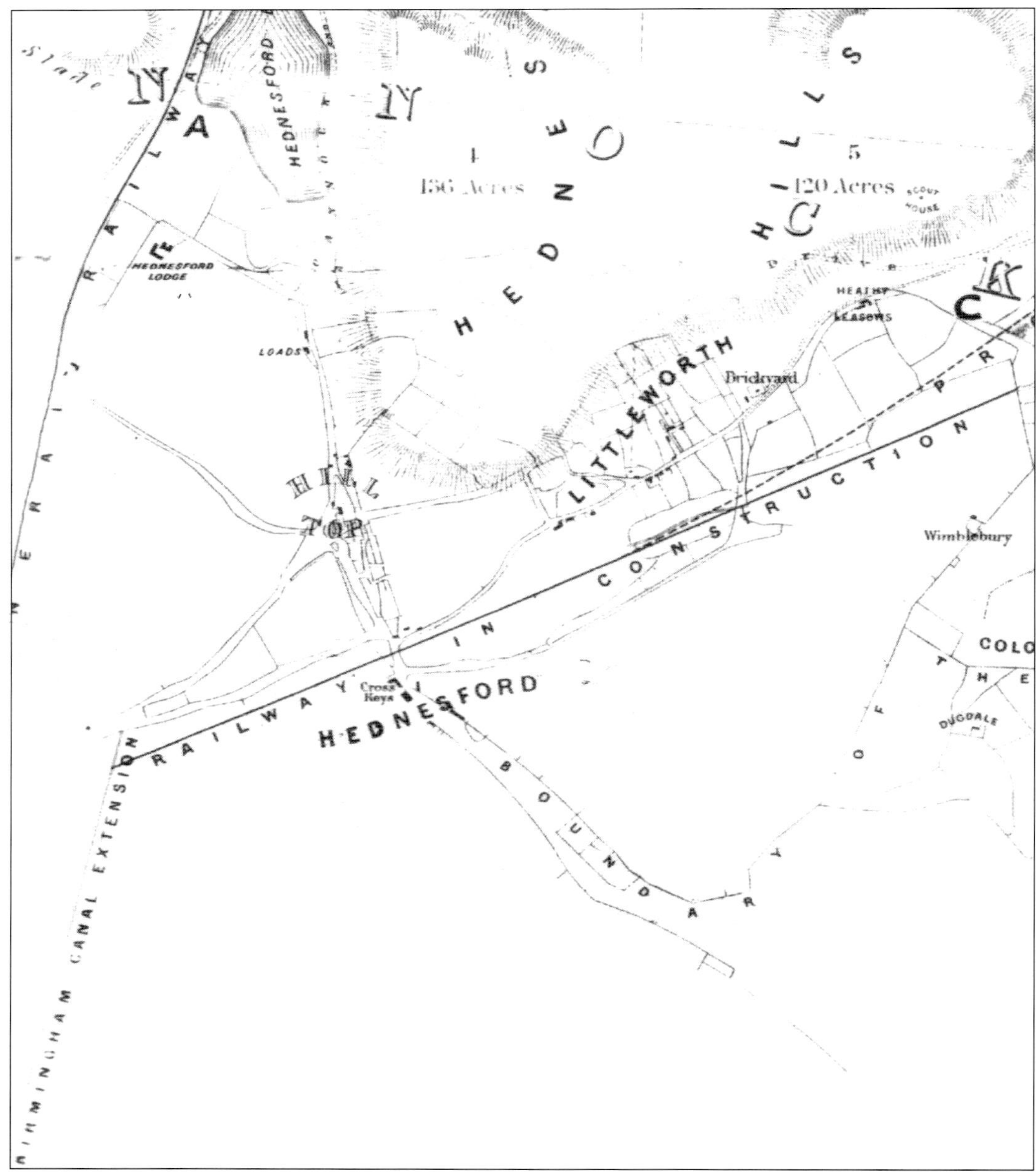

IX. Hednesford district c.1858. Taken from the plan of lands under which the mines were to be let.
(By kind permission of the Friends of the Valley Heritage Museum)

Staffordshire railway line were purely of local significance and primarily canal feeders. However, a through connection between Walsall and Rugeley was formed by the Cannock Branch of the South Staffs. Railway Company and opened in 1858 and north of Cannock by the Cannock Mineral Railway Company in 1859. Hednesford's passenger railway station was opened in 1859 and the line was leased to the L.N.W.R. by 1860.

Francis Piggott had seen the possibilities of growth in the area and had leapt at the opportunity. By 1862 he had been proved right because in that same year the Cannock Chase Railway proposed a new line to be constructed from the Hednesford line to Cooper's Lodge, going through Heathy Leasows. Piggott's mines would then have connections to both canal and main line railway and success and wealth should have followed.

4 Hednesford Railway Station, date unknown

In 1864, with £60,000 capital, he formed the Hednesford Colliery Company, but disaster was soon to strike! Coal was always at the mercy of market prices, obviously cheaper in the summer than in the winter. The cost of drawing coal from the faces, however, remains the same. One possibility, though never popular, was to pay the miners less in the summer months; the other was to cut their working hours. Those solutions were tried in most areas with the inevitable disputes with the workforce. Piggott was under another pressure. He had agreed to pay Levett a royalty of one tenth of the selling price for each ton of coal mined and that would cut his profits even further.

He came up with a cunning solution! He would keep two sets of books – one which showed the supposed "get" or extraction of coal which Levett saw and another book for the actual "get". Obviously the second was the greater amount and he would keep the profits from those undeclared tons. Unfortunately for him he was found out. Who told Levett was never disclosed, but he was taken to court. Despite the obvious deception he argued that if he paid Levett the real amount he would not have enough capital left to cover mining expenses. The case dragged on and in 1867 Piggott issued a Deed of Assignment in favour of his creditors as the yield from the mines had not been adequate to pay "anything like a fair dividend on the outlay". In other words, if his creditors pushed for payments he would simply hand the mines over to them, with all their possible debts.

The ploy worked for a time, but the mines were still in financial trouble. Finally in 1869 Piggott ran out of capital and sold his venture to William Tredwell. However, he only held on to the company until the following year and on June 24th, 1870 he sold the Old Hednesford Colliery Company to the Cannock Chase Colliery Company run by John Robinson McClean. He, together with his partner, William Harrison, had opened their first pits towards Chasetown when they had bought the old Uxbridge Pit from the Pagets, in 1852. Their newest acquisitions were to be named Cannock Chase No. 9 and No. 10, referred to locally as Old Hednesford.

The difficulties met by Piggott were to be encountered again with other colliery companies, but in 1870 they were way beyond the horizon. The future for Hednesford and the surrounding area seemed to offer nothing but growth and wealth.

But not everyone was happy with what was happening to Cannock Chase. In *Our Own Country*, a book describing the best of life in England, the author wrote:- "Formerly there were few more perfectly wild spots to be found anywhere in England. For many square miles the Chase consisted of gravely upland plateau, furrowed by a series of small streams into a mass of low rolling hills. These were covered with heath and heather, with bracken fern and whortle berry bushes, with occasional groves of birch and scattered oak. This moorland was a haunt of scarce birds and insects; black cock and red grouse were plentiful; herds of fallow deer wandered over it. But all this is changing; several new collieries have been opened, defiling the air with smoke, the ground with piles of refuse.... so that soon Cannock Chase will be but a traditional name".

5 Engraving of Cannock Chase c.1850

Whatever the viewpoint progress was not going to be halted.

A TOWN BURSTS FORTH
1870 - 1900

Despite Piggott's difficulties other mining entrepreneurs were not disheartened and the next thirty years were to prove the most dynamic ever seen in the Cannock Chase district and Hednesford was to be right at the heart of the development. Collieries opened and people flooded in from all over the British Isles. Hednesford would never be the same again. For the locals it must have been both exciting and frightening. From a small village to a sizeable town in just ten years was nothing short of amazing.

With the opening of the railway and canal basin situated to the east of the village, speculators realised that a transport system was in place for the new industry. What also helped to boost the area's possibilities was the depletion of the Shropshire and South Staffordshire

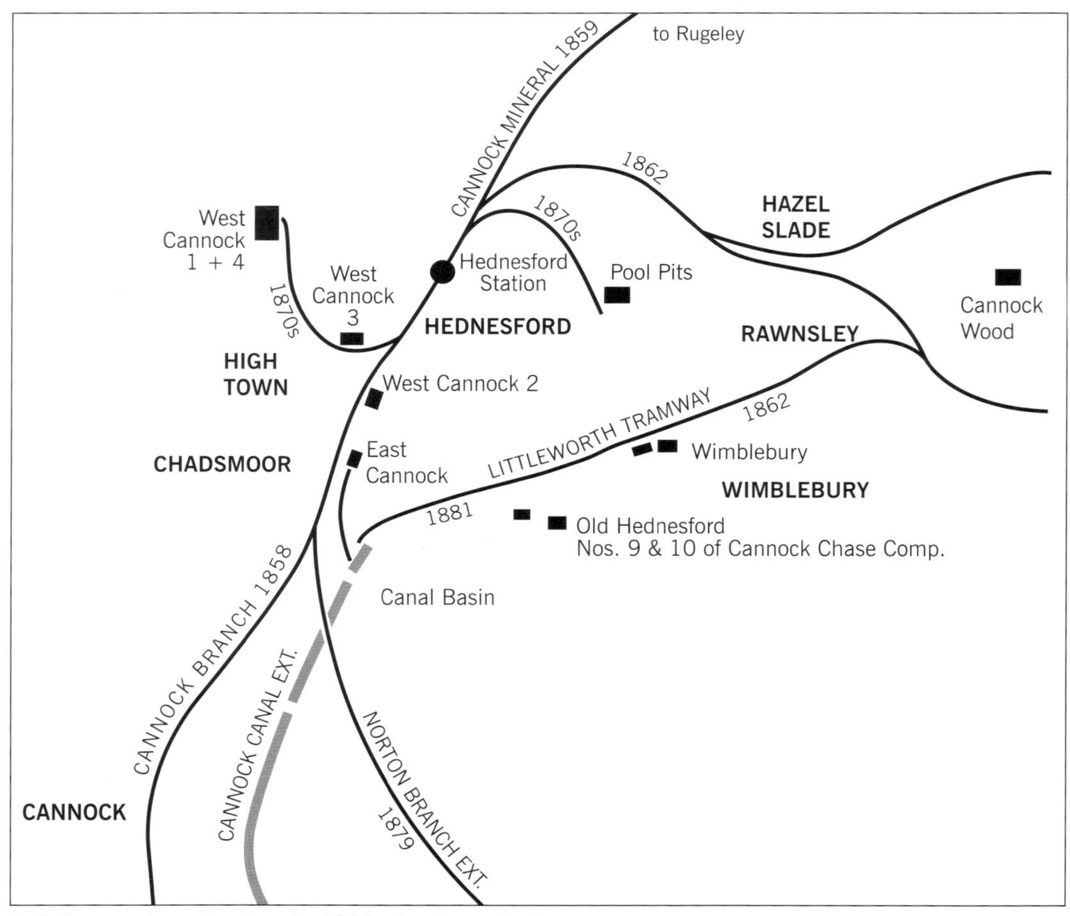

X. Railway and canal system by 1880, showing collieries

Coalfields and their owners were looking for other sources to invest their money.

In 1869 the West Cannock Colliery Company was formed and by the end of that same year it had sunk two mines - No. 1 between today's Green Heath Road and Belt Road and No. 2 between Stafford Lane and the Cannock Road. A third (No. 3 Pit) was to follow around 1870 just opposite High Town and in 1878 they had opened No. 4 just north of No. 1.

By 1870 the East Cannock Colliery Company had been formed and had opened their mine at a cost of £150, 000 where today's Stagborough Estate lies. As already stated William Harrison had bought the mining rights from Piggott in 1870 for the pits close to Splash Lane along with John McClean and by 1872 he had formed the Cannock and Wimblebury Colliery Company separately and had opened up a new mine further up the valley (Wimblebury Pit).

Not content with his holdings in other companies Harrison had also taken part in the formation of the Cannock and Rugeley Colliery Company in 1866 and in 1874 that company had opened the Valley Pit opposite today's park The park was still Hednesford Pool at the time and so the pit was nicknamed Pool Pit. Incidentally it was the opening of that mine which heralded the demise of the Pool. To stop possible flooding of the mine Bentley Brook was diverted and by the 1880's the pool area had started to dry up. By 1900 it was almost nothing but a distant memory.

★The actual history of each of the companies and particular mines has been researched by the Cannock Chase Mining Historical Society and can be read by those wishing a more detailed knowledge of the history. What is of interest is why the colliery companies and their owners took such financial risks in investing their money in the district when all geological surveys before 1870 had suggested that there was little coal below the ground and what was to be found was too deep to be viable for profit.

Their faith in the area was given a large boost by a geological report which came out in December, 1870. Written by Randall, following his survey of the district, he argued that previous Ordnance Maps which had suggested that coal deposits were shallow and any of depth would be under rock formations too expensive to

overcome were wrong. In fact he argued that the ground below was of "loose chips" which could be easily gone through. He also stated the coalfield was far more extensive than had been previously thought - "the great slice leased by the Marquis of Anglesey to the new company of the West Cannock Colliery, who have just gone down through the first three workable coals with their new shafts, was, we believe, not less than 2,600 acres: and the noble Marquis, as well as Lord Hatherton, has plenty more of equally promising ground".

His report continued, "I will conclude by saying I believe the coals all over the Chase, and much of the adjoining district, lie nearer the surface than has been imagined; that the present arbitrary drawn boundary lines of the field are fallacious; and that we may fully expect to see this rich mineral field developed far beyond them in the direction of Rugeley and Stafford. I confidently look for a lower series even of coal to be found than has hitherto rewarded the researches of coal proprietors in this prosperous and highly productive district."

Finally his report adds, "I am of the opinion that ere long a busy population will be found undermining the surface in search of valuable minerals, which far outweigh in value that which any cultivation of the surface can give."

With such a glowing report who could resist investing their money in the new coalfield and who could resist coming to the area in search of work? Few could and soon Hednesford must have resembled one of those notorious gold-rush towns of the Wild West.

6 The Wooton family whose daughter was head of West Hill Girls School. The Wootons had been in the area for many years.

During the first fifteen years of the mining companies there was an explosion in the population. The 1871 Census reported 1,948 people in Hednesford and district (1,081 men and 867 women) – almost quadrupling the population of the 1861 Census. By 1881 it had risen to 6,781 people making their homes in the bustling new town and villages (3,668 men and 3,113 women). The vast proportion of these worked in the mines as can be seen below.

1851	5 miners
1861	36 miners 4 banksmen 2 engineers
1871	249 miners 6 banksmen 4 engineers 9 sundry occupations
1881	1891 involved in mining (over 50% of the total male population)

8 The Denny family - Mary Denny, who was Mary Blewitt, with daughter Gerty and son William.

7 The Drinkwater family. William on the right middle was a miner all his working life.

9 Len Denny with daughters Agnes Morris and Gerty. Pictured at Tackeroo c.1913.

A study of the new streets that had suddenly appeared by 1881 gives an even clearer indication of how many miners there actually were and how many owed their livelihood to coal mining. Husbands, wives and children were all in some way involved in mining.

For example:-
Green Heath area 193 miners
Cannock Road 29 miners
Mount Street 134 miners
High Town 76 miners
Station Road 112 miners

New Street 67 miners
McGhie Street 42 miners
Pie Green 20 miners
West Hill 20 miners
Huntington Road 11 miners
Queen Street 11 miners
Bradbury Lane/West Cannock Colliery Buildings 103 miners.

*Most of these men would have worked for the West Cannock Company in one of their four mines.

A study of the remainder of Hednesford and surrounding villages shows a similar pattern of development. Heathy Leasows, a farm at the top of the hill, had by 1871 become a new village called Rawnsley with 47 occupied houses shared by 193 people, 73 of them miners. Wimblebury, which had just been Dean's farm, in 1871 had 124 houses with 707 occupants, of which 160 men were employed in the mines.

The area around Church Hill, Littleworth, Rawnsley and Wimblebury generally fed the Cannock and Rugeley Colliery Company and the Wimblebury Colliery Company with their workers, while the East Cannock Colliery Company usually took its workforce from "Old Hednesford" itself and the Stafford Lane area. (Obviously men moved from pit to pit, but they were usually very loyal to their own area and mine.)

All of this sudden migration into the district meant that the town suddenly expanded and it was around that time that the expression "Old Hednesford" came into being, referring to the original village. What in 1850 had been a small hamlet expanded beyond anyone's dreams (or nightmares depending on your perspective). Houses sprang up in all directions, some of them built by the mining companies, especially the Cannock and Rugeley Company who had almost 100 homes constructed for their workers by 1890. West Cannock followed suit, but not so profusely. The vast majority were built by private landlords. Some of them still exist today, the oldest probably being Furze Terrace in Mount Street built in 1870, closely followed by those in Church Hill and Uxbridge Street (Buxton Buildings built in 1875.)

11 Furze Terrace, Mount Street, built in 1870

Those terraced houses were built in blocks of threes, fours or fives and were comfortable dwellings for the new workforce, considering what they had probably left behind. The pattern was always the same (probably for speed of erection and cost). They had three downstairs rooms - the living room, parlour and kitchen - with a central staircase leading to three bedrooms, though the small bedroom over the kitchen was only reached by going through the other bedroom. The toilet was outside, sometimes needing a walk down the garden. One real asset for the miners was the ample garden space which most contained, a chance for relaxation and fresh air for those below ground all day or night, though the fresh air might be soured by the cesspit (a sewer situated in the gardens which collected waste from a row of houses).

Interestingly those houses still standing today are regarded as good starter homes, a testimony to the quality of the construction, despite what the Reverend Bullivant had to say at the time when he complained that Simcox, the builder had erected "common collier's cottages"

10 "Old Hedgeford" down by the Cross Keys, c.1910

opposite his church. The Artisan's Dwellings Act of 1875 insisted that set standards were laid down for new homes and so private landlords who had not met those standards soon had to make good their properties or sell them to miners who would improve them. Adverts in the *Cannock Advertiser* frequently show private houses like these for sale.

For example in 1878 the following advert appeared:- "To be sold, 6 dwellings with good gardens and necessary outbuildings on Church Hill. Annual rent £75 (that was for all 6 houses)." These were no doubt some of the cottages Reverend Bullivant so despised.

12 Last remaining terraced house on Church Hill, just above Blagg's shop c. 1980. Built in the 1870's.

And in 1886:- "For sale 4 superior houses situated at Pye Green with large gardens, pigstyes and a separate brewhouse to each with a good supply of water. Low rentals for three of £18 4s per year, the other is empty." Incidentally the tenants of the three occupied houses were William Warrender, Michael Bromley and Thomas Bond. It was not clear if any of them bought their rented house.

Such was the need for new housing that many workers, especially the young men unable to afford their own home immediately, found themselves in lodgings. In 1851 there was only one lodger in the area, by 1861 there were 4, by 1871 that figure had grown to 130 and by 1881 there were over 300. Most of these centred around the Rawnsley, Wimblebury and High Town districts as they grew the most rapidly; in fact before 1870 those districts barely existed at all. The reason why housing could develop so quickly was because of the large amount of land that the Marquis of Anglesey and the Williams family were ready to lease out.

A look at several properties in the area amply shows the problem.

Wimblebury

Richard Weston	Head of house	Aged 63 Coal Miner
Sarah Weston	Wife	65
Delilah Emery	Servant	21
Humphrey Slufess?	Orphan	5
John Stephens	Lodger(widower)	70 Coal Miner
William Blakwell	Lodger	28 Coal Miner
Samuel Boucher	Lodger	20 Coal Miner
Benjamin Clayton	Lodger(married)	37 Coal Miner

That was not unusual for 1871. In many cases whole families had to share homes. By 1881 matters had not got any better as can be seen from the following two households in High Town.

William Jackson	Boarder	24	Coal Miner
Charles Jackson	Boarder	22	Coal Miner
Thomas Jackson	Visitor	26	Coal Miner
James Smith	Visitor	23	Coal Miner
Jesse Smith	Visitor	20	Coal Miner
Henry James	Boarder	29	Coal Miner
Joseph Mason	Boarder	21	Coal Miner

★Must have been quite a household with seven single men living together. Good job there was no noise abatement legislation in those days! But they were not so overcrowded as the house next door, where they had the added inconvenience of both sexes.

John Kempson	Head	53	Labourer
Elizabeth Kempson	Wife	40	
Mary Jane Anslow	Daughter	18	
William Anslow	Son-in-law	23	Labourer
Sharlotte Kempson	Daughter	15	

James Kempson	Son	13	
Elizabeth Kempson	Daughter	5	
Lucy Kempson	Daughter	2	
Thomas Evens	Boarder	32	Labourer
Patrick Ryland	Boarder	29	Labourer
John Moor	Boarder	49	Labourer

★ Even in crowded houses lodgers were often taken in to help pay the rent, but heavens knows where they all slept as those houses were the cottage variety already described.

The situation had not improved much in later years as can be seen from a meeting held in May, 1891 in Mr. Keeling's Field in Bradbury Lane. Between 200 and 300 people assembled to object to the Council's proposal to eject families who shared houses and thus only paid one rent. The meeting was addressed by one "Iconoclast", a local spokesman who frequently wrote under that pseudonym in the papers. He said that "seeing houses were so scarce in the district" the Council should not evict anyone. To back up his argument he quoted various areas where "two or three families lived in one house". In the Green Heath district there were about 40 houses containing two or more families; along Station Road there were something like 26 houses with more than one family: while in the vicinity of the Anglesey Hotel there were 12 containing more than one family.

One case in particular that he quoted was a "two-roomed house, one up and one down, and there were nine in the family – two married couples and the rest, with the exception of the old "granddad", were grown up young men".

That impromptu meeting closed with the crowd voting that the Council should be condemned for applying ejectment orders when it knew that "there were not sufficient houses in the area to supply the demand" and the Council "should give the housing of people their due consideration".

The demand for new housing led to the expansion of specialised tradesmen in the area.

XI. Hednesford Town Centre 1886

13 Webster's Butchers Shop, Hednesford, c.1920

The 1871 Census listed 20 carpenters, 4 plumbers, 23 bricklayers, 2 plasterers and a painter while there were 19 brickmakers, 2 tile makers and 3 sawyers. The Cannock and Wimblebury Colliery Company had taken the opportunity to open a brick and tile manufacturing company just below their mine by 1881 and that was to remain open and producing in Hednesford until the 1970's.

Further industries followed with another brickworks off Mount Street and Station Road, near where the pool is today, and Cannock Chase Iron Foundry opened between the railway line and the Rugeley Road, owned and run by Francis Dickson Bumsted, later to become Bestmore Tool Company. Today a car sales and skip hire firm occupy the site. Midland Railway Carriage & Wagon Company also opened a works making and repairing carriages.

With the massive rise in the population there was the obvious need to feed and clothe them and businesses flocked to the area, setting up their shops in Station Street (now Market Street). It was the obvious site as it neatly sat between the two populated areas of the growing town and because it was close to the railway for transport of goods. Other traders, who mainly sold food and alcohol, opened up their shops in

14 The Queen's Arms was built in 1866.

streets where people lived, hence the growth of the "corner" stores. (As a lad in the 1940's I can remember 9 such shops in Mount Street alone.)

By 1881 there were 25 grocers, 12 butchers, 10 fruiterers, 3 bakers and confectioners, 2 fishmongers and 2 tea dealers feeding the town; while 14 tailors, 12 boot and shoemakers (one making clogs), 2 watchmakers and 3 hairdressers looked after their appearance. For household goods there were 2 furniture shops, 5 drapers and 2 ironmongers. Besides these there were many other traders dealing in anything from fancy goods to picture frame making as well as the workers' Friday night friend – the pawnbroker.

Almost at the centre of these was the Market

Hall which was opened in 1872 for any traders who could not afford the rent on a permanent property or were awaiting a premises, which usually included a home at the rear of the shop. The Market Hall was to remain a feature of Hednesford until the 1960's.

Finally let's not forget the workers' other friends – the beer retailers and the tobacconists. Apart from the Cross Keys, owned by John Knight in 1881, many other public houses sprang up in the district. First was the Queen's Arms in 1866, run by William Winterburn, followed by the King's Arms in King Street, run by John Dean and the Plough and Harrow at Hill Top, run by his brother. (They had sold their farm at Wimblebury and moved into the alcohol trade.)

In Mount Street there was the West Cannock Inn run by Samuel Robinson, opened in 1870, and what was later to become the Globe Inn near the Hednesford Wharf run by Thomas Brindley. In 1870 the Uxbridge Arms at the end of Market Street was opened and run by William Ormson. By 1881 Wimblebury had the Lamb and Flag run by Richard Mason and the Miners' Arms run by Michael Ward. Littleworth and Rawnsley had the Trafalgar Inn run by Thomas Harris and the Littleworth Castle, a spirit merchants under the management of Richard Owen. There were also many "off licences" in the streets which also sold beer and spirits.

15 As it was a few years ago before the alterations.

Alongside these developments there was an obvious need to be part of the wider world, something quite new in Hednesford's history. That commercial growth really began when the Post Office opened its first branch in Station Street in 1862 with John Martin as the first postmaster. One of Hednesford's stalwarts, he had been a wheelwright in the 1850's. By 1870 there were two deliveries and dispatches a day, plus a wall box on Station Road which also dispatched letters twice daily, once at 10.10 a.m. and the other at 7.20 p.m. Other offices and boxes soon followed and by 1900 every village had at least one post office. Pity that today's Royal Mail deems most of them unnecessary!

The banking world was soon to follow suit with Lloyd's and the Staffordshire Joint Stock Bank starting sub-branches in the 1870's which opened six days a week.

16 A Sunday School Rally outside the Anglesey Hotel in 1911.

The town and surrounding area was growing in other ways. Shopkeepers had readily seen to the physical needs of the population and then the church began to meet its spiritual needs. Prior to 1860 there had been no church in Hednesford, but in May, 1864 a congregation began to meet in the newly opened schoolrooms on Church Hill. In 1868 St. Peter's was complete and the Reverend Pauli moved in as the first permanent vicar. Whatever their other failings miners in general were devout people, probably because of the ever present possibility of death in the mines, and so the following years saw chapels and churches springing up all over the district. Besides St. Peter's Church there were no less than 20 chapels, churches or missions built (including those three at Hazel Slade).

Such was the rapid spread of the church that in 1871 Hednesford became a parish in its own right with St. Peter's as the "mother" church. More of that in the chapter on the various churches.

Possibly the most unusual mission was the one at Canal Wharf. The 1871 Census records no less than 56 people living at Hednesford Canal

17 Hednesford Canal, c.1920

Basin on 18 boats and by 1881 that number had grown to 21 boats. Obviously their life was transitory, but there would always be a considerable number of people at the basin at one time. A newspaper report of the time stated:- At Hednesford alone, from April 16th, 1883 to the 21st - not by any means the busiest time of the year - 88 cabins boats, having on board no less than 227 people, passed the toll office".

Gradually housing developed around the area to meet the needs of those families, including Moss's Row and Moss Buildings along the Old Hednesford Road. (John Moss was the farmer who owned the land around White's Hill, where today's Walnut Hill and Mosswood Estate now stand, but in the nineteenth century his land was regarded as part of Hednesford.) Because of the growing nature of the site Thomas Brindley set up his beerhouse there which eventually became the Globe Inn.

The inn could not satisfy the needs of the boatmen and their families "for whose social, moral and spiritual welfare little had been done in that district", especially in the cold winter months. They wanted somewhere warm to retire to from their boats and so in 1883 a meeting proposed the building of a mission at the Wharf at an estimated cost of £1,000. It would offer the people "a suitable coffee and reading room, well supplied with local papers - where men and their wives may spend an enjoyable evening". Also the building would include "a comfortable Mission and schoolroom, where our friends may hear of Heaven and learn the Way". But there would be "no stiffness about the service conducted in the place, but the Gospel of Our Lord and Saviour Jesus Christ will be preached in language which everybody may understand".

Such was the zeal and enthusiasm of the boatmen and their families that by July, 4th, 1885 it was actually opened at a cost of £600 with Mr. P. Worrall as the first Christian Missionary. Friends of the Boatsman's Hall, Worcester Wharf, Birmingham had raised £300 of the necessary money and Messrs. Williams gave the land at a nominal rent.

18 Canal Boatman's Mission, c. 1910

The town's children were soon to be catered for also. In 1870 the Government had passed the first on a series of Education Acts which were to make education compulsory and with the area only recently developed it was relatively easy to select sites for schools (probably much to the dislike of the children). Church Hill already had the beginnings of its school in 1864 and West Hill Boys and Girls (separate buildings) were opened in 1875 and the Infants in 1882.

A small school was opened in Rawnsley in the 1870's for both sexes and one at Hazel Slade in 1884. Wimblebury had its school by 1890 and St. Joseph's Catholic School (all age) by 1898. Most of these schools still stand today, save for Wimblebury and Rawnsley whose children were sent to the surrounding remaining schools.

The School's Report by the Board of Guardians on the 25th October, 1884 had a glowing optimism over the new schools. West Hill had 268 boys and 203 girls on the roll with the Infants having 191; Rawnsley Mixed had 157 children and High Town Mixed had 89. Interesting to note that those numbers altered from day to day as absenteeism was frequent and reasons varied and unusual. But more will be said of that in the chapter on schools.

Hednesford saw other developments as well. In 1872 the Hednesford Gas Company was formed and the building was located at the end of Victoria Street (originally called Gas Home Road), just opposite today's Park. It was run by Alfred Myatt who had brought his family to Hednesford from Bath in Somerset. By 1873 there was gas street lighting for most of the town centre. Towards the end of the decade the Reservoir was constructed on Hednesford Hills with Thomas Marshall as it keeper, living in Reservoir House. Its task was to stop parts of the town flooding in heavy rains while possibly supplying water to some of the homes.

Entertainment was not forgotten either. Not everyone wished to frequent the many public houses, especially the women, and so in 1876 the Public Rooms were opened along the Rugeley Road. It would offer various types of entertainment ranging from concerts to readings catering for the more aesthetically minded. For those interested in sport there was football and cricket and many local teams were started to play friendlies on Saturday afternoons after work. The Anglesey Recreation Ground at the back of the hotel was opened in October, 1881 for just such sport.

Other hobbies that the miners brought with them were also catered for. Gardening clubs and fishing clubs flourished as did pigeon flying and whippet racing. In 1894 the Drill Hall opened where the Hednesford Volunteers, formed in 1882, could practise. It too acted as another venue for entertainment as did the many churches and chapels. More detail can be found in the chapter on Sport and Leisure.

Quite obviously the town resembled nothing like what it had been in 1850, but precisely where had all these people arrived from? Another look at the 1871 Census, involving purely the miners, the men that is, reveals that they came from all over the British Isles, though mainly from the Midland Counties. Perhaps your relatives were among those who arrived?

Besides these men 2 were from both Wiltshire and Yorkshire and one each from Lancashire, Kent, Surrey, Essex, Oxfordshire, Somerset, Herefordshire, Buckinghamshire and Middlesex. There was even one miner from Guernsey.

Such was the spread of the town that at a meeting on June 13th, 1894 there had been a proposal that Hednesford, including Rawnsley, Wimblebury, Pye Green, Chadsmoor (including High Town) and Cannock Wood, should separate from Cannock and become a District Council in its own right. Under the new Local Government Act, which would abolish the local Boards, it had the chance to put its case forward. Mr. Cole told the meeting that he thought that they had "had Cannock rule long enough", while Mr. Joseph Baker thought that if they supplied the Local Board with the money, which they had in huge amounts, then they ought to control their own finances – "they paid the piper and they ought to pick the tune" whereas in the past "they had paid the piper and someone else had picked the tune".

Councillor Stanley told the meeting that as Hednesford held the majority on the Local Board he saw no reason why they should not have their own new District Council and he would "lay himself on their altar to work in that direction which they thought best".

Strange that we are still discussing those same issues today! Even stranger was the position of Hazel Slade. Though counted within the Parish of Brereton at the time, geographically it was closer to Hednesford and most of the people worked in the Rawnsley and Wimblebury area. It would not become part of the Cannock administrative area until the twentieth century.

With all the expansion in the area there was one facility which was lacking –a hospital – especially when the dangers in the mines produced so many injuries. When the miners or any other men were injured they had to face the long and harsh journey to Wolverhampton. Dr. Stead, who had arrived in the town in 1883, witnessed a steady stream of his patients literally being "carted" off to hospital. In fact in his first five years of practice he had attended some 2,000 cases of employed men out of a possible total workforce of 3,500. He had tried to raise interest in the idea of a local hospital, but with little success. However, a meeting in May, 1888,

South Staffs	169	Leicestershire	13
Lincolnshire	4	Staffordshire	74
Wales	10	Northamptonshire	4
Shropshire	63	Ireland	9
Cheshire	3	Warwickshire	32
Worcestershire	9	Bedfordshire	3
Gloucestershire	19	Derbyshire	9

chaired by the Reverend Grier, decided to set up a fund to create one.

By January, 1896 sufficient money, donated by the miners and local tradesmen, had been collected to look to renting out one of the houses in Hednesford. The choice was between Mount Pleasant in Uxbridge Street and Ford House in Littleworth. Eventually it was settled that Ford House should be the site and Mr. Richard Owen, the owner, agreed to let it to the committee at £35 per year, with the possible option of buying it at a later date. That meeting also proposed that the town's workforce should pay 1d a fortnight with boys paying a half penny.

19 Hednesford Accident Home, formerly Ford House.

The Accident Home was opened in 1897 to cater for the less serious cases and employed a nurse and one assistant. By February, 1898 the Home had had 36 cases (it only had three beds at first), 31 of whom had been discharged, 2 had unfortunately died and 3 still remained there. Also those nurses had made 1,253 home visits to 128 cases. Financially it was secure as the balance sheet below shows.

1898

Income

Cannock & Rugeley Colliery	£181 3s 8d
West Cannock Colliery	£ 97 3s 7d
Old Hednesford Pit	£ 25 3s 5d
East Cannock Colliery	£13 15s 2d
Hednesford Foundry	£13 2s 9d
Tileries	£ 4 16s 2d
Subscriptions	£198 16s 11d
Total	**£559 1s 8d**

Expenditure

Furniture	£33 13s 10d
Nursing & General Exp.	£285 13s 5d
Total	**£319 7s 3d**

★Reckoning up is done in old money.

Because the balance was so healthy and looked as though it would remain so for the foreseeable future it was decided to purchase the property outright from Mr. Owen at a cost of £600 – the difference being loaned by the bank.

That hospital would last for well over half a century. For the first six years it was run by Miss Wilkins until Miss Beelestore took over in 1903. In 1907 Miss Anne Blakemore took charge and remained there for 43 years.

So far a very rosy picture has been painted, but progress often has its drawbacks and Hednesford was no exception.

The massive influx of people brought with it the possibility of unemployment as not all men who arrived could find permanent work. At a lecture given by Dr. Stead on August 13th, 1887 he stated that in Hednesford alone there "were over 100 men who were totally unemployed and an even larger number were earning such low wages that it did not amount to one shilling per head per week for the members of the household". The Board of Guardians had instituted relief works with wages varying from 11d per day for a single man to 2s 4d per day for a married man with six children. However, miners were so proud that they "would rather starve" than ask for relief. He suggested that a Relief Fund be set up as "the necessity was only too real".

The sudden growth of the town had brought with it another problem – poor sanitation. Houses and streets had been built so rapidly that an adequate system of sewers had not been properly introduced. Open cesspits were a frequent sight. On February 25th, 1883 an inquest was held into the death of a child in Green Heath due to poor sanitation. In 1884 there were frequent meetings of the Cannock Local Board where the preoccupation of the meeting was the lack of good sewerage in Hednesford, in particular Mount Street and George Street on Church Hill. By 1894 there were still lots of houses where there was only one closet to about five homes and some of those were not guarded from public gaze.

The situation had not drastically improved by the turn of the century and as late as late as 1913 some members of the Council objected to sewers being laid "where there were practically no houses built" and suggested that the situation could be "remedied by the laying of a few drain pipes" which could run into "dumbwells" or cesspits. That was particularly the case for the newly developed Pye Green area which at the time had few houses. At a stormy meeting held at the Anglesey Hotel in June, 1913 Pye Green's case was discussed concerning the "abominable stench" in the area where sewerage was "deposited on waste land opposite the houses". Strangely the Council had installed closets in the new houses, but had neglected to add sewerage pipes.

After a much heated debate the councillors insisted that if work were to be carried out then some of the cost should be met by the residents, "which had been done in the district for years". (Residents of Mount Street and many other streets had received the same answer in the 1880's.)

*Author's note – The first house where I lived in the 1940's over the Common from Heath Street had just such a cesspit which served the five "isolated" homes.

The new workforce brought with them something never experienced in Hednesford before – industrial unrest. The first strains of that began in 1874 when on March 28th miners nationwide decided to strike for better wages and hours of work. It had been the custom to pay the men higher wages in the winter than in the summer for each ton of coal produced, as the trade always took a downward turn in the summer.

For example:-

	Coal per ton	Thick coal wages	Thin coal wages
March 1874	16s 0d	5s 6d	4s 0d
July 1874	16s 0d	4s 6d	3s 3d

However, the men were expected to work just as hard at all times of the year. Also if the trade fell badly the mine owners frequently "laid off" the men for two or three days a week. That meant that families had little income to run the home and pay bills. Hednesford witnessed charity kitchens opened on more than one occasion. What was worse in such a small area as the Cannock Chase Coalfield was that some pit owners "laid off" men while other pits in the district were working full time.

The 1874 strike was to last for sixteen weeks, but much to the dismay and anger of the men the colliery owners forced them back to work with a reduction in wages. The reason for their defeat was that the strike had taken place in the summer months when the owners least felt the hardship of lost production.

By 1880 things had got no better and might even have been worse for the men. At a miners' meeting in the Uxbridge Arms in the January Mr. Southall, the miners' agent, announced that "Cannock Chase Coalfield had been going down since 1877 and reductions in wages had followed until wages had come down to 2s 3d per day for holers. A rise of 3d per day was proposed by the owners, but if coal was selling at 11s per average ton then wages should be at least 2s 9d per day". It would seem that once again dispute was inevitable, but somehow a strike was avoided.

However, another strike did take place in 1886, but with the same result as the 1874 one. In 1888 still worse was to happen. By the summer West Cannock No. 4 Pit was facing the distinct possibility of closure (it probably should never have been opened at all as it was so close to Nos. 1 and 3.) Yet again the trouble was the lack of trade in the summer and the subsequent "laying off" of the men or short time.

Protest meetings were held and even the Reverend Grier, the new vicar of St. Peter's, (Reverend Bullivant had died in October, 1887) spoke out against the "distress in the area which was a periodical, reoccurring at the same time every year". However, as the dispute continued the situation became violent and riots broke out at the pit head. Eventually it was decided to keep the pit open because as winter approached trade once again improved. But it was the first signs that all was not well for the coal mining industry.

In 1893 the problem reared its ugly head again and was to be later called the Great Federation Lockout. Striking miners were locked out of the pits and the coal masters refused to let them near, saying that they could last out until Christmas if needs be – they would not surrender to the workers' demands. The trouble had really begun in 1888 when the miners had received a rise in the region of 40% (the main reason for the idea of closing No. 4 Pit), but that had gradually been eroded due to the drop in colliery profits. In fact they had not paid dividends to shareholders for a couple of years. In some coal producing districts, namely South Wales, Northumberland and the Forest of Dean, miners had actually taken cuts in their wages to safeguard jobs.

At a meeting in the Market Hall, Hednesford in February 1892 miners heard that the Cannock Chase mines were profit-making and dividends to shareholders had risen from 7.5% to 32.5%, but the local miners were still being asked to take a pay cut. Councillor Stanley, agent for the Chase Coalfield, urged the men to take strike action, but acknowledged that "it was a dangerous weapon to use, but employers used the same all the time when they made men play (have time off work) five or six days per fortnight when it suited them to do so. If it was right for the masters to compel men to work, summons them if they did not, or cause them to cease work for a few days just as it was convenient then it was not wrong for the men to cease work if it was in their interest to do so."

Support once again came from the Reverend Grier when he declared that miners were "as important as soldiers" to the welfare of the nation and deserved to be treated well. Discussions between miners and colliery owners continued for another year, but in July, 1893 the strike began. Once again the miners' families suffered badly and once again charity or soup kitchens opened in the town. Charity also came from further afield as the following poem shows.

"Oh friends do show your pity
To us men from Cannock Chase
Who through hunger and starvation
Have to beg from place to place.

There are friendly hearts from Willenhall
West Bromwich and Wednesbury
Who would not turn us from their doors
But supply our wants most free.

★Written by Thomas Thomas, himself a miner, whose family had originated from Cops Maws, Denbyshire, Wales and had moved to Hednesford around 1872. In the 1881 Census he was 25 years old and lived with his parents and 6 brothers and sisters in Green Heath. In that same year he was badly injured at West Cannock No. 1 Pit (see chapter on miners) and possibly never worked in the mines again.

Unfortunately the strike of 1893 was to lead to violence again. On Thursday September 22nd seventeen trucks of slack, purchased by the company for keeping their engines running, were delivered to the West Cannock pits by two engines. Those trucks were stoned and some were supposedly derailed by a group of "unmanly and noisy youths and a few women". Soon a gang of around three hundred gathered in the Huntington Road and the women "gave good evidence of the power of their lungs". Eventually they were calmed down by the appearance of Mr. Stanley and just when all seemed to have gone quiet the "blower" from the West Cannock went "loud and long", indicating that something was wrong. Someone had set fire to a wagon of hay which was attached to a line of empty trucks and "unbraked" the trucks so that they rolled down the rails and crashed off the line.

Whilst causing no real damage, save for the lost trucks, the incident did little to enhance the miners' cause and the local newspapers heartily decried the event saying, "We hope they come to feel as heartily ashamed of the event as we do" and "we hope to do all we can to bring to their senses the real offenders who are the enemies of the miners of Cannock Chase." That event lost the support of the papers and many distinguished people.

Despite all their efforts and sacrifices the strike came to an end on November 25th, 1893 with the miners still having to take a cut in wages.

20 Level crossing near the Cross Keys Inn

One factor the miners could not stop was the possibility of a mine being exhausted and as early as 1881 the owners of the Cannock and Wimblebury Company were facing financial difficulties and offered the pit to the Cannock and Rugeley Company on lease. By the April of that year it was for sale, but it was not bought until 1887 when the mine was virtually exhausted of coal supplies. Rather than close it down it was decided to keep it open and use it to draw coal from the Pool Pits. A tunnel was cut to connect both mines. Technically the mine was saved and the workforce from Wimblebury and Rawnsley did not have to travel further afield to get to work, though quite a number already walked over Hednesford Hills to reach the Pool Pit.

Apart from the coal disputes the area remained a relatively quiet place, only occasionally being interrupted by mishaps. In 1875 Hednesford railway bridge had been built to save the long wait at the level crossing, thus connecting the old and new town. In 1876 the town awoke to a fire at the station and by the time it was extinguished the old station was destroyed. Fortunately the bridge itself was saved and a new station was constructed, that time attached to the bridge itself.

In 1887 at about two o'clock on the afternoon of Sunday, June 11th a serious incident happened at the Reservoir. Without warning part of the embankment collapsed sending thousands of gallons of water cascading down the Common towards the Pool Pits. Luckily it did no damage to the pits, but some of the iron railings around the reservoir were completely destroyed. That relatively minor event left grave doubts as to the future of the reservoir and it was finally abandoned in 1930.

Misfortune struck in other ways. In an effort to bring extraordinary entertainment to the people and liven their humdrum days the world famous Wombwell's Circus was booked. On March 15th, 1892 they set up their tents on the Anglesey Grounds and everyone looked forward the thrilling spectacle. The afternoon performance was so exciting that by the evening the crowds were even larger. Little did they envisage what was to come.

At about fifteen minutes to ten Dallah Montana, an African lion-tamer, climbed up the ladder and entered the cage which contained two bears, one Russian and one American, and one hyena. Unfortunately the ground was frosty and he slipped and fell. No sooner had he hit the ground than the Russian bear attacked him and gripped him by the side. Seeing the attack the hyena leapt into the fray and bit Montana on the head and neck. Almost immediately the second bear joined in the assault and by the time that Montana was rescued it was too late. The animals were destroyed and poor Montana was buried in Burton-upon-Trent on the Friday. The funeral arrangements were made by Mr. Stacey, the local undertaker.

Despite the various setbacks the turn of the century seemed to offer a great deal of optimism. Who on earth could have guessed what was round the corner.

A STEADY GROWTH 1900 AND BEYOND

For the first decade of the twentieth century the prosperity of the area continued to grow. Market Street (the new name for Station Street) was lined with shops on both sides, selling everything the townsfolk could wish for, making sure that trade stayed within the town; in fact it rivalled Cannock for attracting new businesses. Evening entertainment was catered for with the opening of two cinemas and a whole host of clubs and organisations sprang up to occupy the men and women. A stranger to the town would have been pleasantly surprised to see such a bustling and vibrant area.

The once acute problem of housing shortages was gradually being taken care of with the extension of the northern side of Hednesford. Mount Street was extended as was McGhie Street and High Mount Street; Heath Street, Abbey Street and the surrounding Green Heath district was developed; High Town to the south west was being enlarged: while to the east further housing was being constructed in Wimblebury and Rawnsley. In 1899 Cannock and Rugeley Colliery Company had recommended that it build more "cottages" for its workers in Rawnsley and by 1914 it had completed 96. A good number of those still stand today just above the Trafalgar Inn, a testament to their solid construction.

21 Rare picture of Hednesford, c.1910

New landlords were being encouraged into the area in the hope that they might improve existing housing stock, while some occupiers were being encouraged to buy the property. An advert from May, 1900 shows fifteen such houses being offered for sale in Wimblebury. (They were some of the oldest houses in the village.)

"Thirteen freehold cottages, four of which front the main road (John Street) and nine which front Glover Street, together with piggeries, washhouses, stables and outbuildings, now in the occupation of Messrs. Mattheson, Roberts, Ward, Mason and others as weekly tenants with rentals amounting to £110 2s per annum" and "two cottages with large yard, piggeries and outbuildings situated in Glover Street, occupied by Messrs. Witton and Sagar with rentals of £15 12s per annum."

Also in the same sale was The Miners' Arms because its landlord, Michael Ward, had died recently. It comprised of four bedrooms, living room, taproom, parlour bar, a large club room, stable, scullery and outbuildings with a large yard. It was described as a public house with "an excellent trade and situated in an improving neighbourhood".

With such consolidated growth there was a greater need for new public services so that Hednesford did not have to rely on other towns. In January 1912 meetings were held over the possible purchase of the privately owned Gas Company in Victoria Street to guarantee public lighting in Hednesford as well as lighting to many homes. The Council decided that it was too expensive to purchase (a wise decision considering the new advances in electricity), although many homes would still depend on gas lighting for years to come (the author's included).

In the same year discussions took place on the desperate need for a mortuary in the town due to the increasing number if inquests that had to be held after pit tragedies. It was eventually agreed and was certainly up and running by the time of the dreadful Gaskin Murder in 1919 when the unfortunate remains of Elizabeth Gaskin were housed there.

October, 1912 also saw the opening of the New Institute along Anglesey Street by Sir Oliver Lodge, Principal of Birmingham University. Previously the Gas Works buildings had served as the institute for mining. Besides providing a general education for young men it would help in the training of those involved in a trade or profession, particularly mining and engineering. Obviously with mining as the main industry a great emphasis was placed on it and the building contained a model mine in which tests could be carried out to improve safety.

22 Hednesford Institute, much the same today as it was in 1912.

The basement Lodge said, "was the most interesting and, as far as he knew, unique" because it held a collection of "mine testing appliances, aiming at the safety of workers in the industry", including the latest devices for ventilation in the pits. He went on to congratulate Hednesford for its foresight in building such an institute and promised greater links between the university and the town's young men.

By the end of 1912 the area had got what it probably most needed. On December 28th Mr. Joshua Payton was appointed as the resident instructor of the new Mines Rescue Station which would open in the early months of 1913. Somewhat of a legend in the town's history, he was born near Queen's Street, Wolverhampton in the 1860's and like many others had arrived in Hednesford to work in the mines. It was while working at Lea Hall Colliery that he inadvertently became interested in safety issues. As an onsetter it was his job to load the tubs on to the cage and in 1908 he was almost killed when a lump of coal fell down the shaft. Instead it killed his buddy beside him and led Joshua to invent a devise to stop the same thing happening again.

When the Old Hednesford disaster occurred in 1911 he led some of the rescue work and it was there that he came into contact with

Professor Cadman from Birmingham University, a meeting which was to change his life. He persuaded Joshua to run the Rescue Station and helped him with new techniques. At the start of the war he began to train the tunnellers and by 1915, with guidance from Cadman, he had taken the rescue team to Porton Down to train them for gas warfare. When they arrived back in Hednesford he designed a gas chamber for the station and had it built.

23 Mines Rescue men c.1925. Man seated is Mr Payton. Notice the lack of safety helmets.

In later life he helped in the rescue work at the West Cannock disaster of 1933 and in 1939 oversaw part of the operation in the attempt to rescue the 99 men from the ill-fated submarine "Thetis". He died in 1942, but not before training his two sons, Ernest and Albert, to take over. Besides his work with mines rescue he was also Chief of Cannock Fire Brigade for some years. He had been at the forefront of moves to set up Hednesford's own fire station which in 1914 opened on West Hill.

By 1914 Hednesford and district was almost self-sufficient, but there was underlying weakness in its prosperity - everything was based on the continued well-being of the coal industry. So long as that remained strong the area would continue to expand. The old adage of "having all your eggs in one basket" seemed not to be bothering anyone, but cracks were beginning to appear.

Towards the end of the nineteenth century the miners had fought for the eight hour working day and rightly had been successful. During the first decade of the twentieth century they fought for a minimum wage so that families would not continually face the hardships of reduced wages when the summer months arrived. By 1912 matters came to a head and the miners nationally went on strike. Their demands were that there should be set wages for boys and men with various scales depending on the nature of the work and the skill involved, irrespective of the time of year. After a long strike the Government finally conceded and the Minimum Wage Act was passed. However, it did refuse to set a national minimum wage, leaving it to each mining area to sort out it own wage structure.

For the Cannock Chase area it arrived at the following figures:-

Boys 14 last birthday	2s 0d	per day
Boys 15 ..	2s 2d	per day
Boys 16 ..	2s 4d	per day
Boys 17 ..	2s 6d	per day
Boys 18 ..	3s 0d	per day
Boys 19 ..	3s 6d	per day
Boys 20 ..	4s 0d	per day
Boys 21 and until transferred	4s 6d	per day

Increases above those rates were to be governed by the capabilities of each boy.

Dirt fillers and emptiers and other unskilled men	4s 9d	per day.
Datallers and ordinary timberers	5s 4d	per day.
Loaders	5s 6d	per day.
Expert timberers and rock rippers	6s 0d	per day.
Practical workmen in stalls, including holers	6s 3d	per day.
Stallmen	6s 4d	per day.

★If some companies already paid over those rates they were allowed to continue to do so.

The Minimum Wage Act coupled with the Eight Hour working day led some coal masters to wonder if they could continue. The Chase area had another key factor which was making mining very expensive - to keep production at a financially sound level the men were having to travel further and further afield underground.

The eight hour day included that travel. The opening of West Cannock No. 5 Pit along the Rugeley Road in 1914 was seen purely as an attempt to overcome the drop in production in the other pits, but how long would that last? The company already employed around 2,500 men and the new pit was to employ a further 1,000. With it the company also gained an extension of 60 years on the lease.

It may be a gruesome fact, but the First World War solved the coal masters' problem for a while as coal production was stepped up to help industry produce armaments. For its duration the price of coal was kept at a "false" high. After the war production continued at the same level so that by 1921 the industry was experiencing a glut and so prices naturally fell, especially in the summer months. In our own area coal merchants were unwilling to place orders due to their large stocks. Matters got so bad that by October, 1921 the West Cannock Company had to give notice to between 500 and 600 men at their No. 1 Pit. Curiously the slackness in trade only seemed to hit the Hednesford pits whose men were only working three days a week on average, whilst the remainder of the Chase pits were working normally.

Trade did eventually pick up and men were re-employed, but no one could have forecast the Great Depression of 1926. That was to be the final straw for one pit - West Cannock No. 4 which finally closed in 1928. Happily most of its workforce was absorbed into the remaining four mines.

The other pits continued to get by, but nationalisation in 1947 was to see the gradual decline and closure of many. The first to go was West Cannock No. 3 in 1949, but once again most of the 225 men, including 180 underground workers, were redeployed to the other three pits. By 1955 West Cannock No. 2 closed, followed by No. 1 in 1958. The company's workforce could not all be redeployed and so many families who had spent generations in the mines found themselves searching for work elsewhere.

The other mining companies faired no better. East Cannock Company seemed fine in the 1930's under the guidance of the manager, Mr. J. Morris of Cheslyn Hay, and money was actually spent on improving facilities at the mine, including a new canteen for the workers in 1944, the first in the area. However, the end was not far off. In October, 1956 the first stage of closure began with some 100 men being given two weeks' notice. Fortunately most of them found work at the Littleton Colliery in Huntington.

By May, 1957 the pit closed with just 50 men left to carry out the salvage work. Twenty were still working there in December, 1958 when the mine officially closed and in the following year the main 170 foot stack was blown. The site was levelled to await further development (today's Stagborough Estate).

24 East Cannock stack loaded ready to light the wood to bring the stack down, c.1960. The lamp house stands next door.

25 East Cannock and mound just before its demolition, c.1960

26 There she blows

27 East Cannock stack, c.1960. The end.

As for the other mining companies Old Hednesford, owned by Cannock Chase Company, had closed in 1928 and its shafts had been filled in, but the company still worked pits outside our area. Wimblebury lasted one of the longest, finally closing in 1962. The sole remaining pit in the area was West Cannock No. 5, but its days were also numbered.

The end of the nineteenth century had witnessed an explosion in the population, but the first half of the twentieth century saw that diminish to just natural growth. People were no longer flocking to the district, though some did arrive during the First World War to make up for the numbers who had enlisted.

By 1911 Hednesford Parish numbered 11,473, but that had only increased to 11,644 by 1931. As the table below shows, had it not been for Littleworth, Wimblebury and Rawnsley the population may have even fallen.

	Hednesford/ High Town	Little/Wimb/ Rawnsley	Total
1911	5,149	3,849	11,473
1921	5,768	4,381	11,600
1931	5,422	5,366	11,644

*The difference in the figures and totals lies in the fact that Pye Green and other outlying districts were sometimes not counted as within the parish, thus making accurate figures almost impossible.

A word must be added here as to the effect of the First World War. Some 234 young men lost their lives in that dreadful conflict. The vast majority were single or newly married men and so a good percentage of the next generation were obliterated. The consequences for the young women of the parish must have been dire because for the first time in our history the young women outnumbered the young men.

On a happier note, two events happened in the 1930's which unknowingly might have forecast how Hednesford should look to its future. On Monday May 11th, 1931 Hednesford Park was handed over to the Council by the Cannock Chase Miners' Welfare Committee. The money for the park had been raised over the years by

28 Mary Bates who came to Hednesford c.1920. Story has it that "Bobby" Bates. her grandson, met her at the station because she needed protection as her money (gold sovereigns) were sewn into her petticoat. With the money she bought numbers 22 and 24 West Hill Avenue.

placing a levy of one penny per ton on all coal raised in the local mines. By 1930 some £15,000 had been raised and the park could be created. (Incidentally that same committee had raised £3,000 for the Accident Home and a staggering £104,000 for a convalescent home in Weston-Super-Mare for the miners' use.)

Colonel Williamson, chairman of the committee, performed the opening ceremony and declared that he "hoped the ground would be appreciated and be a big success and a blessing to the people of Hednesford". The new park had two bowling greens, eight hard tennis courts, putting greens and a cricket pitch with pavilion and changing facilities. The grounds were laid out with attractive flower borders and various walkways. As users of today's park will see the layout has barely changed.

With the same idea of leisure pursuits in mind the Marquis of Anglesey presented Hednesford Hills to the people in 1933. Sadly in 1909 Beaudesert Hall had caught fire and so much damage was done that, despite attempts to repair it, it was abandoned by the family. Between 1919 and 1930 the Fifth Marquis sold many of his properties in the Chase area and finally the rights to the Hills were transferred.

But the Marquis did not let them go without placing certain conditions on the release. They were for the Chase residents to have "free access to the Hills for walks or anything reasonable and the young people would be allowed to play their games there". That access should be "for all time" and the only proviso laid down was that "it was desired on behalf of the Marquis to make provision for the future enlargement of Hednesford Churchyard". It would be strictly against the bequest for any building to take place on that gift! Those provisos still stand today.

29 Market Street, Hednesford, c.1930

The sale of most of the Marquis' land led to the possibility of redesigning most of the villages which had sprung up around the mines. The late thirties and early forties saw plans drawn up by the Council for major redevelopment, especially in those villages where the housing was considered sub-standard to modern needs. It would mean the inevitable demolishing of the terraced houses and considerable disruption to the communities. Though the end results, which can been seen today, would mean better housing most villagers regretted the loss of their close-knit, friendly neighbourhoods.

One of the first villages to undergo that redevelopment was Wimblebury whose plans were ready by the late 1930's. Comprised originally of just four streets (Piggott, Arthur, Glover and John Street) it was decided to develop the land on the other side of John Street as well and build a new estate. People were moved out of their homes as demolition began and then could move back if they wished as the new houses were complete on the new estate.

Some redevelopment had already begun when most of the houses around The Miners' Arms were demolished. The public house also went later to widen the road. Strangely they were the very houses in the May, 1900 advertisement. Had desired improvements not taken place?

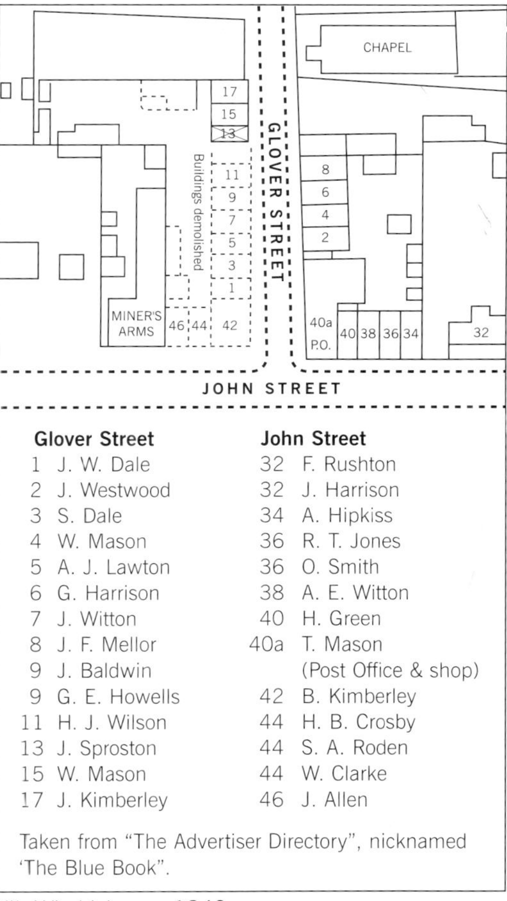

Glover Street		John Street	
1	J. W. Dale	32	F. Rushton
2	J. Westwood	32	J. Harrison
3	S. Dale	34	A. Hipkiss
4	W. Mason	36	R. T. Jones
5	A. J. Lawton	36	O. Smith
6	G. Harrison	38	A. E. Witton
7	J. Witton	40	H. Green
8	J. F. Mellor	40a	T. Mason
9	J. Baldwin		(Post Office & shop)
9	G. E. Howells	42	B. Kimberley
11	H. J. Wilson	44	H. B. Crosby
13	J. Sproston	44	S. A. Roden
15	W. Mason	44	W. Clarke
17	J. Kimberley	46	J. Allen

Taken from "The Advertiser Directory", nicknamed 'The Blue Book'.

XII. Wimblebury c.1940

Denis Gould, who provided much of the local knowledge of the time, was the first to move back into the estate in 1947. He also related many local stories which few but Wimblebury people would know. The village itself was nicknamed "The Holy City" as it had no less than three churches, chapels and missions. St. Paul's Church, which had the school on the same site, stood at the end of Glover Street and was one of the last buildings to be demolished in the 1960's. The Wesleyan Chapel, also in Glover Street, was used as an air raid shelter in the Second World War and opposite was Chapel Yard where Taylor's Bakery started their business delivering bread and cakes with a horse and cart. When the chapel was demolished a pit shaft was discovered underneath which was probably a sample shaft for the original Wimblebury Mine. The remaining religious building was the Pilgrim's Home, a wooden hut at the far end of Glover Street and Arthur Street. It had a sister "home" in Bradford Street, High Town and locals referred to the worshippers as the "Blue Pilgrims". They were strictly tea total.

When the old Wesleyan Chapel was due for demolition funds were raised to have another chapel built just above the Lamb and Flag and foundations were begun. However, those foundations were not strong enough and subsidence ruined the work. What was built was dismantled and was never replaced.

At the end of Glover and Arthur Street stood Nos. 61 and 62 which were the houses of the managers of Hednesford Brick Works. Between them and the Works, where the Wimblebury Club built in 1921 stood, was a pool, known locally as the "Cat and Dog", tragically so named because many unwanted animals were drowned there. The end of the brickworks in the early 1970's saw the demolition of both houses.

Looking down from Cannel Mount, so named because of the type of coal found in the area, and down John Street the first thing a visitor in the 1930's would see on the left hand side of the road would be Clarke's small holding. Mr. Clarke lived in Piggott Street and had a few animals grazing on that land. He also grew crops for his animals and the entrance to his fields can still be seen today just before the turn into Clayhanger Road. Below that was the Lamb and

Flag, owned by Mr. Ashley in 1938, and further down was the Miners' Arms, run by William Wheatley in 1947. It was one of the few pubs in the area to be demolished and never replaced.

At the very bottom of the hill on the left stood The Bungalow which was occupied by George Bates who had been the local policeman for Littleworth. On his retirement he became the watchman and weigh bridge keeper for

31 Frederick Bates, son of P.C. Bates outside "The Bungalow", John Street, Wimblebury, c.1935.

30 Wimblebury from Cannel Mount, c.1930

Wimblebury Pit which was in the valley behind the bungalow. Opposite that was the entrance to Harvey's Farm, the site of the original Wimblebury Farm, and to its side stood a hut for the Bevan Boys who worked in the mine. Going up the hill the Polish refugees had their huts. Almost at the top of the hill was the "Chicken Run" Club, so named because the building was originally a chicken shed before it was purchased in the 1940's. It remained there until the 1970's when it was demolished. At the very top of the hill, opposite the Trafalgar Inn, was the Littleworth Victory Working Mens Club, nicknamed "Bates's".

In the valley was Wimblebury Pit, the sole source of employment for the village men. It had a chequered history right from the start as previously stated, until it closed in 1962. Incidentally it was the opening of that mine which led to the drying up of Riddings Brook which had started its course at the top of Rawnsley and flowed through the valley towards Splash Lane, under the Cross Keys and eventually met Ridings Brook in East Cannock Road. It was over that brook which the famed Heddin had his ford. Close by the pit, during the Second World War, British Timken opened up their factory to produce bearings for war planes and later for Rolls Royce engines. It was taken over by Fafnir in 1960 and after the closure of the mine villagers found work there. Unfortunately it closed in the 1980's.

The reorganisation of Wimblebury in the 1940's and 1950's illustrates what happened throughout the district as other villages followed suit. Pye Green, Brindley Heath, Rawnsley (though not to the same degree) and Hednesford all saw the demolition of most of the terraced housing. Each redevelopment was heralded by an outcry of disapproval from locals who were certain that their beloved community spirit would be destroyed, but perhaps the greatest shout of all came from the inhabitants of Brindley Village.

During the First World War it was decided to build a hospital at Brindley Heath to treat the wounded soldiers and those convalescing as well as any troops that fell ill at the Camps. The wooden buildings, lined with asbestos, were to have 1,000 beds in twelve wards, 208 feet by 20 feet at intervals of 25 feet and connected by a corridor. When the War finished it was taken over by the Ministry of Pensions, still treating troops suffering from shell shock or gas poisoning and had around 600 beds. However, by 1924 the hospital was almost empty and it was decided to sell off the site and the equipment.

32 Brindley Village Hospital Camp, c.1918

West Cannock Colliery Company bought it and began to renovate the huts, gradually moving families of miners in as they refurbished each home. Some of the first families to arrive there were the Baxters at No. 1 on the map inset, the Lowes at No. 4, the Seabridges at No. 8, the Lewis family at No. 2 while the Wainwrights settled in at No. 23 near the entrance to the village; all arrived there by the end of 1924. During the following four years the community grew to 58 families, the take up of the dwellings being as follows:- 1925 - 30 families; 1926 - 6; 1927 - 11; and finally 1928 - 6. So Brindley Village began to flourish.

It was such a close-knit community that was determined to look after itself and so an infants school was started at the rear of the houses in 1925 to save the really young children the journey to the Valley Infants School at Station Road. Despite protests from that school over possible loss of numbers and consequently teachers, the Brindley Village School opened, further enhancing the community spirit.

The miners were not slow to organise their own entertainment either and in the summer of 1926 they opened their own Working Men's Club in the village at the rear of the main block of houses. So successful was it that within the first six months the club had made a good profit of almost £100 and almost £210 in the bank. From those first accounts it is possible to see that the villagers were determined to make a success of their community. The club held social

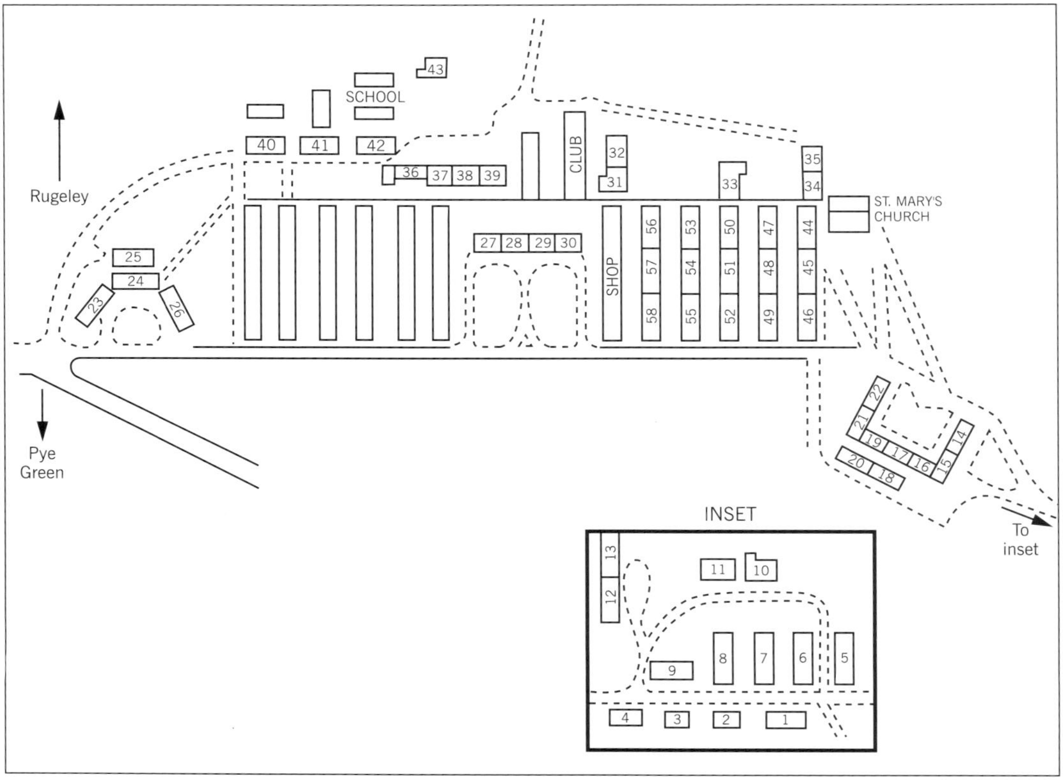

XIII. Brindley Village 1924 - 1955 *(By kind permission of Mr Ken Cavalot)*

33 Brindley Village c.1940

34 St. Mary's, Brindley Village children with Rev. Mellor

evenings where food and entertainment were paramount, including games for the children. At first even a piano was hired for the club, though how it was transported to the village club and back again is not recorded.

The one thing that the villagers did lack at the start was their own shops where everyday provisions could be purchased. However, that was remedied in 1929 when Miss Cantrell opened the first shop in the final ward that was to be converted. She stayed until 1931 when L. Jones took over, followed by Mrs. Shenton in 1935 and finally Mrs. Cox in 1940.

The villagers did not forget their spiritual welfare either because the old hospital chapel was soon converted into St. Mary's Church and eventually they had their own minister in the shape of Reverend Mellor. Once again the villagers were determined to show their individuality and sense of community by setting up a children's altar at the church, the idea being that the children were the future of the village.

For twenty years the village flourished, but the signs began to appear that all was not well, not in the eyes of the villagers, but with the local council who were determined to give the people "better" homes rather than improve those already in existence. (They did not know it then as a council, but the presence of asbestos would have finished the village anyway in the not-too-distant future.) In 1948 the first four dwellings were demolished not to be replaced and by the 1950's news came that the whole village was to disappear. By 1955 the final huts were demolished and the people moved to Erindley Crescent at Brindley Heath. The last building to go ironically was the club, the place which had, more than most, engendered the village spirit.

All that can be seen today of the "lost village" are the odd remnants of tarmac road and the

35 Christmas in Brindley Village.

occasional rhododendron still growing in a long forgotten garden.

A RELIGIOUS NOTE

Throughout Hednesford's early life its inhabitants had relied on St. Luke's Church in Cannock for their spiritual welfare, but with the sudden influx of miners into the surrounding area and the likelihood that even greater numbers would arrive in the near future it became increasingly apparent that new places of worship were needed. So began a period which would see the construction of no less than 18 churches, chapels and missions, not including three at Hazel Slade. To trace the history of every one would need a book solely devoted to that subject and so this chapter concentrates on some of those still in permanent use, but a full list of all the places of worship appears at the end of the chapter.

In 1863 the Second Marquis of Anglesey gave five acres of land at the top of what is now Church Hill to build a school and a church. The school was the first to be completed in 1864 with arrangements to hold religious services there until St. Peter's Church opened. With a stipend of £100 per year, met by the Diocesan Church Extension Society and the Marquis of Anglesey together, the Reverend J. Pauli was installed as the first vicar and he quickly set about raising funds necessary to build the church. Cannock and Rugeley Colliery Company donated £300 towards the building fund and £940 towards an endowment, while Mr. McClean of the Cannock Chase Colliery Company gave £200 towards the endowment plus £100 for the building fund and £150 as a reparation fund. Besides his gift of the land the Marquis also donated £300 towards the building fund.

In April, 1865 the construction began and probably would have been finished much more quickly had it not been for the delays faced with the Enclosure of the Chase (To put it simply

36 St. Peter's Church, c.1940. Notice the graveyard at the side

Enclosure Acts parcelled out the ownership of land and common land. Our Act was passed in 1861, but was not finally ratified until after 1865.) By mid 1868 the church was complete and on September 22nd it was officially consecrated by the Bishop of Lichfield. Such was the desire of the people to have their very own place of worship that on that Tuesday morning the service was "crowded to excess, many being outside the door".

Designed by Mr. Rushfoth of London, it was actually built by Mr. Matthew Anderson of Cannock at a total cost of around £3,000. A description of the church from the *Staffordshire Advertiser* at the time states:-

"The building is of stone." (Donated by the Marquis of Anglesey it came from his quarry at Etching Hill, Rugeley.) "It is in early English style, is plain in parts almost to baldness, but the design is only partially carried out, provision being made for a tower at the west end and the pillars and arches for a north aisle had been built and enclosed with a thin wall which may readily be removed" when the money for the tower was available. "The chancel has a semi-circular design and, having buttresses between the windows, forms outside a very effective feature. There is a

37 St. Peter's Church

south transept for the children and the building will seat 500 people. The inside of the walls as well as the outside is of smoothed stone and the interior effect is everything that could be desired and throughout every part of the building is in harmony and suits the position well."

Within two years of the opening in May, 1870 Hednesford became an ecclesiastical parish in its own right and so baptisms, marriages and deaths no longer had to be registered in Cannock. In fact the first baptism, that of Edward William Degg, had taken place in the school on February 5th, 1865. Dorothy Riley was the first to be buried in the newly consecrated graveyard in 1868, only two days after the ceremony; and on a happier note George Holmes and Annie Butler were the first couple to be entered into the new Parish Marriage Register in 1870.

Throughout the remainder of the century and into the beginning of the twentieth century the beautification of the church continued. In 1872 an organ was added and in the same year the vicarage was completed at a cost of £1,300. Unfortunately Reverend Pauli saw little of its benefits as he was succeeded by the Reverend Bullivant in 1874. In 1876 a stained glass window was placed in the chancel by Margaret Eskrett in honour of her husband, Thomas

38 Grave of Reverend Grier who died in Sept. 1894

Eskrett, one of the first church wardens and a well-known race horse trainer who had passed away on April 25th, 1875.

A description of the church in 1899 says that it "consists of nave, apsidal chancel and transept. There is but one bell, but a very fair organ which has been enlarged and improved" since the original one of 1872. The description also adds, "His Lordship (Marquis of Anglesey) has since given another acre of ground for the purpose of enlarging the burial ground".

On May 18th, 1905 Lady Alexandra Paget laid the foundation stone of the north aisle which was built of Penkridge stone and cost £2,500. It was constructed by Messrs. Davies & Son of Hednesford and completed by 1906. In

39 Inside old St. Peter's Church

1910 a new organ was erected and in 1915 a beautiful oak pulpit was presented by Mr. Ives of Hednesford along with the litany desk, donated by the teachers and scholars of St. Peter's Schools. In May, 1922 the new clergy and choir stalls were added, those of the clergy being canopied.

40 The storm damage of 1931. Thought to be on Churchill

All boded well for the church, but disaster was not far away. The problem lay in the fact that mining areas had a tendency to subsidence, a result of not back filling old tunnels carefully enough. Church Hill was to become particularly prone to subsidence (a fact even modern housing has had to contend with). Shortly after 3 o'clock on Sunday January 9th, 1921 "without the slightest warning the gable end of the church closest to the vicarage fell with a resounding crash on to the footpath below, which is the main thoroughfare to the churchyard" and the cemetery beyond. That collapse rendered the belfry insecure, but fortunately no one was hurt. At the time the cause of the damage was not fully realised, but it cost £800 in repairs and that was merely the start of the difficulties.

By the 1930's subsidence was causing greater concern. Such was the damage in 1934 that "a steel rod, clothed in a rood beam, was placed from wall to wall across the upper portion of the chancel arch". However, by January, 1936 "ominous cracks made their appearance in part of the walls, floor and foundations" affecting the chancel and the transept situated on the south side. At the side of the entrance to the chancel the stone floor had been badly cracked as well as the steps to the sanctuary and its floor. Also the semi-circular wall of the chancel was damaged, the stonework having pulled away from the choir stalls. All of those faults were a repetition of the earlier damage, but on a greater scale.

Reverend Goodin, the then vicar, told reporters of the Cannock Advertiser that "a scheme had been forwarded to the architect" to underpin "that part of the church almost immediately". He also added that "the Vicarage garden was a mess. Running across it was a trough two feet deep in some places. The drive only held up because it was bridged with girders and concrete". He finally said that "they had to face the fact that the property was being very badly damaged by subsidence". That work was done at a cost of some £3,500 and took virtually the whole year to complete.

Further additions were made to the church, namely in 1961 seven panels were inserted in the open-work vestry screen. They were carved emblems representing St. Peter's and its daughter churches. Sadly, all but two of those daughter churches were demolished with just St. Saviour's in High Mount Street and St. Michael's at Rawnsley surviving.

In 1985 the decision was taken to demolish the old church and erect a new building. The final service took place on January 5th, 1986. The new church was consecrated on December

19th, 1987, the service being conducted by the Right Reverend Christopher Mayfield, Bishop of Wolverhampton. It has rafts of concrete to withstand the possibility of further subsidence and the building is mainly of brick with a steel frame. Not to loose sight of the old church some of its features, like pillars, were incorporated into the new building, while at its rear what remains of the old chancel wall still stands.

Methodism had been introduced to the people of Hednesford with the visits of John Wesley in the 1730's, but so small was the population that the idea of building a chapel was out of the question. However, with the arrival of the miners, themselves steeped in chapel going, it was inevitable that chapels would be constructed.

At first they met and held services in their own homes, but eventually eleven members decided that the time was right to start a fund for a chapel and so they set up a subscription list. Once again Cannock and Rugeley Colliery Company came forward with £100 and that was closely followed by West Cannock Colliery Company, also gifting £100. Quickly the fund grew to the point that it was "thought safe to venture on commencing with the erection of a brick building which would accommodate 150 people at a cost of £400". However, to play safe and allow for the increase in costs the plans were slightly modified and a contract for £270 was placed with William Baldwin for a site opposite the railway station along Station Road.

Soon the site was levelled and on Monday May 20th, 1872 the foundation stones were laid by Mr. J Brewer of Walsall and Mr. H. Mills of Bescot. After the ceremony thirty of the new congregation laid the first course of bricks during that evening having donated one sovereign for their own brick. By February of the following year the building was complete and on March 6th, 1873 the official opening ceremony of the Hednesford Wesleyan Chapel took place. So huge was the assembled crowd that the evening service had to be moved to the Market Hall in the town centre as the chapel was not large enough to hold everyone.

By 1880 membership had grown and further accommodation was necessary and so it was decided to build a new schoolroom for the children to hold regular bible classes. Once again subscriptions were sought and in 1881, having raised £200, the land next to the chapel was purchased. By April, 1883 the estimate of £516 was accepted and on June 18th the foundation stones were laid by Mrs. T. Evans and Messrs. G. Steads and A. Baker.

"By three o'clock about 1,000 people had gathered at the rear of the chapel and the splendid band of the Hednesford Volunteers marched upon the ground" and afterwards speeches were given. "In the cavity of one of the foundation stones was placed a bottle containing a copy of the circuit plan, a copy of the Cannock Advertiser and one of the Hednesford Advertiser, together with a circular announcing the day's proceedings. By the kindness of the officers of the Salvation Army the Market Hall was laid out for tea to accommodate 400 people and the Public Rooms along Rugeley Road were also taken." The whole day was considered "the most enthusiastic and most successful ever held in Hednesford in the history of Methodism." The building was fully completed by October, 1883 and opened for use.

41 Station Road, Hednesford c.1920 showing St. John's Chapel on the right

Further additions were made to the inside of the chapel and the outside during the 1880's – orchestra stalls for the choir and a preacher's vestry in 1887 and an external porch erected in the same year. At about the same time an Adult Bible Class was started by Mr. Thomas Evans which he ran until his death in 1893. In 1890 the old organ was replaced and even more extensions were planned. In 1907 the Sunday School Committee offered to be responsible for raising funds for the building of a new room for the Wesley Guild, thus allowing the whole site to cater for the needs of as many of the membership as possible, each having their own rooms.

42 Ladies Sunday School Demonstration on Churchill outside the outdoor beer licence. Bill Haines is the driver. Miss Price and Mrs Garbett at either side and young Harold Haines standing at the side. C.1910

43 Trinity Church, Station Road as it appears today. Little has changed from the original chapel

44 Wesleyan Sunday School Demonstration, c.1920

The advantage of having a site with so many buildings separate to the actual chapel was soon to become obvious when in the First World War the ladies could cook and serve meals to thousands of troops from the Camps on the Chase without disturbing the religious services. In fact it was estimated that during the period they provided such welcome entertainment and food for the men that over a quarter of a million meals were served and over £1,000 was raised for the troops' benefit.

After the war in the 1920's the biggest alterations to the chapel site happened. With the young in mind (today`s youth are tomorrow's stalwarts) the land at the side of the chapel closest to the road was converted into a tennis court. A Guide Company was formed and a hut was purchased from the Rugeley Camp and erected close by purely for the needs of the young congregation. On March 23rd, 1921 a well-equipped Young People's Institute was opened.

The chapel itself underwent renovation, during which time it remained closed. The pulpit and organ, which had originally stood in the centre, were moved to one side creating the chancel with choir stalls at its side. Stained glass windows replaced the old plain ones and electric lighting was installed. All that took time and money, but finally on March 7th, 1927 the refurbished chapel reopened. Those alterations form the layout of the present building.

During the same decade the various strands of Methodism had begun to hold conferences on Methodist Union in the hope that the various groups might eventually amalgamate into one united church. When that happened the local chapels altered their names to show that union. Thus Hednesford Wesleyan Church became St. John's Methodist Chapel, a name it kept until recently when it became Trinity Church. (Around the same time that St. John's began Hednesford Primitive Church along Station Road became Bethedsa Chapel and High Town Methodist Union became High Town Methodist Church. Neither have survived.)

One of the traditions of the Methodist Movement was to show its commitment to religion and the highlight of the calendar was the Sunday School Demonstrations. All the Methodist chapels would congregate in the centre of Hednesford where a service was held and then each chapel would march back to its own place of worship where a garden party would be held. On the May 24th, 1938 St. John's held a bi-centenary service to commemorate the beginnings of Methodism and a celebration rally was held on the Anglesey lawns. All other chapels took part.

The final alterations to the church took place in the 1960's when the tennis court was demolished to make way for a car park which itself was extended after 2000. In 1973 the church held its own centenary celebrations.

Surprisingly what appears to be one of the oldest buildings in Hednesford is actually one of the youngest – that of Our Lady of Lourdes in Uxbridge Street. From the time of Henry VIII Roman Catholicism dwindled in England, but there still seemed to be those who would risk practising the religion. Staffordshire's list of Recusants (those who followed the Papacy) included some Hednesford residents already mentioned, but they were few in number and performed their services in secrecy. Not until religious freedom was granted in the early nineteenth century could they openly worship, but numbers were very small.

However, like other denominations, once the miners had arrived in large numbers it was deemed necessary to establish a church in Hednesford to save them the walk to Cannock's St. Mary's. Whilst the building of the Catholic school of St. Joseph's at Hill Top was in progress one room was set aside for Sunday worship. On Monday August 8th, 1898 the first service was held and the new mission was dedicated to St. Joseph and Philomena.

45 Armistice Day Celebrations at Trinity Church, then St. John's. All present are realtives of P.O.Ws.

By 1907 children baptised in the mission were registered as born in the new parish of Hednesford and by 1911 it had its first priest in Father Boyle. It still had no building of its own, but by 1913 land had been found in Uxbridge Street and by the April negotiations started for its purchase. On a visit to the pilgrimage centre of Lourdes in France in the summer of 1913 Father Boyle made a solemn promise that his new church would be modelled on that in Lourdes and with that in mind he asked the Birmingham architect firm of Harrison's to draw up plans.

47 Cutting the first sod at Our Lady of Lourdes new church. Second from the right is Father Healy, using the spade is Bishop Barratt. C.1927

46 A rare, and damaged, picture of Father Boyle, founder of Our Lady of Lourdes

The War intervened and, although the plans were complete by 1917, it was not until 1919 that the land in Uxbridge was purchased from Mr. P. Williams, who incidentally had sold them the land on which the school stood. When the plot next to it in Uxbridge Street was purchased from Mr. J. Stokes in 1920 the building could start. The parishioners had been without a building since the start of the parish and so in August, 1920 work began on a wooden parochial hall and chapel. Not wishing to waste valuable funds most of the structure came from the German internment camp on the Chase and was constructed by parishioners and skilled men kindly lent by the Cannock and Rugeley Colliery Company. Supervised by Mr. Kenny and Mr. Begley it was finished by the December.

It was at the opening ceremony of that chapel that the new name of Our Lady of Lourdes was adopted. Fate has a way of spoiling things and Father Boyle passed away in April, 1921 with his dream not even started. He was buried in Cannock, but later his remains were transferred to Hednesford.

By June, 1923 the site for the new building was ready, but had to wait until further funds were available (the new priest, Father Healy, wrote all over the world asking for donations). Finally, on August Bank Holiday, 1927 the first sod was cut and excavations began.

Having seen the dangers from subsidence experienced by St. Peter's Church it was decided to make the foundations especially secure and between 1200 and 1300 tons of concrete and 150 tons of mild steel bar reinforcements were used. As an added precaution foundation piers, that were separate from the superstructure and encased in insulating material, were added. That meant that the concrete raft was capable of adjustment by jacks should subsidence occur.

That feature was unique to the British Isles at the time and attracted widespread interest in the architectural world. The *Express & Star* on January 5th, 1933 reported that "during the last few months it has been visited by mining and architectural students from different parts of the country, owing to the unusual nature of the design".

On September 12th, 1928 the foundation stone was laid, but the actual building then stopped to allow everything to settle for almost two years. In 1931 the first stones of the building began to appear and by January, 1933 it was well on the way. By June, 1934 it was virtually ready. Even the frontage that can be seen today was laid out, leading the *Express & Star* to write that "The main approach to the west entrance had been laid out in an elaborate manner. Handsome gateways, extensive areas of slabs, wide tiers of steps and enclosing walls of imitation Cornish granite all contribute to the imposing view". That same month, on June 6th, 1934, the opening ceremony took place with Archbishop Williams leading the ceremonies.

In 1935 the grotto, made from concrete, was finished. It was not until 1957 that the old wooden chapel was demolished, being replaced by the Centenary Hall.

Surprisingly the building is constructed with concrete and faced with white granite, rendered to resemble natural stone. That solved three problems – firstly, funds had not been available to build in brick or local stone; secondly, time had been an essential ingredient; and thirdly, reinforced concrete was thought to be the strongest material against possible subsidence. It was the solidity of the foundations which allowed the architects to incorporate a bell tower of 80 feet surmounted by a spirelet, topped by a gilt crucifix. That tower should have had a clock with 23 carillon and chimes, but it has never been purchased.

Built in cruciform design, above the main entrance in a niche on the west wall is a life-size statue of the Virgin Mary carved from Portland stone. Inside the nave stretches 120 feet and is flanked by vaulted aisles, containing small chapels. The chancel with its aspidal end is probably one of the largest in the country, while the transepts, both north and south, contain further altars made from marble.

The most striking feature of the inside is the main altar. Commissioned for the opening ceremony in 1934 it was delayed while the Sienna marble columns were completed. Above those was erected a canopy of Canadian cedar and mahogany, carved by Bridgeman & Son of Lichfield and costing around £2,000. It was finally finished in 1935. Also on the main altar are three stained glass windows, one presented by

48 The completed building, c.1935

Mrs. T. Davies in 1935 and the other two by the Carney family in the late 1960's. (That altar is not in use today as it was considered too distant from the congregation.)

Though a most imposing building it has not always inspired admiration. Nicholas Pevsner in his book, *The Buildings of England - Staffordshire,* described the building as "amazingly ambitious" and "self-confident", but it was not to his liking. He complained about its "mock 13th century, French style" and the use of concrete. He perhaps forgot that it was supposed to be a copy of the one at Lourdes.

What follows is a list of the other chapels, churches and missions built in the area. Though Hazel Slade is not covered in this book they are also included.

Why so many religious buildings we may be tempted to ask. Miners and their families were always aware of death because of the nature of their work and religion granted some form of solace. Life was not so certain; disaster could be just around the corner as the next two chapters prove.

1850 Methodist Union Chapel – High Town ★
1852 Primitive Methodist Chapel –
      Littleworth (now a timber merchants)
1870 Wesleyan Chapel – Wimblebury ★
1872 Primitive Methodist Chapel – Station
      Road, Hednesford; later the Bethedsa ★
1876 Wesleyan Chapel – Hazel Slade ★
1876 Methodist Chapel – Bradbury Lane,
      Hednesford (now "Ye Olde Birds")
1882 Ebenezer Primitive – Methodist Hazel
      Slade ★

1884 All Saints Church – Hazel Slade ★
1885 Boatmans Mission – Hednesford Canal
      Basin ★
1885 Salvation Army Mission – West Hill,
      Hednesford (dem. 1990. New hall in
      Anglesey Street).
1888 St. Saviour's – High Mount Street,
      Hednesford.
1889 St. Michael's – Rawnsley.
1889 St. Paul's – Wimblebury ★
1889 Brindley Heath Mission ★
1890 Wesleyan Chapel – Hill Street,
      Hednesford.
1892 Wesleyan Mission – Bradbury Lane,
      Hednesford (now a private house)
1894 St. Mark's – Pye Green ★
1899 Congregational Church – Mount Street,
      Hednesford ★
1925 St. Mary's Church – Brindley Village★
1928 Methodist Chapel – Florence Street,
      Hednesford

★Denotes that they no longer exist.

49 The main altar in St. Mary's, Brindley Village

LAMENT FOR THE COLLIERS

"Get up," the caller says, "Get up!"
And in the middle of the night
To earn my babes their bite and sup,
I rise my weary wight.

My flannel dudden donn'd thrice o'er,
I kiss my birds, and then
I, with a whistle, close the door
I ne'er may ope again."

Anon.

Few readers who once had relatives working in the mines would not sympathise with that writer who, despite his loathing of the job, knew that the pit was his only way of keeping his family in food and clothing. Few also would fail to recognise the possible dangers that he would face on a daily basis, never knowing whether that day might be his last. Perhaps many readers, like the author, have stories to tell of disasters or near tragedies which befell their own families, I know that I have. This chapter then is dedicated to some of those men who never came home from their shift.

In October, 1881 a preliminary report from Her Majesty's Commissioners on Mining stated, "The facts detailed by many of the most competent witnesses, and the trustworthy statistics as to the accidents compiled by Her Majesty's Inspectors of Mines, leaves no doubt as to the great amelioration in the safety of mines which has taken place during the last thirty years. On one side, greater attention has been directed to the scientific treatment of the various problems involved in underground operations; on the other, more care and regularity have been exercised generally by the workmen and officials in the daily routine of their work.

If gas be regularly emitted from freshly bared surfaces of the coal it may be dealt with by due and well-understood precautions. The statistics show that a much larger proportion of fatal casualties is due to fall of roof and sides than to any other cause."

50 Valley Pits. Nicknamed "Pool Pits", c.1920. Cannock & Rugeley Colliery Company.

Despite all the precautions taken by the colliery companies and the workforce mining, by its very nature, was still a precarious occupation. The chief dangers, as the report pointed out, were gas and tunnel collapse. The invention of the Davy Lamp had made gas explosions less common, but they still occurred. However, there was little that could be done about roof collapse until hydraulic machinery

51 Miners at work putting trees in

52 West Cannock Colliery No. 3 Pit, c.1930

installed roof supports. In the nineteenth century those timbers, known as "trees", had to be manhandled into position and it little wonder that occasionally they failed.

The following reports of roof collapse and fatalities does not attempt to lay blame on any particular person or company as all local companies had their bad accidents, but merely tries to show the inherent dangers of working in the mines while in some small way honours those that faced those dangers.

In all of those accidents workmates were always ready to try to save their pals and rushed without thinking to the scene of a roof fall. That makes the case of Henry Briscoe particularly tragic. Henry was a tub loader working alongside Henry Teage, a stallman, and Henry Greenway, his "butty" or helper, at West Cannock No. 1 Pit. On the morning of February 15th, 1886 some of the supports or trees started to give way close to where the men were working. As they did so a rock dislodged itself from the roof and hit

Miner	Accident	Company	Date
Joseph Dunning of Chadsmoor	Roof collapse after charge of shot made it unstable.	Pool Pits	June 10th, 1879
John Pritchard	Working in shallow seam when the roof collapsed.	Cannock & Wimblebury	Sept. 4th, 1879
William Brindley	Rock fall at 2.00 a.m. just as he was leaving work.	West Cannock No. 2	Nov. 5th, 1879
Thomas Rowley (aged 21)	Moving a prop when the roof fell.	East Cannock	July 5th, 1880
Andrew Bishop of Hall Court Rd.	Buried alive by a fall of coal. Died later through lung congestion.	East Cannock	Feb. 20th, 1883 June 2nd, 1883
William Smith of High Town	Fall of rock.	West Cannock No. 4	June 28th, 1883
James Gratton	Fall of coal which crushed his head and left thigh.	Pool Pits	Aug. 11th, 1883
Henry Jones	Crushed by a lump of rock about 5 tons. He was prodding the roof to remove rock while fixing new trees.	Pool Pits	Nov. 23rd, 1883

★Taken from just two years newspaper reports it shows how miners daily risked their lives. No doubt a whole book could be dedicated to accidents in the local mines.

Greenway who collapsed under its weight. Without hesitation Briscoe rushed forward to help his mate, but was himself hit by another fall and killed instantly. Ironically Greenway escaped with only a few cuts and bruises.

Roof collapse was not the only hazard in those cramped conditions. At the coal "face" the tunnels could be as low as two or three feet and men were often forced to work without the possibility of standing up, clawing their way through the coal with nothing more than picks. Because of the narrowness of the tunnels there was always the danger of injury and death from the tubs which had to be manoeuvred along the passageways. They were often so close to the tunnel walls that there was barely enough room for the men to avoid collision with them. Injuries caused from glancing blows from the tubs were frequent and death was not uncommon as can be seen from the list below.

case of a death amongst the young workers. Alexander Downes was himself only fourteen when tragedy struck. His main job was working on the screens at West Cannock Colliery, but when he was not required he was often in the habit of "good-naturedly" going to assist the men in moving the wagons to their proper place for loading. At the inquest which followed his death no one could fully explain why his body was discovered lying between two trucks on the morning of June 2nd, 1882. Despite there being few external marks on his body it was obvious that he had been crushed between the buffers of two trucks. What made it more tragic was that his own father was one of those who discovered the corpse.

The inquest held at the Anglesey Hotel recorded "Accidental Death" as was the case with all those men listed above. Strangely, or callously we might think today, Mr. McGhie, the colliery manager, stated at the inquest that the Mines Regulation Act did not require any rules

Miner	Accident	Company	Date
Samuel Rowley (aged 15)	Crushed to death between wagons and tunnel.	East Cannock	April, 1881
Arthur Gent	Horse driver who was run over by the wagons and his leg had to be amputated. He died from the operation.	East Cannock	May 5th, 1881
Thomas Thomas	Horse driver going along the pit "Road" with empty tubs. His horse was startled and a tub fell and crushed him against a load moving in the opposite direction.	West Cannock No.1	Dec. 15th, 1881
James Francis of Green Heath	Dragged 16 yards by his leg which was caught in a tub and hauling rope. Amputation led to death.	Pool Pits	Dec. 4th, 1882
John Smith	Brakesman and shunter who was trapped between the train trucks and wall. He was crushed to death.	Pool Pits	Sept. 5th, 1883
Alfred Brindley (aged 14)	Horse driver who was crushed between a tub and a tree.	West Cannock	Oct. 15th, 1887

Today we would decry the very idea of a fourteen year old working in such dreadful conditions, but unfortunately he was not the only

to be provided for truck loaders, but it was his intention to issue a set of special rules in order to prevent a repetition of such accidents.

53 Miners at work

Fortunately for the Chase area the one disaster that usually plagued coal mining - gas explosions- was not a common event, but when it did occur the consequences could be horrendous with the possibility of many lives lost.

During March 7th and 8th, 1881 gas was discovered near to the working face in West Cannock No. 4 Pit and Mr. McGhie ordered that an extra set of pipes be installed and the men not to be allowed to work until the gas had been cleared. Any shot firing (explosives placed into the coal and lit from the safety lamp) was also banned. The usual test then for any gas present was to take the top from the safety lamp and if none were present the lamp would continue to burn freely. That was ordered and the immediate danger seemed to have passed.

On the night of March 29th George Higginson and Thomas Davis set about their job of charging two holes with compressed powder at the heading or face. John Beard, the fireman, checked them and gave them the tinder to fire the shots. Thomas Davis then fired the shots and all three retired to a safe place. However, as soon as the second shot fired they were all burnt with something which they believed to be powder. All three were able to walk to the pit bottom, congratulating themselves on their lucky escape. Unfortunately days later Davis died.

At the inquest the doctor stated that although Davis had seemingly rallied from the shock of the explosion he had died from congestion of the lungs caused by the burns which he had received during the firing. Higginson told the inquest that he had noticed "blowers of gas" in the head prior to the explosion and thought that Beard had "brushed" or blown away the gas before firing which was the usual practice. He also stated that he had seen gas in a pot hole in the roof nearby about seven hours before the disaster but had told no one.

The coroner, Mr. Morgan, told the jury that if Beard was certain that gas was present at the time of firing he could be charged with manslaughter, but there seemed to be no evidence of that. The jury consequently declared a verdict of "Accidental Death" with the warning to colliery managers that in future only one hole should be fired at a time. Mr. McGhie promised to issue such instructions to his firemen.

If Beard and Higginson were fortunate not to suffer the same fate as Davis then in 1887 men were not so lucky.

During the night shift on September 21st a group of men, namely Joseph Owen, Enoch Owen, Richard Stanley, George Thomas and William Owen, were busy trying to build out a "gob fire" (a fire spontaneously started from the waste products left after mining the coal) in No 1 Stall at West Cannock No. 1 Pit. The usual method was to "stank" the fire or smouldering waste by building up around it a pile of earth and rubble which would stop the flow of oxygen to the smoke. The top was covered with fine dust, about two or three feet deep. Those "gob fires" were a common feature in the mines and not considered dangerous unless gas was detected.

At 10 o'clock the overman, William Guy, checked on the men to see that all was well and, having been assured that it was, he left them at around 10.30 p.m. Tired from their labour the men sat down for a rest, but after ten minutes there was a dreadful explosion and Joseph and Enoch Owen and Richard Stanley were killed by the blast. The other two managed to stagger for help and an immediate investigation began into the cause of the explosion.

At the inquest, held at the Uxbridge Arms, both George Thomas and William Owen were adamant that no one had used matches to light a pipe (strangely miners were known to smoke down the pit even though it was strictly prohibited). Also the two men were positive that no one had attempted to take the top off their lamps.

William Guy testified that he had first known of the "gob fire" at about 9.40 a.m. and had examined the area. Finding no signs of gas or naked flame in the rubble he had decided that it was best to stank out the fire and set the men on doing the job later that night. However, he did inform the inquest that the next morning on examining the men's clothing that was left at the pit he found two pipes and four matches. He did add that he was sure none of the men would have smoked as he had never "found any of the men smoking and did not think the matches in question were taken into the mine for the purpose of being used".

James Williams, the night overman, said that he had examined the waste at 7.00 p.m. On the fatal evening and had found no gas nearby - the

Miner	Accident	Company	Date
John Conway	Run over by tubs and killed.	Cannock Chase No. 9	Dec. 22nd, 1891
Noah Jones	Roof collapsed, caused by a slip in the roof. Crushed bowels causing peritonitis and death.	West Cannock No. 1	Jan. 28th, 1892
James Burns & James Davis	Poisoned by carbonic oxide gas.	East Cannock	April 6th, 1892
John Pointon	Injured himself while lifting a tree alone (his job). Ruptured the pleura which caused death from pneumonia.	West Cannock No. 1	Jan. 2nd, 1894
Isaac Darrall	Fatally burnt in a gas explosion	West Cannock No. 1	Jan. 11th, 1896
Harry Dyke (aged 33)	Pinned to the pit face by an air pipe and suspended by the neck. Death from suffocation.	West Cannock No. 1	May 25th, 1897
George Nicholls (Hill Top)	Roof collapsed pinning his head to the floor.	West Cannock No. 1	Dec. 10th, 1898
Albert Bagnall (aged 18)	Horse driver kicked in the temple by the horse and died.	East Cannock	April 15th, 1899

nearest being over 30 yards away. The final witness was Mr. Scott, Inspector of Mines, and he had not detected gas either. All that he could suggest as a cause was that heated gases did come into contact with the "gob fire" and the explosion occurred. However, he was sure that if "fire damp" or methane were present the explosion would have been far greater. So far as he was concerned no colliery rules had been breached.

In his summing up Mr. Morgan ironically told the hearing that since he had been coroner "fatal accidents in the collieries had marvellously decreased which he attributed to the better management of the collieries". The jury returned a verdict of "Accidental Death" and likewise added that they found "the general conditions of the workings to be very satisfactory".

Despite the optimism of the coroner and jury fatal accidents continued to happen during the 1890's. Listed on the previous page are just a few.

One of the worst disasters to hit our local mines was not caused by a roof fall or explosion, but by an accidental fire. Ironically it happened at the Old Hednesford Colliery near the Cross Keys, the pit with perhaps the best safety record in the district.

Shortly after "snap time", around noon on Thursday, December 14th, 1911, a fire broke out in the bass seam close to the pit head setting fire to nearby tubs. It was later assumed that the fire had started in the lamp house (a timber building) where a quantity of oil was stored for the refilling of the "Shukeys" (oil lamps). Inevitably small quantities were dropped, but a bucket was used to catch these. However, despite that some did fall to the ground. They were usually cleaned up, but the man whose job that was had been off work that day. Unfortunately close by the lamp room were empty tubs whose wheels were heavily greased. The fire, once started, took hold swiftly.

There were 161 men in the mine at the time with 71 of them working in the bass seam. Most got out quickly as the smoke warned of imminent danger, but those working closest to the seat of the fire had the greatest difficulty. They could either risk going past the fire to the shaft or take the long way round, some 600

yards, and risk being overtaken by the deadly fumes. Eleven men, who were working in Two's and Three's Stall, had that dreadful choice. Six of them managed to get past the fire as it raged with one, William Dean, having his head badly singed. Another, W. Tayne, collapsed as he reached the top. The remaining five of the eleven, seeing the extent and savagery of the blaze turned to go the other way, but were overtaken by fumes and perished.

Despite the best efforts of the fire brigades and the rescue teams from Birmingham and Kidsgrove the fire raged throughout the day and it was not until ten o'clock that evening that the firemen seemed to be gaining control. All Friday they attempted to damp down and by the Sunday morning the mine began to clear of smoke and dangerous fumes. Gradually the rescuers came upon the bodies and on the Tuesday they were brought from the pit. William Bradbury (a single man from Wimblebury), Jacob Ward (married from Littleworth), William Baugh (single from Church Hill), William Reeves (married from Heath Hayes) and Tom Stokes (married from Cannock) had all lost their lives.

54 Tom Stokes and his wife. Tom was the hero of Old Hednesford disaster. Postumously awarded the Edward Medal, first class, in April 1912

It was subsequently discovered at the inquest that Tom Stokes had initially managed to escape, but had gone back to help his workmates. He had helped guide men along the return airway to safety and, realising some had been overtaken by fumes about 500 yards from the shaft, had returned to rescue them.

It was because of that tragedy and the time taken for the rescue services to reach the pit that it was decided that Hednesford should have it own rescue services. Two years later the Rescue Station opened in Victoria Street and the following year the fire brigade started.

55 East Cannock Colliery Rescue Brigade c.1925
Joshus Payton second from left on top row,
Ernest Payton is far right

Another two major disasters were to happen during the inter war years. At about 7.20 a.m. on Tuesday June 14th, 1927 the cage with 19 men inside was descending the shaft at Wimblebury Pit, but when it was within a few feet of the bottom it suddenly went out of control and crashed, hurling the men into a shambled heap. Fourteen men were injured, four sustaining fractures of the thigh and one a broken leg. Luckily no one was killed and the casualties were rushed to the Hednesford Accident Home, arriving there within the hour.

Captain Peake, General Manager of the Cannock and Rugeley Collieries, told reporters that in his opinion it was a "pure accident attributed to a mishap with the winding gear". Strangely though the pit had been closed only the week before so that new pit-head gear and more powerful winding engines could be installed. They had been used for the first time on the Monday night shift (those men were still down the pit when the accident happened) and everything was fine.

After the accident the winding gear was examined and proved that nothing was wrong. Whatever caused the accident was never discovered, but one of the men in the cage during the accident, Frank Yates, said, "The cage seemed to catch in something and hang a bit in the shaft. Then it released again and shot forward with great speed". Another, J. Wilding, admitted that he was terrified at the time, but "I will, of course, go down the pit again. It was an accident, and a bit of bad luck. But it's all in the game".

The next disaster happened on May 12th, 1933 at West Cannock No. 5 Pit. At 8.45 a.m. men working at the coal face were suddenly hit by an explosion of fire damp followed by a gust of hot air which raced along the tunnel, burning the men in its path. Within minutes the Hednesford Rescue Station had been informed and as luck would have it they were already kitted out doing a simulated rescue and so arrived at Brindley Heath quickly. Within an hour and a quarter eight injured men had been brought to the surface and rushed to the Accident Home.

However, as the rescue continued dead bodies were discovered. The first was that of Samuel Gwilt which was recovered around one o'clock. Two others were later found, that of Benjamin Cornwall being so badly burned that not even his brother, Jack, who helped to carry out the corpse could recognise him. It was only when the body of Charles Turnock was brought out that Jack realised that the other corpse must be his brother as he was the only man unaccounted for.

The final aftermath revealed that three men had died instantaneously while three others died from their injuries some days later in the Accident Home. They were Joseph and John Williams and William Higgs. Fifteen other men suffered various degrees of burns, but went on to recover. Despite a lengthy investigation the actual cause of the explosion was never detected, but all miners know of the unpredictability of fire damp and the dangers they face daily.

56 Rescuers bring up one of the dead from the West Cannock 5s disaster, 12th May 1933

Dangers were many and few would doubt the courage our ancestors displayed every day as they ventured down the mines. However, there were dangers at the pit top also, but fortunately with few fatalities.

At around three o'clock on the afternoon of April 7th, 1898 at the Cannock and Rugeley Colliery (Pool Pits) Charles Harding climbed aboard the "Beaudersert" engine. Because it had stood aside for some time having repairs done the brakes were stiff and so more lubricant was applied. Finally the train began to push its load of wagons. However, as they went down the incline their speed grew too fast and William Taylor, the brakesman, tried to apply the brakes. He did eventually get some to work but only on one side which served to throw the train to one side, catapulting him from the train.

Fighting to keep the train under control, Harding finally gave up and, along with his stoker, a lad named Charles Moore, jumped from the train. All that they could do was watch as the engine raced towards the main London and North Western Line. Fortunately within a few yards of the main line and opposite the Rugeley Signal Box it hit a number of wagons on the same line. The first simply collapsed "like the closing of a book" while the second was smashed to pieces. The engine itself fell over on the embankment facing the Rugeley Road. Several trucks followed the same fate and were completely wrecked. For once no lives had been lost, but it proved how dangerous mining was even when you did not go down the pit!

57 Colliery locomotive which worked the line between the Cannock & Rugeley Colliery and Hednesford Station

Blame did not always lie with the mining companies and working conditions. At times some miners were their own worst enemy and there are many instances of men being taken to court for breaches of colliery rules.

One Petty Session of the Cannock Court on April 18th, 1885 showed an alarming disregard for those regulations. John Compton was charged by the East Cannock Company with

58 Steam locomotive "Marquis" at the Cross Keys level crossing

taking a tobacco pipe into the pit on March 20th. Whether he intended to use it or not it was still strictly against the rules. Men in the past had actually been caught lighting up in the tunnels despite the possibility of gas and so all forms of smoking had been banned under threat of prosecution. Compton was fined 5s with 10s 6d costs. At the same session John Jones was charged with a similar offence committed on April 1st at the same pit. Knowing that he was in the wrong he had at first denied the offence, but a search of his clothing revealed a pipe. He too was fined 5s with 10s 6d costs.

Again at the same court session Arthur Bradbury was charged with entering the Cannock and Wimblebury Pit on February 14th with a naked light and James Hyde for doing exactly the same on March 9th. Only too aware of the seriousness of the offence, Mr. R.S. Williamson, the colliery manager, pressed both charges and the court fined both men £1 with 10s 6d costs.

Despite those heavy fines (weekly wages were not much more than £1) similar offences were still brought before the Petty Sessions Court. Cannock and Wimblebury Company took Henry Schivers to court for possessing two matches and a pipe down the pit. That pit was considered to contain a "great deal of gas and was worked exclusively with safety lamps". The defendant pleaded partial ignorance as he was unable to read the rules, but he was still fined £2 with 10s 6d costs.

Eventually the men learnt their lesson and instead of carrying tobacco and pipes into the pit (the idea being that a smoke caused coughing which cleared the lungs of filthy dust) most carried "baccy", a stick of raw tobacco rather like liquorice, which they chewed.

Cases did not only involve smoking. In October, 1884 Herbert Armishaw was charged with having his safety lamp within the prescribed two feet of the swing of his pick and thus endangering the lives of his fellow workers. He had actually hit the lamp and pierced it, but delayed taking it to the station to have it changed. He was fined £2, including costs.

Because of the possibility of gas it was necessary to always keep the shafts and tunnels well ventilated and so when men passed through air doors in the return air way it was their duty to close them. Thomas Pearce was fined 10s with 10 6d costs for failing to do so on 12th June, 1886 and John Kelly was fined the same amount for the same offence on 13th June. (Kelly seems to have taken revenge because he reported one Thomas Willis for passing beyond a danger point after a notice had been posted. Willis was fined £1 with 13s costs.)

With the tunnels being narrow in places the dangers from moving tubs was always present, but once again some saw fit to disobey the rules by riding the tubs. In March, 1890 Samuel Higgs was prosecuted for riding the tubs at the "Valley Pit". Once again the manager, Mr. Williamson, asked that the man be made an example of as "boys had been fatally injured whilst riding tubs in the past". Higgs was fined 5s with 11s 6d costs. But that did not deter others and in May, 1890 a lad named Alfred Round was fined 6d with 10s 6d costs for riding on the chains of the tub.

Finally, a lad named William Foden, a horse driver at Cannock and Wimblebury Colliery, was charged with neglecting to place a back-stay behind a tub on April 17th, 1885, thus rendering it unsafe while it was travelling down a steep incline. He was fined 5s and costs, probably a whole week's wages.

59 Canal basin with East Cannock Pit in the background. C.1960

Whatever the cause of mining accidents it cannot be denied that mining was a dangerous life and so it is fitting to end with the writer of the following published in the *Cannock Advertiser* on August 29th, 1891.

The Collier

Only a collier - with horny hands,
His muscles firm and strong;
Who works away in the deep dark pit,
Singing his cheerful song.

He earns his bread through the sweat of brow,
Far, far from the light of day;
Sings as he works - works as he sings,
And he busily toils away.

His Sabbath's a day of holy rest,
From labour and toil he is free;
He sings his praise in the house of God,
A glorious sight to see!

He wears no ring - but he pays his way,
And fears no man to meet;
He can look you firmly in the face,
As he walks along the street.

Oh tell me not, all our heroes great
On the battlefield are found;
For our colliers all are heroes great,
As they work beneath the ground.

There's many a "Gordon" in our pits,
And many a "Stanley" brave;
Who toils for the sake of fellow men,
And works in a hollow cave.

Only a collier - with a grimy face,
Give me the grip of his hand;
The mind is in the standard of Man,
Acknowledged throughout the land.

Only a collier - who knows no pride,
Yet an uncrowned king is he;
He loves his wife - adores his God,
With a conscience clear and free.

Then cheer the colliers with all your might,
In the good old-fashioned way;
For they well deserve your highest praise,
And worthy of better pay.

(Anon)

LEST WE FORGET

The following chapter endeavours to give a flavour of the passion and pride felt by the families and men who fought in the First World War, whilst also showing some of the dread and despair experienced by them and their loved ones. Once again the confines of the book do not allow for all those who gave up their lives to be mentioned in detail, but the Roll of Honour does appear at the end of the chapter.

Our local association with the armed forces began in the 1860's when it was thought that the Chase might make a possible site for an arms arsenal, but it was finally decided by Parliament not to go ahead. However, the value of the site was kept in mind and in 1873 the Army held one of its grand Manoeuvres in the area, based on Hednesford Hills. The headquarters were based on the Hills while two camps, one at Brindley

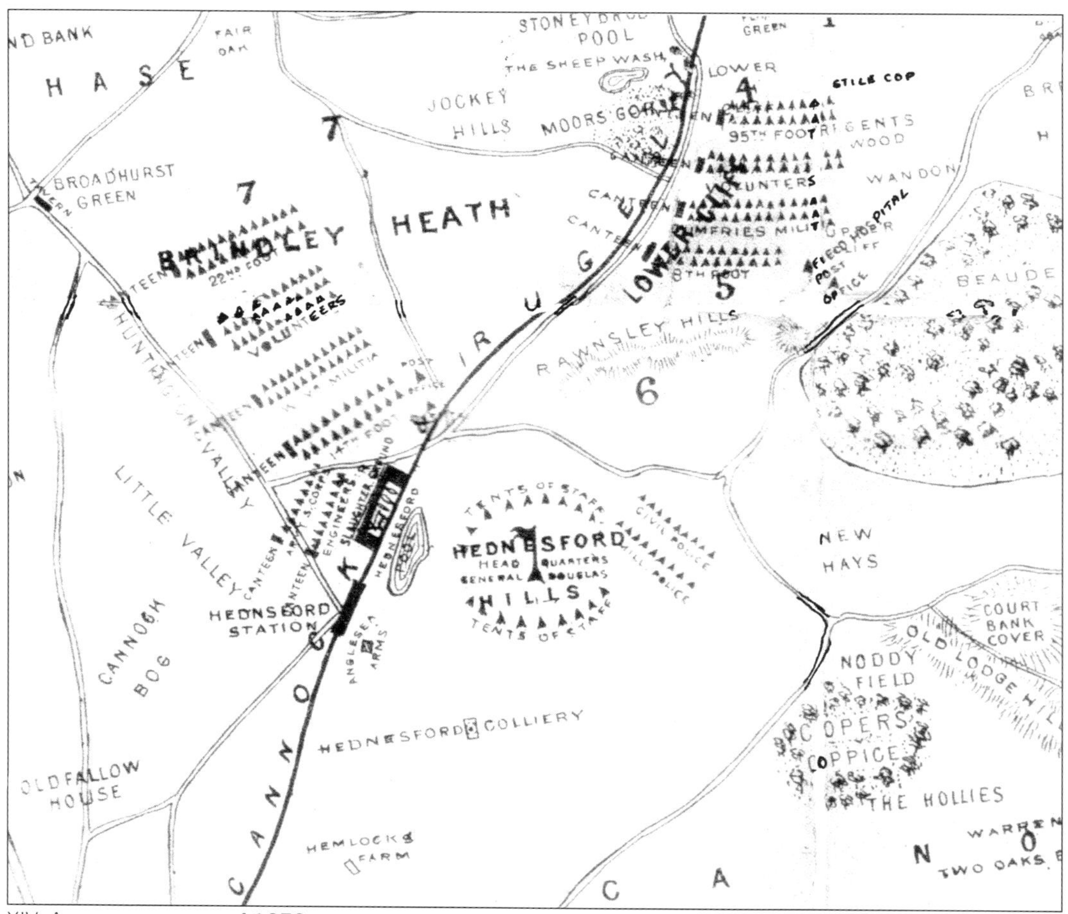

XIV. Army manoeuvres of 1873 *(By kind permission of Stafford Record Office)*

60 Cover of booklet advertising the 1873 Army Manoeuvres on the the Chase

Heath and the other at Etching Hill, played out the exercise.

The exercise must have fired the imaginations of the young men in the area and by 1892 Captain Williamson had set up Company F, a branch of the Staffordshire Volunteer Force. It had one major drawback – the lack of facilities to drill and hold regular meetings, especially in winter months. Undeterred Captain Williamson set about raising sufficient funds to create a permanent home and by July 3rd. 1894 a meeting was held at the Gas Works in Victoria Street where he announced plans to erect a brick hall to accommodate his troops. What probably inspired the locals to act quickly was the fact that another army manoeuvre was held in the area in the summer of 1894, though based more around Teddesley Park.

Land was donated by the Gas Company and building started. By December, 1894 it was complete and the Drill Hall was opened by Mr. Hamar Bass, the local M.P., on December 8th. Funds gathered had not been sufficient to pay for the total cost and some £600 - £700 was still needed, but a bazaar held on that weekend managed to raise over £300 and other donations virtually cleared the debt.

The first troops of F Company, some 116 men, began to use the hall immediately and when it was not in use it was let out for various town functions. No one at the time would realise the advantage of having such a permanent base and Company.

When war broke out in 1914 F Company was being trained by Lieutenant Colonel William Burnett and they were some of the first men to march off to war. Like so many towns and villages throughout England they proudly marched away amidst the cheers of relatives and friends, convinced that they would be home by Christmas having taught the Germans a good lesson.

61 South Staffordshire Regiment at Perham Down 1916

It was that same spirit of patriotism and optimism which led local men to volunteer rapidly. In late August the Drill Hall was a frantic scene of young men eager to fight for their country. Captain Russell, the recruiting officer, was kept busy throughout the weeks issuing warrants and signing up new recruits. 50 young men signed up in one week alone and by the following Monday a further 70 had joined. In fact there was a continual stream of young men and older men who had previously seen service and were anxious to rejoin their regiments.

"In fact I wish I could go with him," exclaimed one enthusiastic lady, in reference to her husband who was leaving to rejoin his old regiment, the Worcesters. While when one miner was asked by a reporter from the *Cannock Advertiser* what regiment he wished to join he responded, "I don't care what it is, anything will do as long as I can have a smack at the Germans!" Ironically that same reporter wrote, "Though cheerful, they fully realise the grimness of the struggle in which they may be called upon to play a part and they are resolved to quit themselves like men."

The newspapers continued to keep up the spirits of those left behind by relaying indomitable cheerfulness from those at the Front and frequently printed letters relating the "good news".

Private Meffen wrote, "We are only about four hundred yards from the German trenches. On New Year's Eve a shrill whistle came from their trenches and a voice shouted over "A Happy New Year to you". One of our Yorkshire fellows replied, "Same to thee". We heard them playing musical instruments and their spokesman shouted "Are we downhearted!" They would have been if they had come over. We are winning and that is the chief point."

Very upbeat considering it was war, but in another letter he writes, "If we took two steps in front of the trenches we should be stuck in the mud" and "If you go to some fresh trenches and think you can have a few hours sleep on some straw got from a hayrick not far away, you find yourself when you wake up trying to equal Captain Webb's feat in the Channel." And Lance Corporal H. Craddock wrote, "I had just come out of the trenches the night before with wet and cold feet and it was nice to get hold of a nice dry pair of socks and also a good scarf" (presents from home).

Those extracts were written in February, 1915 and the true horrors of trench warfare were just beginning to set in. However, so far the Hednesford men had been lucky as their casualties had only been wounded men. All that was soon to change.

Probably the first soldier to die from the

62 Arnold Bishop (South Staffs. Regiment), killed July 1916 at the Somme.

62a Arnold Bishop and his family on the steps of their home in Green Heath, c.1915.

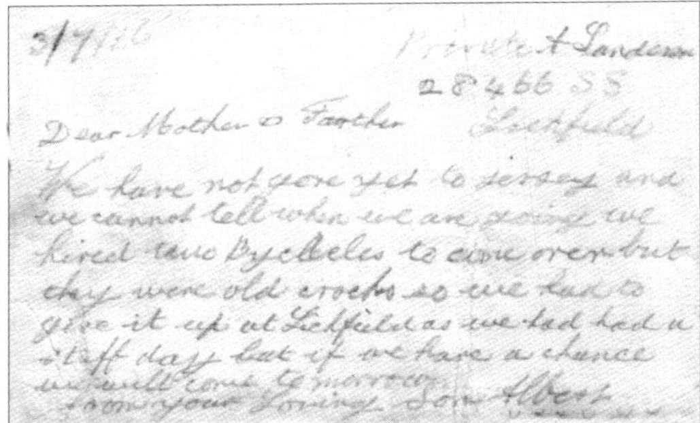
3/7/16
Private A Sanderson
28466 SS
Lichfield

Dear Mother & Father

We have not gone yet to Jersey and we cannot tell when we are going we hired two bycicles to come over but they were old crocks so we had to give it up at Lichfield as we had had a stiff day but if we have a chance we will come tomorrow. From your loving Son Albert

64 Postcard from Albert Sanderson before he left for the front. Sent from Whittington Barracks.

63 Thomas Harper on the left with two unknown pals. Picture taken in France c.1916. They fought in the Battle of the Somme. Thomas survived the war and came back to work at Wimblebury Pit. For a time he lived in "Ghost Row" on Littleworth Road then moved to Rawnsley in 1934. All three were in the South Staffs. Regiment.

65 Private Albert Sanderson taken in Jersey just before going off to the Front in Pate 1916. He died in battle on 23rd April 1917. He served with the 8th Battalion of the South Staffs. Regiment.

Hednesford area was Private Leonard Slade of the Grenadier Guards who had enlisted in August, 1914. So began the dreadful letters from the Front. Mrs. Slade received the sad news at her home in Albert Street, Church Hill in late February, 1915 which read, "It is with deepest regret that I write these few lines to inform you of the death of your son, Leonard, who was killed in action on February 19th by a German shell. I may say that he suffered no pain as death was instantaneous. He had a very nice burial here in a churchyard about half a mile from where he was killed."

Private Slade's death was closely followed by that of Private Alexander Dawes of the North Staffordshire Regiment who lost his life in action at Armentieres on March 12th, 1915. He was a single man who had served three years with the colours and then spent nine years in the reserve. During those reserve days he had lived with his mother at 54 Wood Lane and worked as a miner at Shirebrook when war broke out. He too had enlisted in August, 1914.

The war had finally become personal for Hednesford people, but that did not stop their determination to help their country. Miners had one skill which the army was only too eager to use - their expertise in tunnelling. Mr. Payton, the instructor at the Hednesford Mines Rescue Station, was asked to train a battalion of Headers and Tunnellers from the local mines and by early May, 1915 he had succeeded in training enough men to dispatch 35 of them "straight to where the music is in France". Once again their send-off was enthusiastically cheered away by large crowds at Hednesford Station.

That party consisted of the following:-

Sam Benton	George S. Hickenbottom
David Morris	Jos. Shirley
John Coles	John Hodson
Noel Murray	William Shurety
Henry Corbett	John Thomas Horton
Thomas Newbold	John Slade
*Ernest H. Dando	Thomas Hughes
Chas. Owen	Ben Smith
Chas. Davidson	Richard Jones
Frank Phillips	Joe Smith
Isiah Davies	Reuben Jones
Harry Prince	Thomas Smith
*John Deakin	Samuel Kimber
John W. Ryder	George Whitehouse
George Evans	Joseph Langley
Fred Sheldon	H.W. Wilkinson
John D. Griffiths	John Matthews
Albert Shemwell	

*Of those first tunnellers dispatched only those two men were killed in action.

66 Len Denny c.1915. He was a member of the Royal Engineers and one of the tunnellers in World War One.

With the success of that training Mr. Payton redoubled his efforts and by the end of May, 1915 a second party of 25 men had been dispatched. It was from that second party that the tunnellers had their first fatality. Thomas Archer, a 46 year old father of nine who lived at Brindley Heath, was killed by shrapnel towards the end of June and his wife received the sad news, along with his few possessions, early in July. She must have been distraught because her eldest son, Private Arthur Archer, was serving in the trenches with the South Staffordshire Regiment. Her fears were to be realised later because Arthur also died in action.

Meanwhile the Territorials who had marched off to war in August, 1914 had seemingly faired much better. Despite fighting alongside the Regulars they had not lost a single man. Major Burnett in a letter to a friend, the Reverend Bagnall, says of his troops, "The Hednesford boys are all right. They are in good health and well fed."

A letter from Corporal Pearce from the Front describes their experiences.

"We have been here for four days and nights (in the trenches). This is not for the first time for we had our baptism of fire some time ago. We were sent in with a regular regiment to give us some idea of doing things.

Being under fire for the first time is a queer sensation. Every shot and you think that you're hit. You can hear bullets whistle and scream all round when there is anything like rapid fire being kept up. Shell fire is, of course, the most unnerving of all tests – it is really trying for the first time. The great disadvantage is when they start knocking your parapet about and you have to mend it during the night.

One of our corporals had a lucky escape – it was Billy Pearce (the writer himself). A bullet went in one side of his boot and out the other.

Best wishes from all the boys of F Company."

Printed in the *Cannock Advertiser* on April 17th, 1915 it certainly seemed that the Territorials' spirits were high, but they were to be severely tested in the next few months. On June 6th their luck ran out. Private Dan Seabury was the first Territorial to be killed. He was shot through the shoulder while working in one of the trenches and despite everything they could do for him he died. He was buried in a little graveyard near the headquarters of the battalion where all the Regulars were buried. Two days later Corporal Jack Webster suffered the same fate and was buried alongside Private Seabury.

It was the sad duty of Major Burnett to have to write to the families telling of the losses and they were not the last letters that year. In July Mrs. Dyke of 42 Glover Street, Wimblebury received the dreaded letter informing her that her husband, George, had been killed while on sentry duty. They had been married barely two years and their only child had been born not long after he had left England. In the September Mrs. Oakley of Mount Street was also informed of her husband Samuel's death. She was left to bring up three children.

But perhaps the saddest letter Major Burnett had to write was to Mrs. Stephens of 27 Piggott Street, Wimblebury. Her four sons had enlisted, two of them, Richard (20) and John (23), together in September, 1914. Together they had joined the Territorials and together they had gone to the Front. The other brothers, Harry and James, had joined the Coldstream Guards and Hampshire regiments respectively. On October 13th, 1915 Richard and John were both killed while fighting in the same trench.

But who writes the letter-writer's letter? Lieutenent Colonel Burnett (he had been promoted during the war and put in command of the North Staffordshire Regiment) remained with his beloved Territorials until he paid the ultimate price. On Tuesday July 4th, 1916 news reached Hednesford that he had been dangerously wounded, but on the Wednesday another telegram arrived telling of his passing away. Local "Tommies" who had returned home wounded spoke with pride of his "daring and unconcern" under heavy shellfire and of a commander who led his men "with courage and skill and succoured the wounded at great personal risk".

Despite the loss of men the Government did all that it could to encourage further volunteers and that seemed to include getting those at the Front to write home and chivy up those who had not yet enlisted. An example of one such letter appeared in the *Cannock Advertiser* on January 29th, 1916 and read:-

"There are about thirty Hednesford lads in this battalion and all are doing fine and are "in the pink". Of course we have plenty of water to puddle in, but still I am just as happy as if I were standing at the street corner, and at the same time I have the pleasure of knowing that I am doing my bit.

I think it is a shame that young men, healthy and strong, wont come out and help us to polish these Germans off. We need every man we can get. I have been out here for five months and last week I spent my eighteenth birthday in the trenches with a birthday gift of shrapnel shells from Fritz. Today Fritz has been shelling us for nearly three hours. Our lads, however, send them about three to their one, so you will see that we have a good supply of shells. I hope the slackers will think it over and come and help us to finish this great struggle.

Yours,
Rifleman Jack Porter.
8th Battalion, Kings Royal Rifles."

*Although Jack survived the war he tragically lost his elder brother, Frank, later that year.

67 Private Harold Bailey of the South Staffs. Regiment. He survived the war.

68 Harold Bailey (bottom left) with comrades from the South Staff.s Regiment. Do you recognise any of them? Did they all survive the Great War?

69 Thomas Denny c.1916. He ended up a Regimental Sergeant Major in the war.

The war was beginning to take a heavy toll on the numbers of local lads killed or wounded and was making an equal strain on Hednesford itself. So spontaneous had been the rush to enlist and the continual propaganda to keep getting more volunteers that the local mines were becoming seriously depleted of able-bodied men, especially the young.

Because coal production was a vital ingredient for the war effort in March, 1916 it was decided to review the mines with a possible view to making miners exempt from going to the Front, unless they were determined to volunteer. The shortage of labour soon became evident in our area. Cannock & Rugeley Company revealed that 533 of its men had enlisted, 19.5% of its workforce which had led to over 10% reduction in output. East Cannock had 187 enlisted, 22% of the workforce. West Cannock Company had seen 520 men enlist, but it was more difficult to access its percentage of the workforce as it had four separate mines and men often transferred from one pit to another within the Company. Eventually the Government decided to make the miners exempt.

That was not the only problem that Hednesford people faced. When war broke out the colliery owners agreed to pay the house rent of those employees who had gone to the Front and continue giving the coal allowance. Workmates left at home had consented to donate 6d a fortnight to dependants or 3d if the volunteer's wage was under 20s per week. Despite those generous measures people still found it difficult to make ends meet and soup kitchens and other food donations from local firms and societies had to be a regular occurrence.

But despite its own plight Hednesford was not oblivious to the hardships of others. In the October of 1914 the town welcomed around 50 Belgian refugees who were housed originally in the Mines Rescue Station and Gas Company and then placed into houses in the town. Fourteen actually stayed in Hednesford and were cared for by Mr. Payton. By April, 1915 all had found work and had become self-sufficient, even managing to put by savings for when they returned to Belgium. Asked by a reporter if they would prefer lodgings they said that they wanted to stay together as "nearly all of them came from Bruges and four were brothers". (A few never did return and made their permanent home in England.)

70 Postcard sent to the Front from Agnes Morris to William Morris in August 1916.

71 Postcard from Len Denny from Rouen just before he was moved to the Front in June 1915.

What also must never be forgotten was the mental sacrifice made by those left behind, particularly wives and mothers. Pride and patriotism was always tinged with fear and some families had more than their share. As already seen mothers like Mrs. Stephens saw almost the entire family go to war, only to get the dreaded letter telling of disaster. But one family perhaps needs special mention. Mrs. Dando of 78 Brindley Heath watched as no less than six of her nine sons enlisted, along with her only son-in-law. Richard (43) joined the Notts & Derby Regiment, Hayden (25) the Middlesex, Ernest (28) the Royal Engineers with his brother-in-law, Percy Crowder, while Alfred (34), Frank (23) and George (16) joined the South Staffs. All had worked for the West Cannock Company before enlisting. (The three remaining sons were too young to enlist.)

To mark such an achievement Mrs. Dando received a letter in September, 1915 on behalf of King George V part of which read:-

"The King was much gratified to hear of the manner in which they have so readily responded to the call of their Sovereign and their country and I am to express to you His Majesty's congratulations on having contributed in so full a measure to the great cause for which the people of the British Empire are fighting so bravely.

I have the Honour to be, madam,
Your obedient servant,
F.M. Ponsonby.
(Keeper of the Privy Purse)"

*Remarkably all but Ernest survived.

The First World War perpetrated many horrors and none worse than gas attack. To counter that threat men were trained in the use of breathing apparatus. It was of little benefit if men did not undergo the real thing and so poison gas experiments were assimilated. These were carried out in our area between the Easter of 1915 and 1918 and Mr. Payton, together with Professor Cadman, tested the masks and trained troops in their use.

It was also during that early part of the war that the Government decided to construct military camps on the Chase - the Rugeley Camp and the Brocton Camp (not to be

72 Walter Baker 1917. He was considered too small (being only 4' 1") when he first tried to volunteer, but allowed to enlist when more men were needed at the Front.

73 46th North Midland Divisional Training Camp (1916) before going to the Front. Walter Baker is third from the right at the rear.

74 George Dando 1917. Son of William Dando who started the wholesale fruit and vegetable business in Hednesford. Mrs Reaney who loaned the photograph was his great niece. George died in the 1930's.

confused with the Second World War R.A.F. Camp much nearer Hednesford). The first troops began to arrive in May, 1915 for training before they were dispatched to the Front. The initial idea was to make those camps practically self-sufficient, but the troops needed to get away from the confines of the barracks for some of the time and looked to the local towns for entertainment.

The people of Hednesford welcomed the new arrivals and various clubs were set up to give the soldiers some relaxation after "square-bashing". The Soldiers Institute in Anglesey Street provided "cheap and excellent meals" with facilities for games, concerts, writing and reading, while the Station Road Soldiers' Club, held in the Wesleyan Schools, opened in May, 1915 offering the same recreation. To keep those clubs going financially various events were held in the town. On August 5th, 1916 the first Military Sports was held at Stafford House, Anglesey Street and the proceeds were devoted to providing further entertainment and teas for the troops. At the Christmas the Station Road Club held social gatherings and almost 2,000 troops took part. Though frowned on by the camp commanders for fear of indiscipline, there were always the local inns whose trade had suffered with many miners off at war.

By 1917 there seemed to be no end to the war and more troops were desperately needed. The Government revised its exemption for the miners and in the future men who had entered mining after August 14th, 1915 could be called up along with any unskilled men employed on the surface, providing they passed fitness tests. Also it was to include "men who had persistently worked short time without reasonable cause and so failed to give the National Service for which they were exempted". Just how many men those new rules managed to select was never declared.

As the war dragged on inevitably casualties increased and our local papers bore witness to that. Very few weeks went by without the mention of more men killed in action and few local families escaped the much dreaded bad news. However, at the same time others received good news of acts of bravery and medals of honour. Again those decorated are too numerous to mention individually, but the following bear testimony to the courage of all who took part.

In May, 1917 Sergeant Major E. Martin of the Hednesford Territorials was awarded the D.C.M., the French Military Cross and the French Military Medal in recognition for his bravery on the battlefields of France. No other Territorial had received such high awards. In June, 1917 Sergeant Harvey, who lived at 180 Church Hill before the war and had enlisted in September, 1914, also received the D.C.M. He gained a special mention as he was only 19 years old when the medal was presented. In the same month Private W.T. Buttery of 39 George Street gained the Military Medal for distinguished bravery on the battlefield and his "gallant action was recognised and greatly appreciated". He was promoted to Lance Corporal. Sergeant W.T. Harrison of 28 Anglesey Street was also awarded the D.C.M. in March, 1918 for bravery in rescuing his comrades. At the time the medal was awarded he was in hospital in London having been wounded for a third time.

The first soldier to be awarded the Military Cross in our area was Lieutenant Edward Whitehouse of the Royal Engineers. It was given "in recognition of a piece of daring work in the blowing up of an important bridge in the advance of the Germans in France". It had halted their push forward and had given the British troops time to regroup. Before the war he had lived with his parents at 111 Church Hill and worked at No. 8 Pit of the Cannock Chase Colliery. He had enlisted in September, 1914 first with the R.A.M.C., but later joined the Royal Engineers. In December, 1915 he had been invalided home suffering from shell shock, but six months later he was back at the Front.

At a series of presentations in the area in October, 1918 Private Royden Street of 25 Cross Keys Crossing was awarded the Military Medal "for conspicuous gallantry and devotion to duty. He acted as the bearer officer's runner and did very valuable work under dangerous and difficult conditions from June 14th to the night of June 19th, 1917. On the final night he was carrying stretcher cases through enemy's shell and gas barrage and carried on with great bravery until he collapsed from the effects of gas poisoning".

At the same presentation Captain A.E. Gore of Littleworth was awarded the Croix de Guerre for "showing remarkable bravery during the operations on June 6th, 1918 at the mountain of Bligny. During a difficult situation he rallied the men of his battalion and organised a counter attack which retook all the ground temporarily lost. He afterwards commanded the battalion when his colonel was wounded".

The ultimate accolade, the Victoria Cross, was awarded to Private Thomas Hughes for his bravery in action at Guillemont, France on September 3rd, 1916. Not a native of Hednesford, he had come to live in the town from County Monaghan, Ireland to work as a stable lad and jockey at Rooney's stables down East Cannock Road. He is probably the only stable lad ever to win the Victoria Cross. At the start of the war he had joined the Connaught Rangers and left for the Front in 1915.

On the morning of September 3rd his brigade, along with two others, advanced into the ruins of Guillemont to take out German positions around Mount Street, the main street. Despite heavy firing they succeeded, but Hughes was badly wounded. In his own words, "We went over the top. After being hit in four different places, I noticed a machine gun firing in the German lines. So I rushed up, shot both the chaps on the gun and brought it back.

P.S. I forgot to mention I brought four German prisoners back with the gun."

His citation reads, "For the most conspicuous bravery and determination. He was wounded in an attack, but returned at once to the firing line after having his wounds dressed. Later, seeing a hostile machine gun, he dashed out in front of his company, shot the gunner and single-handed captured the gun. Though again wounded, he brought back three or four prisoners."

Private Hughes was presented with the Victoria Cross by King George V at a ceremony in Hyde Park on June 2nd, 1917. On the evening of Thursday July 11th, 1918 a huge crowd

75 Opening of the Hednesford War Memorial, 9th November 1922. The crowd includes some of the Brown family in front of the pillar.

gathered at Our Lady of Lourdes Church Hall and Colonel R.S. Williamson presented him with £100 in War Savings Certificates on behalf of the people of Hednesford in recognition of his bravery on the battlefield. Unfortunately, due to his injuries he never worked again as a jockey and returned to Ireland where he died on January 8th, 1942, sadly a broken man.

The final word on the war should probably go to the Harvey family who lived in Mount Street. They had the unfortunate distinction of being the last family in our area to lose a loved one in the actual fighting. Lance Corporal Herbert Harvey was killed in action on September 21st, 1918. What was even more tragic was that he was their second son to die. Private Chas. Harvey had died of his wounds in July, 1916. (See comment in the Roll of Honour) A third son, Private John Harvey, had lost his right leg and was still in hospital in Colchester at the time peace was declared. Like so many families the war had torn apart their once happy life.

Once the war ended something had to be done to commemorate the sacrifice made by so many local lads. Late in 1918 a public meeting was held at the Drill Hall to discuss possible ideas, but unfortunately it floundered due to lack of real organisation. However, on May 31st, 1920 a new committee met at the Soldiers' Institute and three possibilities were put forward. The first suggestion was the building of a public hall to commemorate the dead; the second was the

76 Hednesford War Memorial, c.1930.

conversion of the old Pool site into a lake or park with an adjoining monument; while the third was a monument on Hednesford Hills.

As we know the last idea was the one chosen and the Marquis of Anglesey was approached for the necessary plot of land. On September 24th, 1920 he gave two acres on the Rugeley Road. On October 22nd the tender of Messrs. Fraley &

Sons of Birmingham was selected. The monument was to be constructed in grey granite with various bronze embellishments and the names of those fallen inscribed in bronze panels on the sides. The total cost was to be £1,215.

It was decided that those names to be included would be from the Parish of Hednesford which included Rawnsley, Littleworth, Wimblebury, High Town, Pye Green, Brindley Heath and Hednesford as well as including those from Hazel Slade. The memorial was finally completed in 1922 and was unveiled on November 9th by Alice, Countess of Athlone, who was accompanied by her husband.

A smaller brown, marble monument stands in John Street, Wimblebury to commemorate 19 village men who gave up their lives in the war.

and it includes two names which do not appear on the Hednesford Memorial. (See Roll of Honour.) Perhaps the village which suffered the most was that of Hazel Slade which saw 26 of its young men never return - around twenty per cent of its able-bodied, young men!

Over the years more names have been added because of further conflicts, especially the Second World War, but as this history only reaches as far as 1940 they will not appear on the Roll of Honour. However, one final word - moves to relocate the memorial to the centre of Hednesford have recently been muted because of its isolation and the difficulty older people have in walking to its site. Whatever the outcome of discussions we must never forget the price paid by our ancestors.

77 Hednesford War Memorial, 2002.

Adams, Frederick Harry	Driver, R.F.A.	418 Littleworth, Hednesford	
Allen, Walter	Private, Dublin Fusiliers	52 Market Street, Hednesford	
Archer, Arthur	Private, South Staffs.	Brindley Heath	
Archer, Thomas	Sapper, R.E.	Brindley Heath	May, 1915
Baker, Ralph Joseph	Lincolns	54 Bradbury Lane	
Ball, Albert	M.G.C.	Stafford Lane	
Ball, George	Private, W. Yorks	Mount Street, Hednesford	1918
Ball, James	Private, South Staffs.	Mount Street, Hednesford	
Barnett, Joseph Edward	Private, South Staffs.		
Barton, Ralph	Private, Canadians		

Name	Rank/Regiment	Address	Date
Baugh, George	Driver, R.A.S.C.	Clifton Terrace, Littleworth	
Bayliss, Alfred William		417 Belt Road, High Town	Dec. 1917
Beddow, Enoch	R.N.D.	73 Hill Street, Hednesford	
Beddow, John William	Private, South Staffs.	73 Hill Street, Hednesford	Jan. 1918
Benn, George	Sergeant, M.G.C.	Sedgwick's B'ldings, Mount St.	
Birch, Henry	Private, Notts & Derby	4 Heath Street, Hednesford	
Birch, Oliver	Norfolks	Church Hill, Hednesford	
Bishop, Arnold	Private, South Staffs.	97 Green Heath,	July, 1916
Bond, James	Shropshire L.I.	Pye Green	
Borton, Thomas F.B.	Corporal, R.F.A.	Pool View, Hednesford	
Bott, Eli	Northumberland Fusiliers	Hill Street, Hednesford	
Bourne, Fred	Corporal, Royal Fusiliers	West Hill Ave, Hednesford	Oct. 1915
Bradnock, Thomas A.	Bombadier, R.G.A.	33 Cross Street, Hazel Slade	
Brookes, W. Harold	Private, W. Yorks.	Platt Street, High Town	
Brown, Fredrick	W. Yorks.	Green Heath, Hednesford	
Brown, Howard	L. Corporal, Royal Scots	12 Bradbury Lane, Hednesford	Late, 1916
Brown, Percy	L. Corporal, South Staffs.	Old Hednesford	
Buckley, Thomas	Private, South Staffs.	Bradford Street, High Town	
Burnett, William	L. Colonel, South Staffs.	Rawnsley	July, 1916
Byford, W.	Stoker	Market Street, Hednesford	
Caddick, Walter H.	Private, Worcesters	Station Road, Hednesford	
Calladine, William A.	Private, Lancs. Fusiliers	485 Littleworth Road, Hednesford	
Cathcart, George W.	Private, Durham L. Infantry	34 George Street, Hednesford	
Clarke, John	Private, 3rd. Worcesters	Chapel Street, Hazel Slade	
Clarke, James I.	Private, South Staffs.	Hazel Slade	
Cooke, George	Private, South Staffs.	9 Burgoyne Street, High Town	
Cooke, Francis	Sergeant, Liverpools		
Cooksey, Henry	Rifleman, K.R.R.	Station Road, Hednesford	
Cooksey, Richard	L. Corporal, Bedfords	Burgoyne Street, High Town	May, 1915
Cooksey, Thomas	Private, South Staffs.	Burgoyne Street, High Town	
Cosby, Joseph	Private, Yorks & Lancs.	Brindley Heath	
Craddock, Jonas	Notts & Derby		
Crutchley, Albert E.	Private, Royal Scots	Hazel Slade	
Cund, Edwin	Private, South Staffs.	10 Abbey Street, Hednesford	
Dando, Ernest	Sapper, R.E.	78 Brindley Heath	
Davies, Henry	Private, South Staffs.	37 George Street, Hednesford	
Davies, Thomas R.	Private, R.W. Fusiliers	Hazel Slade	Late, 1916
Dawes, Alexander	Private, North Staffs.	Church Hill, Hednesford	Mar. 1915
Dawes, Samuel	Gunner, R.F.A.	Church Hill, Hednesford	
Deakin, John	R. Engineers	Station Road, Hednesford	
Degg, John Henry	Private, South Staffs.	Bradford Street, High Town	July, 1916
Dennis, Fred	Private South Staffs.	Burgoyne Street, High Town	
Douglas, William	Gunner, R.G.A.	Market Street, Hednesford	
Dowding, George A.	Private, R.W. Fusiliers		June, 1916
Downes, D.	Private, K.O.Y.L.I.	Green Heath, Hednesford	
Drury, William	Corporal, Australians F.F.		
Dudfield, Edwin	Private, South Staffs.		Ap. 1915
Dukes, George	Private, South Staffs.	11 Littleworth Road, Hed.	
Dunkley, William	Royal Welsh Fusiliers	Hazel Slade	
Dyke, George	Private, South Staffs.	Glover Street, Wimblebury	July 1915

Name	Rank/Regiment	Address	Date
Edwards, John		Green Heath, Hednesford	
Ellis, George	Private, Oxford & Bucks.	24 Ebenezer Street, Hednesford	
Ellison, Charles		Market Street, Hednesford	1916
Emery, Frank B.	Royal Welsh Fusiliers	Hazel Slade	
Espin, John	Private, Coldstreams	Green Heath, Hednesford	
Evans, James	Private, Labour Corps.	Station Road, Hednesford	
Evans, John T.	Private, Welsh Fusiliers	Church Hill, Hednesford	
Foster, Edgar Rowland	L. Corporal, South Staffs.	Bradford Street, High Town	1918
Foulk, Edwin Joseph	Private, D.L.I.	Littleworth, Hednesford	
Freeman, Arthur	L.Corporal, R.E.	Brindley Heath	
Gardiner, Joseph	Royal Welsh Fusiliers	Hazel Slade	
Gibbon, James H.	Private, Hants.	Heath Street, Hednesford	
Green, Alan E.	Lieutenant, South Staffs.		
Guy, Enoch	Rifleman, Rifle Brigade	Platt Street, High Town	
Guy, Thomas	Sapper, R.E.	Bradbury Lane, Hednesford	
Hallum, John Alfred	Private, South Staffs.	Brindley Heath	
Hammond, Frederick	Leading Seaman R.N.D.	Rugeley Road, Hednesford	1917
Harding, Charles	Private, South Staffs.	Brindley Heath	
Harley, Samuel	Private South Staffs	Wimblebury	
Harrison, Charles H.	Private South Staffs.	4 Albert Street, Hazel Slade	
Harrison, James	Private, South staffs.	Church Hill, Hednesford	Nov. 1918
Harvey, Herbert	L. Corporal, Essex	18 Mount Street, Hed.	Sept. 1918
Hawkins, John Henry	L. Corporal, South Staffs.	Bradbury Lane, Hednesford	
Haycock, Chas. C.L.	Private, Royal Lancs.	1 High Mount Street, Hed.	Oct. 1916
Haycock, Richard	Private, South Staffs.	Brindley Heath	Ap. 1915
Haycock, William	Private, K.O.Y.L.I.	Brindley Heath	
Haywood, Arthur	Private, East Kents	485 Littleworth Rd. Rawnsley	
Hendy, Joseph			
Higgs, Thomas	Sergeant	Bradford Street, High Town	
Hill, Frederick	Private, Royal Welsh Fus.		1916
Holmes, James V.	Private, Duke of Cornwalls	103 Mount Street, Hed.	
Holt, Frank	Private, Essex	Hazel Slade	
Hornblower, John L.	Bombadier, R.G.A.	Church Hill, Hednesford	
Horton, Ernest Wm.	Private, R.A.M.C.	4 Chapel Street, Hazel Slade	Mar.1918
Horton, Richard	Private, Royal Scots	Bradford Street, High Town	
Houghton, Harry	Corporal, East Yorks.	4 Cross Street, Hazel Slade	
Hughes, Harold	Private, R.A.M.C.	Rawnsley	
Humphries, George	Private, R. Engineers	36 McGhie Street, Hed.	
Hyden, Henry	Sapper, R. Engineers	Rawnsley	
Illsley, George	Private, R.W. Fusiliers	Bradbury Lane, Hednesford	
Ivatt, Harold Alfred	Captain, South Staffs.		
Jackson, William	Private, R.F.A.	Brindley Heath	
Jennings, Joseph	Private, Grenadiers	Rugeley Road, Hednesford	Sept.1916
Johnson, Arthur J.N.	Bedfords	Market Street, Hednesford	
Jones, Benjamin	South Staffs.	Abbey Street, Hednesford	
Jones, Herbert		View Street, Belt Road, Hed.	
Jones, Isiah	Private, R.W. Fusiliers	Church Hill, Hednesford	
Jones, John	South Staffs.	Hazel Slade	
Jones, Joseph	South Staffs.	James Street, West Chadsmoor	
Jones, Robert		Cross Street, Hazel Slade	
Jones, Robert Elijah	Private, D.L.I.	Providence House, High Town	

Name	Rank, Regiment	Address	Date
Jones, William	Private, South Staffs.	7 Burgoyne Street, High Town	
Jones, William Daniel	Sergeant, South Staffs.		
Jukes, Job	Private, R. W. Fusiliers	Churchill, Hednesford	
Kenney, Hubert	Grenadiers	The Cottage, Hazel Slade	
Kent, Cyril James	Private, R.F.A.	Station Road, Hednesford	
Kilgallon, William O.	Private, Irish Guards	Cannock Road, High Town	
Kimberley, William H.	Private, South Staffs.	New Buildings, Rawnsley	
Langley, Leonard	L. Corporal, Northumberland Fus.	Hazel Slade	
Lanigan, John			
Lawton, Albert Henry	Private, South Staffs,	11 Glover St. Wimb.	
Leighton, Aaron	South Staffs.	29 Queen St. High Town	
Lewis, John Edward	Northumberland Fusiliers	113 Belt Rd. High Town	
Lewis, Reuben	L. Corporal, Leicesters	Cannock Rd. High Town	
Lewis, Thomas	Private, Liverpools	Platt Street, High Town	
Lockett, Albert H.	Private, South Lancs.	79 Blewitt Street, Hed.	
Longmoor, Henry	Private, South Staffs.	Burgoyne St. High Town	
Lycett, Walter James	Private, Kings Royal Rifles	Hazel Slade	
Marsh, Ralph	Private, Sherwood Foresters	Hed. Road, Rawnsley	Sept. 1916
Marston, Albert J.	Private, South Staffs.	Station Road, Hednesford	
Martin, John	Sapper, R. Engineers	Hazel Slade	
Martin, Thomas	Sergeant, Canadian Sportsmen	Hazel Slade	
Mason, Roland	Worcesters	Wimblebury	
Mason, Walter	Private, Kings Royal Rifles	Hazel Slade	
Matthews, Jack	Private, South Staffs.		June, 1917
Matthews, Harry	Corporal, Irish Guards		Nov. 1917
Maund, John	Private, South Staffs.	51 George Street, Hed.	
Mears, Fred	L. Corporal, Duke of Cornwalls	Abbey Street, Hed.	
Mears, Thomas	Private, South Staffs.	Abbey, Street, Hed.	
Merrick, Alfred	Private, South Staffs.	34 Glover St. Wimb.	Nov. 1915
Merrick, James	Private, South Staffs.	34 Glover St. Wimb.	
Millington, Albert	L. Corporal	Littleworth, Hednesford	Sept. 1916
Moore, Arthur	Northumberland Fusiliers	Bradford St. High Town	
Moore, B.	Corporal	Bradford St. High Town	
Morgan, J.C.	M.G.C.	Hazel Slade	
Morris, William John	Private, M.G.C.	Brindley Heath	
Mottram, James	Sergeant, South Staffs,	Simcox Street, Hed.	
Neville, James T.	Private, South Staffs.	Cannock Wood	
Nicholls, Herbert	Private, London Regiment	Littleworth, Hed.	
Nicholls, Joseph	L. Corporal, Royal Scots	Mount Street, Hed.	Mar. 1918
Noble, John	Private, North Staffs.	High Town	July, 1916
Noble, John T.	Sergeant, Kings Royal Rifles	Mount Street, Hed.	
Oakley, Samuel	Private, South Staffs.	Mount Street, Hed.	Oct. 1915
Oswell, Percy V.	2nd Lieutenant, Surreys	48 Green Heath	
Owen, Arthur R.	Private, South Staffs.	Cannock Rd.High Town	
Parker, Charles	Corporal, Northumberland Fus.	Platt St. High Town	Sept. 1915
Parton, Norman A.	Private, Worcesters	Station Rd. Hednesford	Nov. 1916
Peake, William	Private, Coldstreams	Littleworth, Hed.	June, 1916

Name	Rank/Regiment	Address	Date
Pearce, William	Private, Warwicks	Reservoir Road, Hed.	July, 1916
Pearson, George	Sergeant, R.W. Fusiliers	Cross St. Hazel Slade.	
Porter, Frank	L.C'poral, Kings R'l Rifles	McGhie Street, Hed.	Aug. 1916
Postings, Joseph	Corporal, M.G.C.	63 Bradford St. High T.	
Postings, Leonard	Gunner, R.G.A.	63 Bradford St. High T.	
Potts, George	Private, South Staffs.	Rugeley Road, Hed.	
Powell, George	Private, North Staffs.	Wimblebury Rd. Hed.	
Poyner, John Henry	Private Royal Scots	Bradbury Lane, Hed.	
Preece, Joseph E.	Corporal, South Staffs.	47 Arthur St. Wimb.	
Prince, Arthur	Private, R.F.A.	Reservoir Rd. Hed.	Mar. 1918
Pritchard, Charles G.	Private, South Staffs.	880 Pye Green , Hed.	
Proverbs, Frank	Private, South Staffs.	Rawnsley	Oct. 1915
Purcell, George	Private, South Staffs.	83 Platt St. High Town	
Purcell, John	Private, South Staffs.	83 Platt St. High Town	
Rawlings, Percy	A.B. Seaman	McGhie Street, Hed.	
Richardson, Albert W.	Private, 8th D.L.I.	19 Abbey Street, Hed.	
Roberts, Walter J.	Private, Notts & Derby	219 Littleworth	
Robson, Frederick	L. Corporal, South Staffs.	23 Mount Street, Hed.	
Roden, John William	Private, South Staffs.	Wood Lane, Hednesford	
Rogers, Frederick C.	Gunner, R.G.A.	Church Hill, Hed.	
Rogers, William H.	1st Class Stoker	Church Hill, Hed.	Ap. 1915
Roper, Bert	Leicesters	213 Rawnsley Rd. Hed.	
Rowley, Wallace			
Rowley, William	Corporal, R. Engineers	7 Holly St. Belt Road	
Rushton, Fred	L. Corporal, Kings Royal Rifles	Wimblebury	June, 1917
Russell, Charles	Private, Royal Fusiliers	23 McGhie Street, Hed.	
Sanders, Edward	Private, Royal Fusiliers	Hazel Slade	
Sanders, Joseph	Private, South Staffs.		
Sanderson, Albert E.	Private, South Staffs.	Cannock Rd. H'ton.	Ap. 1917
Sargent, Wallace	Private, Royal West Kents	Hazel Slade	
Seabury, Daniel	Private, South Staffs.	Rawnsley Rd. Hed.	June 1915
Scott, Alfred		Littleworth	
Shemwell, William H.	Private, South Staffs.	Mount Street, Hed.	
Simister, Arthur	Rifleman, Kings Royal Rifles	High Mount St. Hed.	
Simmons, William	Private, South Staffs.	90 McGhie St. Hed.	Oct. 1915
Sishton, George	Private, South Staffs.	Cannock Rd. High Town	
Slade, Leonard	Private, Grenadiers	Albert St. Church Hill	Feb. 1915
Smart, Henry A.	Corporal, 5th South Staffs.	Eskrett Street, Hed.	
Smith, George	Private, Lincolns	George Street, Hed.	
Smith, John	Private, South Staffs.	West Hill Ave. Hed.	
Sockett, W.H.	Private, South Staffs.	High Town	
Spencer, A.	R.I.R.	High Town	
Spinks, F.	Private, Lincolns	Bradbury Lane, Hed.	
Spruce, Albert J.	Royal Fusiliers	Station Road, Hed.	
Stanier, George	Private, South Staffs.	Clifton Ter. L'worth	1916
Stanley, Dennis H.	Trooper, Yeomanry	Booth Street, Hed.	
Stanton, Frank	Private, 14th D.L.I.	Western Road, Hed.	
Stephens, John	Private, South Staffs.	27 Piggott St. Wimb.	Oct. 1915
Stephens, Richard	Private, South Staffs.	27 Piggott St. Wimb.	Oct. 1915

Name	Rank/Regiment	Address	Date
Stevens, E.	Private, South Staffs.	Piggott Street, Wimb.	Nov.1915
Stokes, Alfred	Com. Sergeant Major, South Staffs.	118 Station Road, Hed.	
Stokes, Harold B.	Corporal, Royal Fusiliers	Station Road, Hed.	
Suffolk, Oliver Wm.	Private, South Staffs.	Piggott St. Wimb.	
Suthard, Frank	Steward's Assistant, R.N.	Market Street, Hed.	
Talbot, Uriah	Private, South Staffs.	72 Brindley Heath	1916
Thacker, Thomas	Corporal, Kings Royal Rifles	Piggott St. Wimb.	
Thomas, John	Private, Tyneside Scottish		
Thomas, Joshua	Oxford & Bucks.	Wimblebury	
Thurstance, Edward	Corporal, Royal Scots	143 Station Road, Hed.	
Tolley, George T.	Notts & Derby	Littleworth	
Tolley, Samuel	Corporal, R.W. Fusiliers		
Tomkinson, Edmund	Private, South Staffs.	29 Piggott St. Wimb.	May,1915
Tomkinson, Joseph	Private, South Staffs.	29 Piggott St. Wimb.	1918
Tortoishell, Albert	Private, South Staffs.	Hazel Slade	
Tranter, Ernest	Driver, R.F.A.	West Hill, Hednesford	1918
Tranter, William	Private, Royal Scots	50 George St. Hed.	Sept.1915
Wadeley, Ben	Sergeant, South Staffs.	Church Hill, Hed.	
Walters, Harold	Private, South Staffs.	Florence St. Hed.	1917
Ward, George		Wimblebury	
Ward, James	Private, South Staffs.	Chapel St. Hazel Slade	
Wassell, John	Private, K.O.Y.L.I.	Queen St. High Town	
Webster, John	Corporal, South Staffs.	Green Heath Rd.	June,1915
Wells, Frank H.		Station Road, Hed.	
Wilde, John R.	Private, North Staffs.	Abbey Street, Hed.	Mar.1915
Whilton, Ernest R.	R.A.F.	Cannock Road, Hed.	
Wray, Frederick G.	Worcesters	Church Hill, Hed.	

*Added to these are:-

Name	Rank/Regiment	Address	Date
Harvey, Chas		18 Mount St. Hed.	July,1916
Pritchard, W.H.		39 Hill St. Old Hed.	Dec.1915

Their names do not appear on the memorial, but they were living in the area. There are many such people throughout the country and the War Graves Commission are trying to remedy such errors.

The Wimblebury Memorial also includes the names of S. Barratt and H. Witton who do not appear on the Hednesford Memorial.

SNAPSHOTS OF OUR SCHOOLS

Today we realise that the success of our future lies with the young, but the Victorians were slow to see that and it was not until the Education Act of 1870 that provision was made for their education and even then it was not universal. Beforehand the only youngsters who received learning were those of the moneyed classes whose parents could pay for it as well as a very few gifted children who may be given a chance by the church. Those privileged few were taught in "dame" schools, so named because they were run by middle-class ladies or very occasionally gentlemen who were socially minded.

The 1841 Tithe Map of Hednesford shows one such school run by Edward Selman, but exactly what he did or how many youngsters he educated is not known. In fact very little is known of Hednesford's dame schools despite there being quite a few. There was one at the top of Hill Top, now Carmel Cottage, and one run by a Mrs. Meek, an experienced and certificated mistress, who opened a ladies' school on Rugeley Road. Even as late as 1882, when the local School Board had been set up, dame schools were still popular as can be shown from one report of the Board which suggested that absence from its schools was accounted for by some children "having gone to dame schools" in the area.

But what of the schools which now started to replace them? With his usual foresight Reverend Pauli could see that the area was growing quickly and no amount of dame schools would suffice. In 1863 he persuaded the Lichfield Diocese to invest in a school building and a church at the top of what is now Church Hill and the Marquis of Anglesey gave sufficient land to build both. The school was the first to be finished and in 1864 St. Peter's opened. It must have appeared quite isolated at the top of the hill as one visitor who came back to the school in 1920 from the United States remembered that there were "no houses built on the hill in 1868, just the schoolhouse".

Those attending the new school had to pay a small fee to enable a teacher to be employed and the buildings to be administered. By the turn of the century the Government paid a considerable grant to the school, though a fee was still necessary. The headmaster had to estimate his grant by averaging the yearly attendance and then request a grant for each pupil taught (infants were granted less than those in the mixed school). The School Managers then supplied one twelfth of the grant and the Authority the remainder.

The first master employed was William Hawkins, who with his wife, Mary, had come from Warwickshire and settled in a house close to the school in Church Hill Terrace. He was to remain at the school until 1885 and not only was he in charge of the school but he also became choirmaster and organist at St. Peter's Church. Such was the popularity of the school that in 1883 a further large classroom was added and in 1888 further additions were made costing hundreds of pounds.

To begin with the school was all-age (5 year olds to 13 year olds), but not many infants attended. Compulsory education was difficult to enforce as there were so few schools and places available that parents had ready made excuses not to send their younger children. But on November 3rd, 1892 St. Peter's opened its Infant Department at a cost of over £600 and Enoch Orton, who had been appointed headmaster of the whole school in October, 1890, handed over charge of the new school to Marion Sylvester. There would be no excuse not to send infants then.

78 St. Peter's School c.1945/50.

Enoch Orton remained in charge of the Mixed School until March, 1921 when he retired. His entry in the school log book dated March 24th, 1921 shows his affection for both school and children. It reads:- "I completed my record of thirty one and a quarter years as Headmaster of these schools and lay down my charge with much regret." (The new headmaster would be Mr. Owen.)

Both schools continued to expand, certainly in numbers attending. Accommodation in the Mixed School in 1895 was supposed to be 145, but 159 actually attended. The Infant School had opened with around 70 children, but by the end of the first year over 150 were attending. By 1900 the average attendance for both schools was 350 which only reduced to 345 by 1912. It was apparent that further rooms were needed and so temporary accommodation was found further down Church Hill. Eventually an old army hut was salvaged from the Camps and erected in 1926 for the children of Standard V. It continued in use until 1938 when Littleworth Secondary School was opened and the older children were transferred to there. The "Brotherhood Hut" as it was known was then demolished.

St. Peter's continued as a Voluntary Junior and Infants Mixed School until 1953 when it was finally decided to relinquish its voluntary status and join the State schools. In 1955 the Infant School was enlarged and modernised, adding electric lighting throughout in 1957. Due to the age of the building and the probable cost of repairs it was decided to erect new classrooms and so St. Peter's closed temporarily in the winter of 1962/63. However, by October, 1963 the new buildings were ready and the school reopened. Since then there have been further stages of improvement, notably the addition of new kitchens and classrooms.

79 The staff of St. Peter's School, c.1920.
Back row: Mr Bailey, Ruth Helena Pickerill, Marjorie Cotterill, ?. Seated: ?, Mr Orton, Headmaster, Mrs Bailey.

79a Mr Orton, Headmaster of St. Peter's School.

St. Peter's School was initiated by the church and maintained by various grants. In answer to the Education Act state school began to emerge run by Local School Boards. Unlike St. Peter's the State had total control in matters of finance, teachers' wages, buildings and stock needed to run the school, such as books, as well as the appointment of staff and matters concerning attendance. The Cannock School Board met regularly and was comprised of leading members

80 Church and school service at St. Peter's.

of society from each of the towns. They also visited schools often and inspected what was happening, both to the buildings and children. Instances from their reports show their overall control.

An Attendance Officer's report from November, 1882 shows that he had made 450 visits both to homes and schools, "380 to homes of children reported absent". His report continued that "for the whole of the area the number of children on the books was 2294" but the average attendance "up to last Friday was 1437, against 1572 in the preceding month". The Board members were shocked, until it was found that many reported absent had left the area or had gone to dame schools.

The reasons for lack of attendance were many, but the Board did its best to improve standards by taking parents to court. In October, 1884 no less than seven fathers were taken to court for neglecting to send their children to school and each were fined 5s including costs. In December, 1884 79 further summonses were issued "out of which 73 were convicted, 2 cautioned and only 4 cases withdrawn". The "wag man" was certainly out to improve attendance figures!

But as late as May, 1912 the Board was still worried by poor attendance. Mr. Shaw reported that "in his district (Rawnsley and Wimblebury) the percentage of attendance for that month was

81 Attendance certificate from 1916.

92 against 90 the last month and 94 in the corresponding months of last year". Mr. Purslow reported that several children who were the requisite age had not yet commenced to attend school". (Incidentally today's percentage attendance figures in most schools are not any better and in some cases worse.)

One major reason for absenteeism was the poor health of many of the miners' children caused by inadequate housing, irregular wages in the summer months and poor diet. Entries from St. Peter's Mixed School log book as late as 1918 regularly mention illness. For example:-

April 19th — *Thomas Roberts died this morning from diphtheria, two other brothers are down with the same.*

April 26th — *Measles seems to have developed in the district. There are several cases this week.*

May 10th — *Measles seems to be very much on the increase this week and the attendance has dropped rapidly day by day.*

May 17th — *Measles is spreading fast, however, mostly among the infants causing the elder children of those families to be excluded from school.*

May 31st — *Measles and mumps are very bad throughout the lower Standards.*

June 7th — *The measles seems nearly exhausted, but is followed now by the mumps.*

July 8th — *Average attendance this morning 69 (out of a possible 213). School closed for the week by the authority of Medical Order.*

Those entries might seem out of the ordinary, but log books frequently have similar series of entries. Schools were, and really still are, breeding grounds for illnesses and with children in no way as fit and healthy as those of today they were ready-made targets for any bugs and diseases.

In an attempt to overcome those problems the Board instigated regular visits by a doctor and nurse. West Hill Schools had fortnightly visits and those were inevitably recorded in the log books. For example, in 1914 Dr. Clendinnen and Nurse Webster paid their visit and "examined several girls", while in 1916 the same doctor "used the school kitchen to examine infant children and boys who had been thoroughly inspected a little time ago". Perhaps many readers will vividly remember the "nit nurse" and foot inspections as well as the dental nurse. However, despite their attempts ill-health remained a serious problem, mainly due to the poor standard of living lots of children suffered.

Grace Bertram, headmistress of the Valley Infant School, knew how poverty and poor education went hand in hand. She wrote in her log book:- *"I have been examining the work of different classes. Am sorry to report that since the strike several of our children are ill-clad and ill-fed. No doubt this accounts for some of the backward ones. The dull children are all from the very poorest homes and to be severe with them would be inhuman for owing to their lack of nourishment it is impossible for the brain to work like other children."*

Shows that not all modern thinking is that new!

As for wages, the Board had control over any extra money which might be paid to teachers. Monitors, past pupils who stayed on at school to assist teachers, had their pay regulated by the Board. In 1882 it was decided to pay them £6 to £7 per year providing they kept their contract for the year. If they continued in their position then men got £11 for the second year and women £8 - a strange discrepancy which remained well into the twentieth century.

Also in 1882 the Board considered a request by a Miss Turnbull to teach the children of Rawnsley School sewing on three afternoons a week for £12 per year. The Board "thought that too high and offered her £10". It was not recorded whether she accepted or not.

As for the cost of running the various school buildings headmasters had to place requests with the Board for ongoing repairs or alterations. The strangest request perhaps was from Mr. Whitfield at West Hill who asked that the teachers' homes, which were part of the school building and still exist today, should be redecorated at the Board's expense. His request was denied.

Another area for the Board to look after was the actual buildings and their upkeep and inspectors made frequent references to the state of the schools in their reports. On the opening of the Valley Infants School in 1903 Mr. Cornes, the Sub. Inspector, said, "The admirable, well-warmed, well-ventilated new premises are a great boon to both children and teachers", but "the cellar is not properly drained and steps should be taken to remedy this defect as during the winter it may be impossible for the caretaker to light the fire. Already she has to make a plank bridge over the pool of water in order to reach the heating apparatus". By the March of 1904 it had not been fixed and was still a problem in 1915.

In 1908 at West Hill Girls School Mr. Jackson reported that "some of the rooms are still without a sufficiency of guarded inlets for fresh air. In these parts of the school the teachers and scholars are exposed to draughts. Apparatus for the extinction of foul air is still wanting in some of the rooms. The urinal space is still inadequate." By 1912 it was again reported that "extractors for the removal of foul air have not yet been provided".

82 West Hill School c.1910.

Hednesford's first Board School was West Hill which opened in October, 1876 at a cost of around £3,500 and with the capability of having 350 boys, 226 girls and 150 infants all housed in the same building. The actual numbers on opening were 117 – 96 attending on the first day and a further 21 in the days following. Its first headmaster was Joseph Whitfield, accompanied by Emily Wood, who had charge of the girls, and Elizabeth Whitfield, his wife, who was in charge of the infants. Mr. Whitfield was assisted by William Aitkins, pupil teacher for Year Three and Charles Lindley for Year Two.

However, it soon became clear that the building would be too small for the large numbers supposed to attend and in 1877 it was decided to enlarge it. To make that possible the Methodist Chapel at High Town was rented out to take the girls and infants and they moved there in 1880 and stayed until 1885. By 1881 the girls section had been started and was completed in 1883. The infants was finally completed in 1888 and opened in the following year on January 7th with Mrs. Whitfield taking charge. The building, which still stands today, was built by Robert Barton of Hednesford at a cost of £1,400.

83 Games lesson at West Hill Girls School c.1955.

The *Cannock Advertiser* described it as "Gothic - the main building roofed in one span". The main room was 74ft by 22ft with a revolving screen across, making it possible to have two separate rooms. It was heated (something quite modern) by Grundy's Patent Apparatus to 70 degrees and easily maintained at 55 degrees.

Strangely there had been objections to spending so much on a new building by some of the Board members owing to the decline in fortunes of the local coal industry and the possibility that families might move away from Hednesford. As will be seen later schools often reflected what was happening in the community.

The Whitfields remained in charge of the schools until 1913 when they both retired and handed over well-established and flourishing schools. Mr. Hickson took over the boys school while Mrs. Wooton was in charge of the girls. Unfortunately disaster was to hit the buildings on August 31st, 1919. At around 9.30 p.m. a passer-by noticed smoke billowing from the girls' area and almost before the alarm could be raised the whole roof was ablaze with flames shooting out of the steeple or belfry. Despite valiant attempts by the fire brigade and local people to quench the fire the whole of the girls' school was gutted. Fortunately the boys section and the teachers' houses were saved because the wind blew in the opposite direction.

For the next few years the girls were educated in the new Belt Road Schools where there were spare rooms. Strangely the building was almost empty except for some families who occupied it because of scarcity of housing. Some 350 girls remained there until West Hill Girls School was rebuilt using temporary huts from

84 West Hill School c.1950 gardening lesson. The photograph faces onto McGhie Street, in the background is the "temporary classroom".

the disbanded Camps. (They were to remain on site well after their supposed expiry date.)

The present school opened on April 6th, 1995 after much refurbishment with the amalgamation of the Infant and Junior schools.

West Hill was only one of the schools catered for by the Board. In 1877 Rawnsley Mixed School was established for 200 pupils and was enlarged in 1895 for a further 50 children. Again in 1903 more buildings were added, but by 1924 it was so overcrowded that some children were transferred to Hazel Slade. Unfortunately after the appearance of Littleworth Senior School it was no longer viable and in 1942 it was closed and the remaining junior children were dispersed between Hazel Slade and Heath Hayes.

The same fate was to happen to the Wimblebury school. Wimblebury Infants opened in 1890 with 68 children and by 1900 it had become a mixed aged school with Miss Woodcock as Headmistress. With its fate so heavily dependent on miners' children it always struggled to gain further admissions because with the unsure future of the mines new people were reluctant to stay. By 1912 it still had only just over 100 children on roll and its future looked unsafe. It finally closed in 1940, the remaining children being transferred to Heath Hayes.

The fate of both schools had been dealt a severe blow by the opening of Littleworth Secondary School in 1938 because all children in the area over the age of eleven were accommodated there. It left the area with too many schools, most of which were half empty and with no likelihood of future expansion. They were simply uneconomical to keep open.

Although strictly not in our area Hazel Slade's school needs a mention just because some children were transferred to there. Because of its unique geographical position, it was quite isolated, its future was secured, mainly because the young children would have had to travel too far to go to other schools. Originally it had been decided that the village needed its own school and the church was asked to donate funds. The site was given by the Marquis of Anglesey and in 1884 the building was erected as a day school and church combined. In 1892 it was given a Parliamentary grant as an infant school with an average attendance of 132 pupils.

In 1912 it became a Mixed and Infants School with around 110 attending. Older children were transferred to Rawnsley around 1920, but by 1924 that had reversed. It was eventually taken over by the School Board who then decided that it was much more of a necessity than the other mixed schools in the area. By 1936 a new school had been built and it was further enlarged in 1948 with the addition of wooden buildings, formerly part of Rawnsley's school. Its numbers increased when Rawnsley closed. Today it is still a vibrant village school.

Another new school in Hednesford was St. Joseph's Catholic School at Hill Top built in 1895 and initially run by a lay Headmistress, Miss Callan, who was assisted by the religious order of the Sisters of the Convent of the Holy Rosary based in Cannock. The Sisters eventually took over the administration of the school in 1920 after the Order had purchased Mount Pleasant in Uxbridge Street and moved some of the nuns into that house.

By 1900 the average attendance was 183 and continued to grow. By the late 1940's Mount Pleasant was in dire need of repair owing to subsidence and so, rather than spend money on it, the Order moved into York House in Anglesey Street (Mount Pleasant was demolished). In 1954 the school became an aided one and until 1961 it remained an all-age school, the last in the area. After the building of Cardinal Griffin in Cannock the older pupils moved out and St. Joseph's became a Junior and Infant School, which it is today.

Bradbury Lane Temporary Infants School, so named because it started in the Bradbury Lane Methodist Chapel and remained there until the Valley Infants School was completed, was begun in 1895 to relieve the pressure on West Hill Infants School and took most of it children from the Bradbury Lane and Brindley Heath area. High Town had had a school in the 1870's, but by 1882 it had become purely an infants school with children over ten being placed at either West Hill or Chadsmoor Board School on Cannock Road. By the turn of the century the High Town school had been "mothballed", luckily for West Hill when they had the fire in 1919. Yet another school was the Primitive Methodist School in Hednesford, but its history was to be very short. It seems to have started in 1868, but lasted only until 1876 when most of its children were transferred to West Hill.

Another infant school had been proposed in November, 1882 to be in the Littleworth area as "there was not sufficient school accommodation for young children in the neighbourhood of Church Hill". There were three possible offers for a premises – the Primitive Methodist Chapel in Littleworth; the Public Rooms on Rugeley Road; and an "extensive shop" on Church Hill. Eventually the chapel site was chosen, but the Board heard in July, 1883 that it would need alterations. The ceiling was eight inches lower than the lowest measurement allowed by the Education Department (it must be no less than ten feet eight inches and was only ten feet in height). The Board thought the chapel trustees might be persuaded to lower the floor and add more windows. However, it seems that negotiations never went any further and the proposed school was never built.

So much for the actual buildings, but they tell little of the life of a school. One thing that the Board insisted on was the keeping of a school log book which recorded what actually happened in the school. They vividly reflect both the school and its children as well as acting as a social record of events within the school's catchment area. Fortunately some have survived and what follows is a glimpse of three schools as they journeyed through some of Hednesford's history.

West Hill Infants – 1876 – 1878

October:

Elizabeth Whitfield, Class 2 mistress, opened the school with the assistance of Ada Johnson, monitor. Miss Elizabeth Burford started as an assistant mistress. Small attendance in the afternoon of October 30th because of the "Wakes".

(Hednesford had its own carnival day each year around the end of October which lasted well into the twentieth century. Almost everyone in the town attended.)

November:

Children allowed to have their dinner in the classroom because of the cold weather. A very rough day and attendance small.

December:

The smallest attendance since the school opened, only 83 in the morning due to bad weather. Miss Bartlett appointed.

February 1877:

Messrs. Gwynne and Jones (Inspectors) arrived to see children go through their kinder garten exercises.

(Kinder garten was the latest thinking in educational circles and centred around manipulative skills like drawing and sewing.)

March:

Rearranged the school into three sections according to the child's age. Upper Section under Miss Bartlett with Miss Voden to assist (she was a monitor); Miss Burford to take the Middle Section (5/6 year olds); and Lower Section (4+ year olds) to be taken by A. Johnson.

(That organisation may have sounded wonderful but remember there was only one room. Only when the new infant school had been built would that arrangement have been adequate.)

April:

Ada Johnson left the school as her parents were leaving the district.

June:

A child was sent home with chicken pox. Next day others sent home with the same. Two children sent home with ringworm. Made an examination throughout the school.

(Ringworm was a skin disease which came out in a circular rash, brought on by poor diet and hygiene. It was readily transmissible.)

October:

Had to talk seriously to the children about throwing stones at each other. Half day holiday because of the Hednesford Wakes.

January 1878:

Agnes Pedley (monitor) obtained a prize from "School Magazine" for her needlework which was sent up. Ellen Coltman (monitor) got a prize for papers sent in on grammar.

(Local and national competitions were frequently entered to show a school's prowess in teaching. All children were actively "encouraged" to enter them.)

April:

Many children are leaving the school through badness of trade causing their parents to leave the district.

(The miners had not fully recovered from the 1874 Strike and many just had had enough and left the area.)

May:

Attendance gets worse and worse. Only 25 present on Wednesday on account of the stormy weather. Between the badness of the weather and the badness of trade the number of children for presentation will fall very low.

September:

Met with several parents on Thursday who are in arrears with their school funds.

(Despite education supposedly being free in state schools parents were expected to pay into a school fund. It could be as low as one penny, but when money was tight and work unsure even that might not be affordable.)

St. Peter's Infants – 1892 – 1893

Although St. Peter's was a church school it still had to follow the same type of lessons as the State schools. What follows initially is a plan of the lessons given under the kinder garten scheme (have they changed much from your experience of infant school?). Besides these the 3 R's were practised daily.

Object Lessons

Natural History

The rat, the ostrich, the elephant, the dog, the squirrel, the bee, the lion, the robin, the frog, the spider, the duck, the rabbit.

Common Objects

The hand, ship, lead pencils, slate, pins and needles, glass, ink, and the kettle.

Phenomena

Clouds, winter and hail.

Vegetation

Potato, apples, oranges, wheat, cocoa, nut and the garden.

Employments

The postman and the grocer.

November:

The school opened as a separate institution. Staff appointed were Marion Sylvester, head, with Miss Eugenie Williams and Miss Jane Stacey as assistants. Beatrice Jones as monitor. I sent two girls home for their pence.

(Unlike the State schools all children had to pay an amount for the privilege of attending. That could lead to some parents deciding not to send their very young ones to school at all.)

Drill was taken for the first time. Space was sufficient for drill to be attempted in the old school

(done in the classroom behind the forms or desks).

December:

A holiday was given in the morning, there being a

heavy snowstorm. Many children are dangerously ill. Four absent with fever. Received school apparatus, including musical bells, reading books, pencils and scarves.

February 1893:
Vicar visited the school this afternoon.

(As a church school the vicar saw it as part of his duty to regularly visit the school and inspect the work taking place.)

March:
Several girls sent home for their school fee. Three boys were punished for playing truant. They had left the school and followed a threshing machine. Holiday was given on the afternoon of the 7th in order that the children may witness the circus procession.

April/May:
Mr. Jarvis (inspector) visited and saw an object lesson. He commended the children on speaking distinctly.
I examined the Babies Class and found that the recitations were said very distinctly. Took the First Class in Stick Laying (Do you know what that was? I have no idea.) *and they answered intelligently.*

Having mentioned recitations the log book listed the things children had to learn off by heart. These included:-

    1. When I am a Woman.
    2. Pussy's Tea Party.
    3. The Queen of the Buttercups.
    4. The Little Lazy Boy.
    5. Little Chatterbox.
    6. Sleep Baby Sleep.

As well as those there were the following songs:-
The Peasant, Sundown Shadows, Naughty Jack, The Seasons, Little Soldier, My Doll, The Shop, Echo, Baby-bye, Alphabet Song and finally London's Burning.

Any readers remember these?

June:
I sent several children home for their fee. Although only a small fee I have considerable difficulty in getting them to pay as they are in great poverty at the present time. Very poor attendance. There are 67 children absent with measles. One of our little scholars has died with the measles.

As with all schools in the area the autumn of 1893 proved very difficult because of the Great Federation Lockout. Many entries in St. Peter's log book show the desperation families must have experienced at the time.

September:
There is great distress in most homes owing to the strike. I do not deem it advisable to press them for fees, consequently arrears must increase. Several children have gone to pick coal from the canal which has been emptied purposely to relieve them.
The vicar visited the school today and expressed a desire that all children in want should be fed before lessons every morning. I distributed bread and cheese as the children entered the school. A dinner of soup has been provided for the infants, they seemed to eat quite hungrily.

October:
Attendance continues to be good. This I attribute to being fed constantly at school. It is becoming painfully apparent that many are relying solely on the generosity bestowed on them at school.

November:
A dinner of soup is given to the poor children. I understand this will be the last time we have to feed children at school.

(The strike was over and the miners were back at work. The log book then returned to its usual entries concerning weather, attendance and sickness.)

Bradbury Lane Temporary Infants 1895 – 1897

Remember this school was temporarily housed in the Bradbury Lane Methodist Chapel until the Valley Infants opened in August. 1903.

December 4th:
This school opened today with 50 present in the morning and 63 in the afternoon. The staff are Elizabeth Marsh, head, and Laura Mellor, monitor. Number increased to 76 and despite the cold and stormy weather 72 were present. Admitted another 11 scholars making a total on roll of 87.

January 1896:
Received coloured beads and needle threaders. Commenced to teach babies Needle Drill and bead threading.

March:
School closed this afternoon by order of the Medical Officer on account of an epidemic of measles in the district. School reopened after the Easter Holiday.

September:
Elizabeth Marsh left to take up another position at Five Ways Infants in Heath Hayes and Grace Longstaff started.

January 1897:
Took babies for their recitation and then for Needle Drill and Form. Object lesson on the "Candle" this afternoon while I had the babies.

July:
Inspectors Report on the school.
The children are in excellent order and lessons are well taught. The school accommodation at present is insufficient for the average attendance. This should at once be remedied or the grant next year will be endangered.

(It was clear that the school was too small for the number of children attending, but unfortunately the Board did nothing about the situation, hence:-

February 1898:
Had a letter from the Board directing me to transfer on March 1st such a number of children to West Hill as would reduce the number on book to 75.

(How those children were chosen was not recorded, but one presumes that those nearest West Hill were the first to go.)

Another inspection in the same month said the school "is hampered by poor and insufficient accommodation. The children have to perch on forms turned down and are crowded uncomfortably. There is not sufficient cloakroom accommodation."

That unfortunately was to be the history of the small school and despite its popularity it would eventually lead to its closure, but not until 1993.

Infants schools may seem rather dull to us in those early years, but children were frequently taken out of school to visit various things in the area. At the Valley Infants it was recorded that they were taken to see Mr. Harding's corn fields; had walks around Brindley Heath to observe trees in autumn; visited the new Sinkin Colliery where they examined pit lamps and watched the cages going up and down; went to the Canal Basin to see the boats; and visited the blacksmith to watch him at his forge. In fact school was so popular that the Valley Infants was often full to the brim. In 1905 the head was directed to take "no child under four and only those under five whose parents had made an application in advance".

Once children had reached the age of seven they moved to the "big" school, invariable on the same site, and there they stayed until they left. That was usually at thirteen, but there was a chance to leave earlier at twelve. During a chat with William Drinkwater (now over 100 years old) he related how at twelve he was sent by his teacher from West Hill Boys to Burns Street School in Chadsmoor to take the "Labour Exam". If you passed you were allowed to leave school if your parents agreed. He passed and had to go to the Workhouse in Cannock to get his pass which allowed him to start work. His father was none too happy with him leaving school so early, but gave in once William got a job at a local colliery. Although boys were not allowed to go down the pit until they were fourteen, he was employed on the bank going various odd jobs.

Once children entered the Mixed School the subjects taught were increased. In a inspector's report at St. Peter's in the 1910's the subjects were listed as:- English, Mathematics, History, Geography, Science, Drawing/Art and Engineering (that meant Woodwork for the boys and Needlework for the girls). To enable the girls to become good housewives in the future Cookery was also added to the timetable. In 1914 West Hill Girls recorded 17 girls being sent to the local cookery school until eventually the school had its own lessons. Physical Education or Drill was not commented upon in the report, but played a necessary role in the school. Strangely Mr. Orton was for a long time the only male teacher at St. Peter's (1904 records himself and seven female teachers). He must have been very fit if he had to take every boy for physical education each week! But perhaps not, as Drill was very much on army lines and performed in military rows while the teacher shouted instructions from the front.

Whatever we might think of those rather crude attempts at physical education it taught the boys the rigours of discipline so much so that during World War One no less than 160 old boys from St. Peter's enlisted. 5 were promoted to commissions and 2 gained military medals. Sadly Mr. Orton had to record 18 deaths from amongst the lads he had taught, including the Stephens brothers. The names of those fallen appear on a Roll of Honour in the school.

In mentioning the great war schools were

85 West Hill Girls School. Games on the field. In the background is McGhie Street c.1955.

86 West Hill Boys School P. E. lesson. In the background is High Mount Street c.1955.

not embarrassed about "waving the flag". There was no need for political correctness. West Hill Girls School records that on Empire Day in 1916 "the girls assembled in the yard and in separate classes saluted the flag. Seven Empire songs were sung and oral lessons on the Empire were given during the day". In 1917 "the timetable was not strictly adhered to as the girls marched around the yard, sang their Empire hymns and saluted the flag".

During that war the children were actively persuaded to help their country financially. In November, 1916 Councillors Willets and Mason visited West Hill School to speak of the War Savings Scheme in which money was donated to the Government to help the war effort. Certificates were given in exchange for money and they could be reclaimed after the war. As rewards for their donations they were granted half day holidays. By March, 1917 West Hill Girls had donated £84-1s-10d and 108 certificates

were handed out. When they reached the £100 they got their holiday. The log book shows that the girls managed 5 such holidays during the war. The teachers themselves also showed great patriotism and many of the male teachers volunteered to fight while the women gave up time to distribute literature in connection with the Savings Scheme.

Rewards of holidays were not only given during the war, but for other major events in the area. Already mentioned was Hednesford Wakes and in 1913 the Valley Infants closed for the day to allow the children to go to the Chadsmoor Police Sports. In 1915 West Hill closed for a half day to let the children visit Sangers Circus in Cannock.

Overall, despite the relatively poor conditions within the actual school buildings, it would seem that our ancestors enjoyed their schooldays: they really were the best days of their lives.

SPORT AND LEISURE

Whilst everyday folk had very little time for relaxation and sport, save for the occasional fair and holy day (hence our holiday), the eighteenth century gentry had a great deal of time on their hands. Horse racing, along with hunting and shooting, were ways of passing that leisure time. Beginning, one supposes, with landowners betting on who had the finest and fastest horses, the sport gradually evolved into race meetings. Readers may be surprised to learn that Hednesford and its surrounding Hills was well-known throughout England for its good training ground and seems to have been started right at the beginning of the racing business.

Exactly when the first race horse trainers appeared in Hednesford is not known, but Samuel Johnson recorded his trade as a horse-breaker in 1759. By 1760 it would seem that some stables had already been established, probably run by James Lord, Senior. That early date is confirmed when examining the Marriage Banns from the 1760's when St. Luke's at Cannock records no less than three marriages involving jockeys. In 1764 Joseph Sprat married Mary Linsdale, in 1766 William Wood married Sarah Benton and in 1770 Humphrey Kellham married Jane Harris. These lads were employed at Hednesford stables, proving that the business was already well established. Further evidence of stables in the area is recorded with Mr. James Lord winning a £50 stakes at Grantham in Lincolnshire in June, 1774 with a bay horse called "Gift", a considerable purse at the time.

By the mid 1770's further trainers must have been in the area, (quite possibly members of the Saunders family), because in 1775 Lord Henry Bayley Paget felt the need to complain that there were so many horses being trained on Hednesford Hills, part of his estate, that they were frightening off the deer and spoiling his grounds and hunting and he was determined to do something about the numbers.

In a letter to the courts it is written:-

"About fifteen or twenty years ago one or two particular Gentlemen sent a running horse or two to stand at Hedgeford and to be co-trained upon that part of the Chace (as it was then spelt) bordering thereupon which before observed there is fine turf. The practice has of late greatly increased" and instead of *"about four or five horses only which ever used to border training there that number now amounts to between thirty and forty and many of them belonging to gamblers"* and there are *"a boy to every horse and a man to supervise every three or four boys. A great number of people are employed who by their riders, morning and evening continually drive his Lordship's deer from a very large extent of ground."*

Such was his annoyance that Lord Paget threatened to cause *"trenches to be cut across the rides or plough them up and thereby render them useless for horse training"*. The trainers replied by seeking an injunction to stop that happening. However, a supporter of Lord Paget wrote that *"Lord Paget has a right to dig in the soil of that waste and he may cut trenches across the rides or plough up part or this as agreed. He may enclose it by the decree and he has absolute right to enclose and make coppice for nine years"*. Fortunately for Hednesford and the trainers a compromise was reached and training continued. Obviously ploughing up the land would have made it useless for everyone concerned.

But what made the area so popular and well worth fighting over? An article by one "Cecil" in the *Sporting Magazine* of 1839 describes the Hills as *"well adapted for spring work. The subsoil is gravel, with good turf on the surface. Consequently they are never deep (boggy), but in dry weather they become very hard."* He also writes that *"the turf is preserved with care,*

RULES
AND
REGULATIONS
RESPECTING THE
TRAINING GROUND,
To be observed by the
TRAINERS, JOCKEYS, HEAD BOYS and BOYS,
At Hednesford, in the Parishes of Cannock and Rugeley. -1857.

RULE 1-Any Trainer intending to have a trial, is to send a written notice to all other Trainers, and in their absence to the person in charge of the stables ; to state he is going to have a trial the following day between the hours of eleven and three o'clock ; such notice to be delivered before six o'clock on the Evening preceding the day he intends trying. Should two or more Trainers want the ground on the same day, they must arrange amongst themselves as to the hour they will be on the ground.

2- If any Trainer, Jockey or Stable Keeper, is convicted of watching a trial, when notice has been given to the Trainers, they shall pay a penalty of Ten Pounds.

3- All Grooms or Boys who are convicted of watching a trial, (notice of it having been given,) shall be discharged by their Employers, and not be again employed by any Trainer or Stable Keeper in Hednesford, under a penalty of Ten Pounds.

4- Should any Boy, Groom or Servant, who has been convicted of watching a trial, prove that he was ordered to do so only by his Master, he shall be acquitted, and the Master shall be fined Ten Pounds.

5- If either Jockey, Trainer, or Stable Keeper, takes any person into his service who has been convicted of watching a trial and discharged from his situation, he shall pay Ten Pounds.

6- Every Horse that is trained upon Hednesford Hills, and others which may come to any Stable in Hednesford, and are exercised on the Training Ground, shall pay ten shillings towards the Training fund, &c., if only for one day. Every Trainer, Jockey, Groom or Person is requested to make an honest return of the number trained or exercised by himself, or by his directions. For every horse in excess of his return, he shall pay One Pound.

7- All strange Grooms, who may come to any stable in Hednesford, shall be made acquainted with the Rules, and in case they or any of their Boys under them shall watch any trial, notice of it having been given to the parties, such Jockey or Groom, shall pay Ten Pounds, if they or their Boys under them are convicted. No Groom, or Jockey objecting to these Rules, to be taken in by any Trainer, Stable Keeper, &c. in Hednesford. Trainers, or Stable Keeper, at whose house strange Grooms may stand with Horses, to be responsible for the penalties being paid on conviction.

8- If any Tradesman or Labourer in Hednesford or in the Neighbourhood is found lurking or watching a trail he shall not be employed by any Trainer, Jockey, or Stable Keeper, in Hednesford ; and if proved that such person is employed, the person dealing with, or employing him or them, shall pay Ten Pounds.

9- If any Trainer, Jockey, or Groom, shall open the preserved ground by removing any Hurdles, Dolls or Gorse, (except for a Trial,) or galloping over the Gorse in any way whatever, they shall pay Five Pounds; and unless the Hurdles, Dolls, Gorse, &c., be replaced within two hours after the trial, he shall pay Two Pounds ; should any Boy remove any Hurdles, Dolls, Gorse &c., he must be discharged by his employer ; and any Trainer, Jockey, Stable Keeper, employing the said Boy, shall be fined Five Pounds.

10- That in case any Boy should leave his Master, and apply for another situation, the person so applied to, shall make enquiries respecting his character, and if he has served the time engaged for, and not to take him into his service unless he receives a proper character from his last employer.

11- That if any Trainer, or Jockey, engages a Boy, and continues to keep him in his service, after it is proved that he has left his Master without fulfilling his agreement, let the term be what it may, when it is proved that he has done so, the person engaging him shall be liable to a penalty of Ten Pounds ; also the case and the names shall be published in the Racing Calendar, and Bell's Life, and the expenses of advertising to be paid out of the Funds of the Hills.

12- That in case any Boy leaves his Master and the Neighbourhood, without fulfilling his agreement, he shall be published in the Racing Calendar and Bell's Life, and at the same time, the cause of his leaving, to caution other Trainers and Jockeys from employing him.

13- If it can be proved that any Trainer, Jockey or Groom knowing that a Boy's time of service is nearly expired, should encourage and tempt the Boy, by offers of higher wages, or the said Trainer, &c., employ any person to hold out those temptations, before the Boy has left his situation, they shall pay a penalty of Five Pounds, and the name published as above.

14- No alteration to be made upon the Training Ground without first obtaining the consent of the Marquess of Anglesey, and a majority of the Trainers respectively. All fines and regulations must be strictly observed.

15- Any Trainer, Jockey, or Stable Keeper, having a dog on the hills, and not taking immediate steps to remove him, to pay Ten Shillings.

16- Should any complaint be made against the person in office, or any person under him, the case to be heard by the said Trainers and Jockeys who are in Hednesford, and the case to be decided by a majority of them ; but the Trainer in office not to have any voice in deciding the matter.

17- That the gallop called Peel's Gallop, and part of the Copy Gallop, and the new Two-year-old Course Gallop, shall be closed from the first of November in every Year till the first of April in the next Year, except when any of these Gallops shall be required for a Trial, the opening of which shall be governed by Rule No. 1. Any Trainer, Jockey or Groom, infringing this Rule, shall be fined Five Pounds.

18- A meeting of the Trainers to be held in the first week in January in every year, and the manager for the year to pass his accounts to be examined, and any balances in hand to be paid over to the Trainer elected to be in Office the following year ; such manager to have the entire control of the ground, to hear all complaints and decide as to the penalties, &c.&c., to collect all payments for the maintaining the ground, and to do his utmost to improve and keep the ground in good order.

We the under-signed agree to the above Rules.

THOMAS FLINTOFF, Manager for the present Year, 1857.

WILLIAM SAUNDERS,	**WILLIAM BURBRIDGE, for E. R. CLARKE. ESQ.**
ROBERT DENMAN,	**JOHN WILKINS,**
THOMAS CLIFF,	**SAMUEL SMITH,**
JAMES DOVER,	**CHARLES MARSON.**

J. Simpson, Printer, Upper Brook Street, Rugeley.

87 A facsimile of the 1857 training ground poster explaining the rules and regulations for the year

affording in the Spring of the year a fine, spongy surface".

He adds that "within the last ten years certain rules have been drawn up and agreed by every person using the exercise ground for the purpose of keeping it in good order. Each trainer takes it by turns for a year to superintend the rolling and such repairs as may be deemed requisite. A subscription is paid by the owner of each horse trained there, which subscription forms a fund for the payment of necessary expenditure."

To make sure that those rules were strictly abided by the trainers met each year, elected their new "Manager for the Year" and had rules for the training grounds printed and posted around the Hills. In that way they tried to ensure that the exercise grounds were kept in the finest condition. Posters for the years 1852 and 1857 show that William Saunders and Thomas Flintoff were the respective managers in those years. Those efforts by the trainers obviously satisfied the Paget family and by the 1830's Henry William Paget, First Marquis of Anglesey, actually sponsored one race, the Anglesey Stakes, held at Hednesford Race Course. In 1841 Sarah Massey, landlady of the Cross Keys, entered her horse "Crafty" in the race and it came fourth.

In the same article by "Cecil" he mentions the trainers at Hednesford at the time of his visit in 1838 and a previous visit, probably in the 1820's. On his first visit Mr. Mytton had "a long string of horses" at Hednesford as did Mr. Giffard (both well-known race horse owners). However, on his return both had retired from the racing business, the former dying and the latter seemingly having lost interest. The trainers on the second visit were:- Samuel Lord who trained for Mr. Edmund Peel of Hednesford Lodge; Mr. Moss; Thomas Carr who owned the oldest establishment; Thomas Flintoff of Prospect House; Mr. Walters; and finally William Saunders. Henry Arthur who had had stables in Hednesford had moved to the Cannock area and had stopped training, though he intended to start again. Richard Spencer, who had had a stables at Littleworth, had passed away leaving no one to continue his work. His stables had been taken over by the Saunders family.

Those trainers also employed three noted jockeys of their day who lived in Hednesford.

Listed below are some of the successes of the various trainers, jockeys and horses.				
Trainer	Jockey	Horse	Race	Year
Thomas Flintoff	Pat Conolly	Birmingham	St. Leger	1830
Thomas Flintoff	S. Darling	Independence	Chester Cup	1831
Thomas Carr	E. Wright	The Cardinal	Chester Cup	1834
Samuel Lord	John Spring	Tanworth★	Chester Cup	1836
John Fobert	Charles Marlow★★	The Flying Dutchman	Derby Stakes	1849
William Day	George Palmer	Haco	Cesarewitch	1853
William Saunders	Charles Marlow	Goldfinder★	Chester Cup	1853
William Saunders	Charles Marlow	Polestar★	Staffs. Stakes	1850's
John Balchin	Joseph Kendall★★	Jealousy	Grand National	1861
Thomas Cliff	Henry Taylor	Croagh Patrick	Stewards Cup	1861
William Saunders	George Ashworth	Wynyard	Liverpool Cup	1871
William Saunders	George Ashworth	Indian Ocean	Liverpool Cup	1872
William Saunders	George Ashworth	Indian Ocean	Shrewsbury Cup	1872
William Saunders	George Ashworth	Playfair	Cambridgeshire	1872

★ Tanworth or Tamworth belonged to Sir Edmund Peel, owner of Hednesford Lodge.

★ Polestar and Goldfinder were both owned by the notorious Dr. Palmer who regularly met his trainer at the Cross Keys.

★★ The jockey, Kendall was Hednesford's only connection with this race.

★★ Charles Marlow was Hednesford's only connection with this race.

88 The stables of Alf Newey at Prospect House, previously occupied by Thomas Flintoff, Thomas Cliff and Frederick Hassall. C.1920

George Whitehouse rode for Peel; Charles Marlow rode for Saunders and had married his daughter; while John Dodgson represented another stable which may have been at the Cross Keys.

In fact the reason why "Cecil" visited Hednesford in 1838 was possibly due to the success that the various stables were having around the country. In 1830's were the heyday of racing at Hednesford and it actually boasted its own race course. Unfortunately where it was situated is not known and it only lasted for a few years from 1835 to 1842 when it was abandoned, probably due to lack of outside support.

Success in the 1830's added to the reputation of the Hednesford training ground and new trainers were not slow in moving into the area, including Thomas Eskrett who came all the way from Yorkshire around 1848. The 1841 Census reveals that no less than 84 people were directly involved with racing, an unbelievable 29% of Hednesford's population and that did not include such people as blacksmiths, farriers and nailers.

Another reason why Hednesford was so popular with horse owners was that, being centrally placed in England, it was within easy walking distance of many race courses. Yes, walking distance! With little transport, save for coaches and canals, race horses had to be walked by the stable lads to the courses - and woe betide any stable lad who rode the horse, his reward would be a severe whipping and instant dismissal. Sometimes they rode on a "hack", leading the race horse, hence "Cecil's" statement that "Liverpool, Manchester and Newton are hence supplied by horses (from Hednesford) without more than two hours walking on the road" and Chester was "within moderate distance".

In fact Thomas Flintoff had his stable lad, George Kent, walk "Birmingham" all the way to Doncaster in 1830 and the horse still won its race. "Independence", another of Flintoff's horses, in 1832 walked to Doncaster, then on to Manchester and finally to Chester winning all its races at those meetings. In 1839 "Cecil" described that horse in affectionate terms – "He (Flintoff) has got old "Independence" as a pensioner. The poor old horse is fortunate in having a good master, who only uses him to ride about home."

By the 1850's there were at least six racing stables in the Hednesford area. William Saunders was at Hazel Slade, Eskrett at Hednesford Lodge, Thomas Flintoff at Prospect House, Samuel Lord on Rugeley Road (now Uxbridge Street), James Hopwood down East Cannock Road and George Palmer near the Cross Keys. Flintoff retired sometime in the 1850's and Prospect House was taken over by Thomas Cliff.

Most of these had their horses shoed at John Wright's forge at Hill Top. He had taken over from the Bentons and became a real local character. Stories have it that he called himself the "King of Hednesford" and at the Hednesford Wakes used to arrive in a coffin from which he suddenly sprung to lecture the good people of the village. In an interview with 84 year old John Craddock in 1927 he said that he remembered "Jack" Wright well and often the blacksmith would arrange for races between horse and man. In one such incident on Hednesdord Hills the foot runner, Will Humphries, was matched against one of Wright's own horses for a wager of £5. Humphries was allowed a certain distance, but the horse still won. Unfortunately as so often happens with local characters as time evaporates they lose their appeal and poor, old John Wright later became the object of ridicule by local children (see chapter on Crime).

The demise of the racing stables began with the rapid development of the coalfields in the area. Why is not clear, but by the 1900's only three stables were left, those of Lawrence Rooney at Red House, East Cannock (opposite where the Globe is today); Tom Coulthwaite's at Hazel Slade; and the stables at Prospect House, possibly run by Alf Newey (Frederick Hassell had retired in 1902). Even then success was still to be had. In 1924 Robert Denman Junior trained "Sir Galahad the Third" to win the Lincoln, while Tom Coulthwaite won the Grand National on three occasions. In 1907 "Eremon" ridden by A. Newey won; in 1910 "Jenkinstown" ridden by R. Chadwick; and finally in 1931 "Grakle" ridden by R. Lyall. The 1931 success was even more spectacular as Coulthwaite had announced his retirement from the sport in 1930 and decided to give the race just one last try.

The arrival of the miners in our area coincided with the birth of another sport, football, which was to readily occupy the needs of the less well-off for a leisure pursuit. In the 1870's many local teams were started, such as Hednesford Rovers, Hednesford Britannia, Hednesford Unity, Hednesford Strollers and Hednesford Swifts and they played one another in "friendly" games. The mining companies they worked for or local rivalry between rows of houses might be just the catalyst to start a team and there was ample space behind the rows of

89 Cannock Chase Colliery F.C. c.1936.

houses or on colliery ground to play the matches.

In 1879 the idea for a Hednesford Football Team was first muted and by 1880 two local teams had amalgamated. They were the Red and Whites who played at West Hill and the Hill Top team (also known as the Hednesford Hills) who played in Reservoir Road and wore white shirts and dark blue shorts. It was decided to adopt the colours of the Hill Top team and they would play their matches at the Anglesey Hotel Ground, known locally as "The Tins" because of the metal sheeting around the ground. The first captain of the new club was Mr. A. Freeman and the secretary was Mr. J. Taylor.

In the beginning only friendly matches were played against other local clubs, but gradually the team was entered into cup competitions in the county. Soon they had quite a following, gaining the nickname of the "Lily Whites" (the "Colliers" or "Pitmen" came much later). By way of her appreciation for the increase in business on match days at the Anglesey Hotel, Mrs. Eskrett provided a supper for both the cricket and football teams after their first season.

Such was the success of the football team that in the 1890's they joined the Walsall and District League, finishing third in the 1902/03 season. Although on the surface it would seem that everything was highly organised matters were not really the case. For instance matches rarely started on time, either due to the late arrival of opponents or even their own players who had worked down the pit in the morning. One game started late because Small Heath had their photograph taken before the kick-off and on New Year's Day, 1887 Stafford arrived an hour late and it was agreed to play just twenty minutes each way. Sometimes the referees never appeared

90 The Keys Ground. Centre is Mr Pointon and his son, William Ernest, with the tray. Even the lads wore flat caps.

and club officials took over. All that must have made the matches something of a lottery for spectators, but where possible games began at 4.30 p.m. on a Saturday, except in the depths of winter.

By the turn of the century the Anglesey Ground was proving too small and so in 1904 the team moved to a new ground behind the Cross Keys. There was also so gentle financial persuasion as Noah Corbett, landlord, had promised to pay off the club's debts of £40 if they moved. Those debts seemed to hound the club for years, but the move seemed to have made financial sense as over 900 spectators saw the first game at the Cross Keys.

By 1908 the team had joined the Birmingham Combination League and to comply with that league's regulations the pitch was widened and two turnstiles were added. The expenses for the alterations were met by a local firm, Butler & Co., and once again Noah Corbett wrote off a debt. Over 2,000 saw the first game and by the 1909/10 season the team were proving almost unbeatable at the Keys, eventually ending the season by winning the league. Their record for that season read:-

P	W	D	L	F	A	Pts.
30	24	3	3	98	39	51

All should have been secure financially (over 4,000 saw them play Darlaston in the English Cup, forerunner of the F.A. Cup), but war clouds were gathering and even though they completed the 1914/15 season the team was disbanded for the duration of the conflict. However, some friendly games were still played by a Hednesford Colliers team.

By 1919 the club was reformed and joined the Birmingham League. To put itself on a sounder financial footing (a ruling for that league) it was formulated into a limited company and 3,000 shares were sold at 10 shillings each. It was contracted to pay over £900 in wages for the season and takings were estimated at £1,500. Travel to away games would cost around £350, leaving around £150 profit for the season. Butler & Co. gave them a good start by promising to "practically agreeing to them having the ground free".

At first all went well for the club and in the 1921/22 season they reached the first round proper of the F.A. Cup losing 3-1 to Southend in a thrilling game. However, money was always to be the main problem and year after year the club struggled to keep its head above water. The 1937/38 season saw it almost bankrupt. So low were the funds that in January, 1938 the team could not afford to travel to Oswestry to play the match, despite the Shropshire club offering to pay some of the cost. On February 24th a letter of resignation was sent to the league. All seemed lost, but somehow the Hednesford Football Club was formed by the next season and the club was saved.

What had led to those problems over the years? Quite simply its success attracted the attention of bigger clubs and players who could have won Hednesford trophies transferred to teams like Aston Villa and Wolves. As early as the 1890's players like Jack Devey, Steve Smith and Orlando Evans (who later returned to keep the Plough and Harrow) went to the Villa, while Tom Picken and Jack Nicholls moved to Albion. Jack "Tosh" Griffiths, perhaps the finest centre forward Hednesford ever had, went to Wolves in 1913 and the leakage continued throughout the inter-war years. In the 1922/23 season Teddy Bowen and Alec Talbot moved to Villa and Jack Harrington to Wolves. In the 1930's Jackie Maund and John Martin went to Villa, Jack Shelton to Wolves and Harry Nicholls to Sheffield Wednesday.

Obviously no one would blame players for wanting to better themselves, but it left Hednesford struggling in their own league (in fact they never won the Birmingham League during the inter-war years despite most supporters considering that period as Hednesford's finest). So with the lack of success gates fell and the finances dwindled – a feature of the modern game all supporters of small clubs know only too well.

But it would be wrong to end without a mention of recent successes. In January, 1997 Hednesford reached the Fourth Round of the F.A. Cup where they played Middlesborough and almost upset their illustrious rivals, only losing 3-2 in a thrilling game. In 2004 they won the F.A. Trophy beating Canvey Island 3-2.

91 Wimblebury White Star F.C. 1936

92 Belt Road Rovers 1949/50. In the background is West Cannock No. 3 Pit.

By way of other leisure pursuits for those less physically active the miners brought with them an institution quite unique to the working class – the working men's clubs, of which there are still at least five surviving in the area. These were places where men could go to relax after a hard day's work in the pit and they provided social contact with workmates as well as quiet reading rooms where newspapers, too expensive for the miner to afford, could be used. These clubs were run by the members themselves by way of an elected committee and they organised the club life and finances. That included various sports to be played between the clubs and darts, dominoes, bowls and cribbage (a card game) soon became a major attraction so that most miners had at least one good reason for leaving the family at home one night a week. Most of those inter-club competitions still survive today.

But the family was not totally forgotten and committees arranged trips and days out to places like Llandudno, Rhyl or Blackpool which were paid for by the weekly subscriptions that each member paid. Though women were usually not allowed into these clubs on weekends rules were relaxed if there was a concert provided.

There was another attraction which made these clubs popular – cheap alcohol. Because of the numbers which supported the clubs the committees were able to do deals with local breweries who sold them the ale at lower prices than paid by the public houses. Surprisingly that did not affect the public bars which still flourished, much to the probable dislike of the local police force and magistrates who witnessed a rise in cases involving drink.

It would seem to suggest that all miners did to relax was drink, far from it! Methodism was very strong in the area as was the Temperance Movement and a great many miners found other ways to enjoy themselves. After a long shift in the bowels of the earth many welcomed the chance to get fresh air and hobbies like gardening flourished. You just have to take a look at a typical miner's cottage with its enormous plot of land at the rear to realise that gardening was very popular. Most were dug and planted out each year. Such was the popularity of gardening that Hednesford formed its own Horticultural Society in 1881 and in 1886 the Hazel Slade and Rawnsley Horticultural Society was formed and held annual shows and competitions.

Another fresh air sport which miners loved was pigeon flying, while the keeping of fowl and banty rearing was widespread. In 1879 the Hednesford and Cannock Chase Poultry and Pigeon Society began and held its first show on February 21st, 1880.

For those with a more artistic leaning there was the Hednesford Amateur Minstrels (sometimes called the Charity Minstrels) and the Hednesford Town Band gave regular performances at the newly built Public Rooms on Rugeley Road or even on the lawn outside the Anglesey Hotel. When Hednesford Football Team arrived home after drawing with Burslem Port Vale in the final of the Staffs. Junior Cup in the 1897/98 season the Band greeted them at the station and when the Great War began the Band gave its final performance on the Anglesey lawns before marching off *en masse* to enlist. They became the band battalion of the 15th Service Battalion of the King's Royal Rifles. The Minstrels also gave regular performances, like that given at Rawnsley in March, 1890 in the Cannock and Rugeley Working Men's Institute.

93 Alan Cobham's Air Circus c.1930 pictured near today's Jubilee Inn. It was 5 shillings per trip in the plane. Mr Frederick Sanderson is standing next to the plane.

But what of entertainment for the ladies and young children - those not already at work. Sadly there was not a great deal – the Victorian and Edwardian idea being that a "woman's place was in the home" and children were hardly in the equation at all! But there were some ways to escape the humdrum of the home. Churches and chapels had choirs which performed music and drama (usually of a religious nature) and the Public Rooms played host to musical evenings, recitals and lectures. Mutual Improvement

Societies, held at the various religious venues, gave talks which were aimed at helping the aspiring ladies lead better lives and improve their education. For example, one evening held at the Wesleyan Chapel in 1881 gave a lecture which illustrated the "Struggles and Triumphs of the Gospel in England". That talk was "assisted by a large number of magic lantern views" and references were made to John Wesley's two visits to Hednesford. Another talk advised housewives on "How to construct a healthy home".

Occasionally the women and children were treated to a day trip by the men's employers, made that much easier by the expanding railway network. In 1879 the West Cannock Company took a party of workers and their families to Aston Park and Grounds; on July 29th, 1882 Cannock and Rugeley Company took around 2,000 to Liverpool; and in 1887 East Cannock Company took a trip to Southport. Gradually those outings became annual events for the mining companies. Other businesses followed suit and Stantons Bakery held its annual day trip well into the twentieth century. The railway companies also encouraged days out with cheap fares an example of which was on Monday July 11th, 1881 when they advertised a day out to Alton Towers for 2 shillings third class.

As well as those chapels and churches organised days visits, usually organised for the congregation and friends. For instance St. Peter's Church took a party of Sunday School Teachers and friends to Malvern by train in June, 1891, while Littleworth Methodist Choir and teachers went to Sutton Park for the day in the same year.

Possibly the highlight of the nineteenth century for entertainment came with the Jubilee celebrations. However, Hednesford "was far behind its neighbours in celebrating the Queen's Jubilee" and many townspeople went elsewhere. The Cannock and Rugeley Company did give its workforce and families a treat on the colliery cricket ground. The men were treated to 900 pounds of best beef, 420 two pound loaves and 300 gallons of ale, while the women and children had 20 pounds of tea, 60 pounds of sugar, 1,000 buns, 100 one pound cakes, 250 pounds of seed and currant cakes and 750 mugs with the portrait of the queen and Jubilee on them. The local *Cannock Advertiser* reported that "the conduct of the men was admirable and the bulk

of the women behaved well, but a few were somewhat difficult to manage". (More of female behaviour in the chapter on crime.)

But if women were treated like second class citizens then children were even worse. It seems that the old adage of "children should be seen and not heard" very much applied. The only possible outlet for their undoubted energy, apart from school and a backyard kickabout, seems to have been the Hednesford Athletic Club, but even that probably only accounted for older boys and men and it was gymnastics rather that athletics. One of its performances in January 1891 under the captaincy of Mr. C. Greatorix was described as exercises on vaulting horses and parallel bars. Those were interspersed with routine "exercises with wands" and "the running maze", both of which were aimed at showing how disciplined the members were in their timing and skill. The event also had a boxing display "executed in a gentlemanly and scientific manner".

If boys had very little except for football, the girls had even less. They found themselves very often helping mother and learning the skills of being a good housewife.

However a little female emancipation did occur with the arrival of Hednesford's first cinema, though it was still considered "improper" for a lady not to be escorted there. On January 12th, 1910 "The Rink" in Anglesey Street opened its doors, at first purely a skating rink, but by December 12th it was showing films. It underwent a refurbishment in 1912 because of its popularity and changed its name to the "Electric Palace" and pictures were shown on Monday, Tuesday, Thursday and Saturday, while Wednesday and Friday saw dancing and other activities. (Notice Sunday entertainment was strictly forbidden.) In 1932 it changed hands with Frank Williams as the new manager and became the "Tivoli".

Such was the popularity of that new venue that it was quickly followed suit by the Public Rooms in 1911 which opened as the town's second picture house, the "New Empire". After a somewhat shaky start it fully opened in the new year of 1912 and produced both films and stage plays. By 1914 it had become the "Empire Picture Palace" and then in 1917 it was refurbished and renamed as the "Hednesford Picture House". By Feburary, 1933 it had become "The Empire". By the early 1960's both cinemas had closed due to lack of local support.

94 Joseph Baker dressed as a pageboy for Hednesford Carnival c.1930. He took part for three years.

Finally there was one local event which everyone looked forward to – Hednesford Wakes. Held at either the Anglesey or the Cross Keys in late October or early November such was its popularity that businesses and schools closed down for at least a half day. It was an occasion for everyone to take part in games and entertainment. The one held on November 1st and 2nd in 1880 at the Cross Keys had prizes for the 100 yards foot race, quoits and "many other English sports".

95 A float at Hednesford Carnival c.1930. Some were on loan from Pat Collins Circus for the event.

However, so eagerly was the event anticipated and so ready were Hednesford people to "let their hair down" that occasionally the organisers were let down by bad behaviour. A few went too far causing embarrassment all round. In 1881 the *Cannock Advertiser* wrote that "The Wakes this year have not passed away so quietly as on previous occasions, in fact there seems to have been a determination on all sides to revive the old custom and provide for the popular taste of the people". A quaint way of referring to the drunkenness which led the reporter to continue that he blamed it on "plentiful work and wages". A strange reaction when miners were still forced to work long hours and be laid off in the summer months!

By the turn of the century the Wakes had almost been replaced by the Hednesford Carnival which took place in the summer months. A more sedate affair it had its carnival queen, selected at the Tivoli on the previous Thursday, and then processions and floats on the Saturday. Rather than just a fun day it attempted to raise money for local charities. There has over the last few years been an attempt to revive these events and long may it continue.

BUSINESS IN BYGONE DAYS

With the rapid development of shopping centres and the inevitable decline in local small businesses one part of our history which might be readily forgotten is the shops and trades which flourished in the past and have disappeared over time. Fortunately some have survived, but they are very few. This chapter hopes to revive memories of some for those who may have worked there or for the people who may have used them.

The oldest surviving firm in Hednesford is Stacey's Funeral Service on West Hill. Joseph Stacey and his wife, Jane, moved from the tiny village of Orslow near Gnosall to Brocton in the late 1860's and then on to Hednesford around 1877 where Joseph set up his wheelwright and carpenter's business in a small cottage on the brow of West Hill, in the exact spot where the funeral service is today. A small workshop was built next door and trade began. Quite naturally as a carpenter he was occasionally requested to make coffins and so gradually he began his own undertaker's firm. To allow the firm to be completely independent he also established a blacksmith's workshop next door (where the parlour of the Chapel of Rest stands today). The 1881 Census still lists him as a wheelwright and carpenter, but by the 1891 Census he was solely an undertaker.

Perhaps the member of the family we most remember is George Stacey who was one of the eight children born to Joseph and Jane and the only one to remain in the business, some of the others emigrating to America. Born in 1881 it was George who really expanded the firm. He bought a house opposite in Booth Street and purchased the land below for his stables, whilst also having fields on today's Sunrise Hill to exercise the horses.

Those horses were always Belgian Blacks, renowned for their placid temperament and regal appearance. Perhaps you may have seen that breed pulling a hearse recently as they are still the preferred horse. George always chose his own horses and most years he travelled to the Liverpool horse sales to purchase replacements. Once back in Hednesford they were cared for by his own staff, making sure that they were well turned out for a funeral. The blacksmith shoed them and the family watered, fed and groomed them. At any given time there were six to eight horses which had to be looked after, four ready for a funeral and four on stand by.

It is no wonder then that most funerals took place in the afternoon, usually around 2.00 p.m. as it took most of the morning to get the animals ready for the hearse. They had to be exercised to guarantee that they were placid, then fed and finally groomed. After all that they were dressed and attached to the hearse. It was policy that on no occasion would a horse be allowed to take part if any slight imperfection was found.

96 George Stacey 1881-1956

97 A funeral procession through Chadsmoor.

At one time Edward (Ned) Marshall worked as the blacksmith. He was employed at the West Cannock Colliery Yard, situated on the Cannock Road behind where the garage is today and next to the railway. There he repaired wagons and made iron work necessary for the mines and afterwards he would assist Stacey's with shoeing the horses and making brasses for the coffins and horse bridles. George Massey, who lived in a cottage at the top of Sunrise Hill, cared for the horses while they were in the field behind his home and helped stable them each evening.

The coffins continued to be made on site and elm was the chosen wood unless a customer requested otherwise. That stayed the same until Dutch Elm disease in the 1980's when mahogany was then chosen. The wood was purchased from Wootton's Timber Yard close to the Hollies in Cannock and arrived ready sawn. Once there it had to be planed and the shoulder bend, near the head, was achieved by pouring kettles of hot water over the cuts to allow the wood to bend without cracking on the outside. It was then sealed and three coats of French polish applied – a fourth if George was not satisfied. It is no wonder then that funerals were expensive affairs.

Most funerals started from the home of the deceased where the body had been laid out in the parlour some days before for those interested to pay their last respects and then it was collected by the undertakers. Tradition had it that neighbours closed their curtains as a sign of respect. When the undertaker arrived a small service was held in the home and everyone then left for the church. The idea of a Chapel of Rest only took on when central heating became the norm, making the home unsuitable for keeping a body for days.

In the 1930's the business began to change with the introduction of cars. Around 1935 George had an Austen 18, but his personal favourite was a Chevrole which could hold both the coffin and close relatives. The horses were still available if requested.

When George died in 1956 the business was taken over by his daughter, Vera, who had married Ralph Poole. Their children, George, Robert and Anne, eventually took over and still run the business today.

Another business which still survives today from the nineteenth century is that of Pointon's, the sweet wholesalers, though originally they made their own. William Pointon arrived in Hednesford from Tipton around 1875 with his wife, Julia, who had been born in Codsall. He was a coal miner and like so many others came to take advantage of the new coalfield and its prospects. However, while still working in the mines he recognised a possible outlet for one of his hobbies – sweet making. (Lots of families made their own goodies.) Sometime before the 1881 Census he had moved into premises on the Cannock Road and there set up his business in buildings at the rear of his home. At one side of the factory he made sweets and at the other end he carved wood, another of his trades. In the beginning the sweets were sold on a stall in the Hednesford Market, but by 1890 he had opened up the shop on Cannock Road where the business was to remain until the 1980's, though the market stall was kept for quite some years. The hundredth anniversary of the firm was held at the shop in Cannock Road.

98 Pointons on Cannock Road.

In 1917 the shop was taken over by William Ernest Pointon who ran it until 1947 when his son, Bertram, took over. However, Ernest's wife,

Eleanor, remained in partnership with her son, Bertram, and her other son, William John, until well into her nineties. Finally the firm was taken over by the fourth generation in the 1980's though Nita, Bertram's wife, still plays a very active part.

In an interview given to Shugborough in 1967 Bertram described his days as a young lad in the factory and later the shop. From Monday to Friday he started work at 8.00 a.m. and finished at 7.30 p.m., while on a Saturday the hours were from 7.30 a.m. to 9.00 p.m. If he worked hard his grandfather gave him a penny for "being a good lad" and another penny if he took his spoonful of oil every week. (Remember a penny bought quite a lot in the 1920's.)

Gradually the business expanded and William bought sweet rollers and machines to mass produce the confectionery. At its height there were 60 sweet rollers and 15 machines. Besides those there were 5 copper boilers which operated on average two days per week and made around 7 hundred weight of sweets, though in full production between 3 and 7 hundred weight could have been made per day.

Once the mixture was boiled and then rapidly cooled it was turned out on to a marble slab where it was kneaded. At that point the flavouring was added. The process took twenty minutes to boil the mixture and fifteen minutes to create the sweets. It was kneaded for around six to seven minutes until it reached a manageable temperature. From there one man handled the mixture on the marble slab while another operated the sweet rolling machine.

Like most sweets of today there were always the popular varieties and best sellers. Horehounds and Pointon's Pink Ones were the favourites and made every week. Horehound or hoarhound was a downy herbaceous plant with small white flowers and contained a bitter juice tasting like cough medicine (chemists often sold a tincture of horehound). William grew the plant on his allotment beside the railway line and in his own garden. It was harvested, dried out and then infused when needed for the sweet making. Four pints of the herbal mixture were added to forty pounds of the sweet mixture. Pink Ones were made with capsicum and aniseed flavourings. Other popular brands included cough sweets, sweet fish, pear drops and sugar pigs.

The flavours which could not be found locally were obtained from Bushes of London, though it obviously made the finished product more expensive. For example, aniseed in the 1930's cost 7 shillings per one pound jar. (At one time a lot of flavourings were by-products from coal, but the government eventually made that illegal.) The white and brown sugar was purchased from Tate and Lyle's, "Tate's Farths" being the nickname for the brown sugar for making the cough sweets and humbugs. In the 1930's sugar cost 28 shillings per hundred weight and was delivered in 8 hundred weight bacon casks packed into 2 hundred weight bags.

Eventually in 1954/55, because of the expense, Pointon's stopped making their own and the business became purely a wholesale one which it still is today, trading just off the Rugeley Road. Locals still refer to the firm as "Sucky Pointon's", "suck" being the old Hednesford word for sweets.

Besides those two businesses there are those which have sadly closed down, but will remain in the memory for many years to come. The first of those was the Bee Hive Corner Stores at the junction of West Hill and Cannock Road. Instantly recognised because of the bee hive above the entrance, it is not exactly clear when the shop first opened, but in the 1870's it was owned by Wigham's and was probably the first general store in the town. By the time of the 1881 Census it had changed hands and was run by Edwin Harris who had moved from Birmingham with his wife, Anne. Although they were to have eight children none of them seemed interested in the business and so Harris went into partnership with Horton and Heath who owned other shops in the area. Harris himself retired from the business around 1890 and managers were put in charge.

99 Tokens used by the Beehive Stores for customers to buy and use at Christmas, c.1880

The longest serving manager was Clem Taylor who arrived in 1905. He was born in Alrewas and was one of eleven children. Eventually he bought the shop in 1928 and it remained in the family until its closure in the 1960's. One of the first things that Clem did was to have the shop repaired and repainted in the original gold leaf colour at a cost of £30.

The shop itself covered almost the whole of the downstairs, fronting on to both West Hill and Cannock Road, with store rooms and a kitchen at the rear. Behind the shop were the stables where the three horses were kept and pigs and fowl were also reared there. (Hednesford's newly created fire brigade was just beyond the shop and often had need of Taylor's horses.) The horses were a necessary part of the business as all deliveries were made by pony and trap and it was not a help to the business when they were commandeered during the First World War.

100 The Beehive Stores c.1910.

Rhoda Taylor, one of Clem's two daughters, in an interview related how her regular job at the store was to deliver orders throughout the district. People had to place an order at the store by 9 o'clock the day before and it left the shop neatly wrapped in brown paper tied with string. On Mondays Rhoda drove the pony and trap to Gentleshaw and Boney Hay; Tuesdays to Huntington, the outskirts of Cannock and Cheslyn Hay; Wednesdays to Cannock Town centre; and Thursdays to the Green Heath area. The remaining two days she worked in the store. That same pattern of work happened to Tom Fowler when he was a delivery boy, only by 1938 he had a bicycle.

Another of Rhoda's tasks was to collect debts. Unlike today people were allowed to "run up a bill" or have things "on tick" with the shop and pay at the end of the week. That was fine until events like the miners' strike of 1926 occurred when Rhoda found herself with embarrassing experiences at the doors of the desperate miners' wives. In sympathy Clem would often give food to the children of striking miners and "forget" the bill. (Many shopkeepers and publicans in the area did the same, caring for the poorer children in times of crisis.)

Perhaps the most evocative memory of the Bee Hive Shop was the inside of the shop. Butter and sugar were sold loose and if you were lucky enough you could watch the assistants pat the butter as you waited. Coffee was ground on the premises one morning a week filling the air with its aroma while wood was chopped into sticks for firewood round the back (Tom Fowler's job on a Saturday). But to a youngster the most fascinating aspect of the store had to be the money chute. In the left hand corner of the shop stood the office where the manager sat. Your money was paid at one of the two counters, one opposite the main door, the other to the side, along with a list of your items purchased. Those were placed into a metal container which was loaded on to the chute. A button was pressed and the container shot round the room and into the office. Any change came back the same way. Quite a fantasy world for your author in the 1940's and early 1950's!

101 Thomas Brown, fruit and veg' salesman with his first van which delivered orders around the district c.1930.

Up the hill from the Bee Hive Shop was Stanton's Bakery, in Western Road. Born in Coseley Samuel Joseph Stanton moved to Hednesford in the late 1880's with his wife, Eliza and set up a small baker's shop in Market Street, next door to Moore's Clothing Factory, close to where the library stands today. There he and his wife, together with Alice and Joseph Hindley, Eliza's sister and brother, began to produce home-made bread and cakes. Next door they had a butcher's shop and their own piggery at the rear, producing the meat for their own pies.

The business soon flourished and by 1905 new premises were needed and so they moved to Western Road where it would seem that they bought an existing bakery site, probably the one established by Charles Elks in the 1870's and sold to one William Bales in the late 1880's. By 1913 the bakery was so successful that it was decided to build a new bakery on the site and in May, 1914 it was opened. A report on the building stated that "no expense had been spared in an endeavour to secure the best hygienic conditions for producing bread and those dainty confections which appeal alike to the eye and palate".

On the ground floor was the packing and dispatching departments, together with the bakery. The new machinery included a dough mixer which was fed by a sifter erected on the second floor which allowed only the exact amount to flow to the mixer. It was fitted with a brush arrangement which ensured the removal of any possible fluff and dust which might contaminate the flour. There was also a machine which divided and weighed the dough into nearly 1,500 loaves per hour. On the second floor was a cake mixer capable of dealing with one and a half hundred weight of cake whilst nearby there was a fruit cleaning machine capable of cleaning 40 pounds of fruit per minute. The new ovens could hold 180 loaves which passed through the oven on a roller. Also on the second floor were stores for flour and sugar, the former holding 600 sacks. Finally on that floor were rooms for icing and chocolate work on the confectionery.

Outside the bakery new stables were erected which, besides the animals, housed the horses-drawn vans, two of which were new, having been purchased from Messrs. Mellor and Sons of Hednesford. The horses were grazed at the side of the bakery or on Sunrise Hill and were shoed at the blacksmith's on West Hill where some bakery carts were stored on occasion. In all the new bakery was one of "the best equipped in the district".

Such was the reputation of Stanton's that in 1926 Samuel put forward entries for the London Bakery Exhibition and with every entry he took first prize along with a gold cup. When he died his two sons, Harold and Rowland, continued the business together with Frank, Harold's son. (A third son of Samuel, Frank, had unfortunately been killed in the First World War in 1918.) The business continued to keep its reputation for high quality so much so that in 1955 Allied Bakeries bought it, though it still traded under its original name well into the 1980's. However, with economic trends leaning towards vast sites it was considered too small and with no possibility of expansion it eventually closed in the 1990's. The land has now been developed by Persimmon for houses.

One of the oldest businesses in Hednesford, and only recently finished, was Blagg's Ironmongers at the corner of Churchill and Rugeley Road. In 1865 George Blagg moved to Hednesford from Leek where he had already had an ironmonger's shop. There is some uncertainty as to exactly when he opened the shop in Hednesford, but he was definitely trading in the late 1870's as can be seen from the *Kelly's Directory for Staffordshire* and adverts for the business in the *Cannock Advertiser*.

With the enormous expansion in housing in the area in the 1870's his shop flourished, selling everything necessary for the new home. That included hardware, tools, plumbing equipment, gardening tools and any horticultural sundries. He also sold leather goods which were manufactured in his workshops at the rear as well as repairing household goods. Strangely his store also sold alcohol (above the entrance used to be a plaque which displayed "George Blagg - licensed to sell alcohol"), though most likely customers had to take their own jugs to be filled until bottled beer was introduced.

When George died his son, also George, took over with his wife, Gertrude. The business became a private limited company in 1947 with Gertrude becoming chairwoman after George died. Their daughters, Margaret and Pauline, were directors of the firm. Margaret married Mr. N.S. Kimberley and he became the company secretary and chief executive in 1954. The shop had been so successful that a further shop had

102 Market Street, Hednesford looking from Churchill c.1920. Blagg's shop is on the right.

been opened in Rugeley and a trades depot in Brereton. Mr. Harold Evans was the general manager of the Hednesford shop, the headquarters, and by 1978 he had worked for the firm for over forty years. He was awarded the British Empire Medal for his services to the trade in 1971 at an investiture in London.

By the late 1980's the family interest in the business was sold and despite attempts by several new businesses to continue trading the shop in Hednesford eventually closed its doors in 2003.

The final business studied did not begin in Hednesford but Wimblebury – that of Tranter, the butcher's shop. Mark Tranter was born in Bickenhill, Warwickshire in 1845, one of thirteen children. In the 1871 Census he was still living there as an agricultural labourer with his widowed mother, but by the end of that year he must have moved to our area with another brother, Abraham, a coal miner, because on October 1st, 1872 he married Elizabeth Tye at St. Peter's Church, Hednesford. After the wedding the couple lived in John Street, Wimblebury and some time before 1880 he had started his butcher's business there. (*Kelly's Directory of Staffordshire* lists him as a butcher in Wimblebury.) The 1881 Census lists Mark as living in John Street with his wife and four children and a maid, Emma Jennings. They were

103 The Tribali family with Anna, Aldo and Iris c.1940. They owned the cafe in Market Street near Tranter's shop.

to have a further eleven children, though not all born in Wimblebury as by the 1891 Census the family were living in Cannock Road, Hednesford.

Due to the size of family they had moved into Anglesey Drive by 1901, but the business still continued in Cannock Road. Besides having the shop Mark reared his own pigs at the rear of the premises and also travelled around the district to people's homes to slaughter animals and cure them. Around 1905 the business moved to 16

Market Street, Hednesford where it was to remain until its eventual closure. His descendants are not sure if it was Mark or his son, George, who opened that shop.

George Tranter, Mark's fourth child, was born in 1878 in Wimblebury and as a young lad often accompanied his father around houses to slaughter animals. Like many children of the period he left school at twelve, possibly to join his father. However, his first job seems to have been with a local chemist, Mr. Ellison, who wanted George to take up the profession. Unfortunately due to George's lack of an extended education the lad felt it was not really his future and so he finally joined his father. Once his future was settled George married Mary Jane Hubble in 1901 and they were to have six children.

The Market Street shop started with just two pigs, but by the time of the First World War George found himself working sixteen hours a day just to keep up with supplies of sausages and other meats for the hospital and prisoner of war camps at Brindley Heath. Such was the shop's reputation for good quality meat that the business expanded to include a stall in Cannock Market by 1930.

*Footnote – In Edwardian England a stranger could have distinguished a gentleman's status in society by the hat that he wore and possible accessories. Working classes had their flat caps, tradesmen in industry had their bowlers and businessmen had their trilbies and "swagger cane". George was never seen out unless he was smartly dressed and carrying his cane, though he did not need it to aid walking. It could be used to tap someone on the shoulder if they were letting the side down by slouching.

George died on December 3rd, 1937 and was buried at St. Peter's. The business was then carried on by his wife and two eldest sons, William and Charles. Such was the continued success of the shops that in 1959/60 a new slaughter house and boiler room was built at the rear of the Market Street shop next to the old slaughter house which had a cast iron plaque on the side inscribed Registered Slaughter House

No. 41. (The family took that plaque with them as a memento when the business closed.) The old slaughter house then became the "fasting pen" to house the animals before slaughter. At the same time a bakehouse was also built.

What were all those buildings used for? Tranter's was a traditional butcher's which meant that they killed the animals and made all their own produce which was sold in the shop. In a chat with Philip Tranter he said that they regularly made over 300 pork pies each week besides trays and trays of faggots, pigs pudding and polony. Also they did all their own roast meats, pressed brawn and tongue as well as sausages and home fed bacon. Obviously that meant a ready supply of fresh meat was needed and so animals were delivered every week and slaughter took place on a Monday.

The fourth generation to keep the shop were the four brothers, Bert, Paul, John and Philip, and sister, Pat. Bert and Paul had retired through ill health just before 2000 and Steve, John's son, had joined the business. However, it was the pressure of being a traditional butcher's shop which was to finally see the end of the business. Towards the end of the twentieth century the government decided that every butcher's shop had to be licensed and before that could happen everyone in the trade need to pass a certificate (it was the era of form filling which saw so many "old hands" in many professions decide to retire). As Philip told me they simply did not have the time or the inclination to go to college and as some of them were nearing retirement anyway they regretfully decided to close the business down. The shop finally shut its doors on October 28th, 2000.

104 Bridge into Hednesford c.1910 showing the station building and Beehive Corner on the right.

LAW AND ORDER

With the sudden arrival of so many new people in the area it might be expected that serious criminal activities might increase as perfect strangers tried to sort out their new pecking order. It had happened in areas like North Staffordshire and the Black Country when their industries had begun and great masses of people had been lumped together in overcrowded places. However, our area seems to have avoided that and dreadful crimes like the Gaskin murder and the Catherine Dooley manslaughter stand out like sore thumbs because they were so rare.

Our criminal past centred round petty crimes, such as drunkenness and minor "scraps", but they give the reader a better understanding of the nature of life for some in nineteenth century Hednesford and its surrounding villages. Life was hard and making ends meet a constant battle. Some people sought desperate measures to ease their poverty, like "coal picking" or poaching; others tried to forget their situation by drinking heavily; and others gambled to win their fortune. But let's not forget that when talking of crime it only involved a small percentage of the population.

*Unlike other chapters this one deliberately omits the names of offenders, unless the crime was severe, so as to spare any embarrassment to readers who might just recognise one of their ancestors.

With the rise in population and the expected "crime wave" that might follow Hednesford got its very own police station in 1877, along the Cannock Road (the building still stands today as flats). The 1881 Census records four officers working at the station, some of them actually living there. Fifty eight year old Eric Baldwin from Gloucestershire was the chief officer, along with Sergeant Henry Grupie, aged 37, and

105 The Police Station on Littleworth Road c.1910 with P.C. Bates on the doorstep.

Constables Samuel Gibbs (19) and William Wood (22).

That decision seemed to have been justified when on October 13th, 1877 William Watkins, a groom, was savagely attacked whilst driving his master's dog cart towards Cannock Wood. It was his job to take the money bags which contained the miners' wages to the various pits of the Cannock and Rugeley Company. His attacker, one Simeon Bird from Birmingham, had leapt into the cart and beat Watkins with a cudgel. Watkins had fought back, but eventually passed out and the money was stolen. Bird was captured and in 1878 was jailed. The police must have thought that Hednesford was going to be a tough place to keep in order.

However, that was to be their only sensational crime for almost twenty years. In the meantime they had to busy themselves with the local weekend habit of drunkenness. "Work hard all week and play hard all weekend" seems to have been the motto for many miners and Cannock Petty Sessions were always dealing with people who had overstepped the mark. Most landlords had frequent skirmishes with men who just refused to believe that they had had enough. William Ormson, landlord of the Uxbridge Arms, had quite a fight on his hands when he tried to bar one belligerent customer, while in the same weekend in November, 1880 James Jones, landlord of the Cross Keys, had exactly the same problem. Both men were fined 20 shillings with costs (a very expensive night out). In the following year nearly every public house had the same problem and "Refusing to Quit", as it was called, became a regular case at the sessions.

Those that did not cause a disturbance in the public houses often fell foul of the police while they were trying to get home. P.C. Hope of Hednesford Police was regularly in court with a string of offenders who could not go home without creating a nuisance. However, on April 26th, 1886 he might have thought better of it later when he interrupted a fracas outside Ghost Row in Littleworth. A crowd had gathered and a neighbourhood row had broken out (drink often fuelled old animosities) when P.C. Hope arrived and dispersed the crowd. As he walked away up Church Hill he was followed and then attacked from behind. The assault was so bad that he had to have six weeks off duty. In court the offender was given eighteenth months hard labour while the judge commended the police for the "very unpleasant and dangerous duties they had to perform".

Attacks on the police were rare as most people respected the job that they had to do and most drunks, though they might not like it, willingly accepted their punishment. One man even thanked the court on being fined 13 shillings with the words, "Very much obliged to you, sir," which created a deal of laughter.

The last word on drunkenness must go to John Wright, "The King of Hednesford". P.C. Robinson had come across John drunk in charge of his horse and cart in the East Cannock Road at 2 p.m. on May 14th, 1887. They was a crowd of children around John poking fun at him, a usual occurrence, and he was blaspheming at

106 Thought to be the local Police Force c.1920. Can you recognise anyone?

them. The constable tried to persuade John into his cart, but himself received abuse and so he arrested John. In court (it seems he was quite a regular attendant) he was fined 20 shillings with costs to which he replied, "I wish the police would see after my turnip fields. (He had had trouble with people stealing his crop.) I've got no money, send the policeman for it." It was not recorded whether the fine was collected!

Besides drunkenness the police and courts regularly had to deal with fighting, but strangely few cases amongst the men, who probably sorted out their differences without police involvement. As already shown miners' wives were not slow to back their husbands in mining disputes and equally were not slow in settling neighbourhood arguments. The police frequently had to separate fighting housewives and the following cases are just from one year – 1886.

On April 13th two ladies, both from West Hill, were walking home from Hednesford Market when one spotted the other from across the road. Without speaking the one ran across the road and attacked the other with a stick and might have continued the assault had not John Nuttridge intervened. The assailant then fled the scene, but was arrested and taken to court. There she defended herself by saying that her victim "had pushed her with her basket first". She denied having a stick, but "struck her with my fist and I did not give her half as much as I ought to have done". Because of her lack of remorse (often the case with women) she was fined 10 shillings and 17 shillings and 6 pence costs with the option of 28 days hard labour.

On August 4th William Noake, a waggoner, witnessed a fight at Hill Top. He told the court that he had seen two families standing together outside their homes when the one woman suddenly struck her neighbour, the man, three times. His wife tried desperately to get him indoors, but the woman then struck her in the eye. In her defence the assailant admitted hitting her neighbour, but said that it was an accident as "the blow was meant for her own husband" who had just merely stood by when her neighbour had called her "a ----- monkey". She was ordered to pay 5 shillings towards the costs.

On September 12th Sergeant Whalley was called to a serious fight amongst feuding neighbours at Church Hill. (As this case was quite complicated let us call them X and Y.) At 2.00 p.m. X had threatened Y with a chisel and pulled hair from Y's head. Y's daughter had intervened and stopped the fight and X had returned home next door. Then Y, with her sons, had broken window panes in X's home before smashing down the door and beating up X, rendering her senseless on the floor.

Jonas Ellington, a court witness, said that he had seen Y fetch X "out of her house by the hair of her head and afterwards throw a stone through her window". X's husband had raced for the police and when Sergeant Whalley arrived he found two or three broken panes of glass and X "very much exhausted and badly bruised". X said that Y and her sons had done it to her.

In her defence Y said that on the night before X and X's husband had been quarrelling because they were both drunk and they were "killing" themselves. All X's bruises came from that argument as did the broken windows when the two had thrown goods at each other. The court did not believe the story and she and her sons were each fined 21 shillings with costs.

107 Constable George "Bobby" Bates who was Littleworth and Wimblebury officer, pictured c.1900.

Occasionally the women were not averse to having a go at the men either. In November, 1881 one lady was in court for two separate offences. She had first attacked a lad and when another man intervened she turned around and attacked him. While in 1886, our notorious year, a lady from Church Hill took her neighbour to court for assault. His defence was that he only attacked her because she had "aggravated him and struck him with a poker" first. He was fined 11 shillings with costs, she got off with a caution.

It was not only for fighting that women found themselves before the courts. To make ends meet many housewives went to the local colliery to collect coal scraps. The colliery companies were at pains to try and stamp out that practise which they regarded as stealing and frequently took people to court. In May, 1879 three women were taken to court by the West Cannock Company for stealing 160 pounds of coal, value 1 shilling. P. C. Blackshaw stated that he had found the defendants at No. 4 Pit with two bags of coal and two large lumps which they had got from underneath a wagon. Mr. McGhie who represented the company pressed charges saying that "something should be done to put a stop to the unlawful carrying away of company coal". It was - the women were each given seven days imprisonment!

In December, 1879 five women were charged by Sergeant Brookes with stealing a quantity of coal from the East Cannock Company. Despite the defendants pleading poverty and ignorance of doing anything illegal by picking coal from a waste mound they could have all gone to prison. They were saved that fate because Mr. Green who represented the company preferred not to press charges. Instead they were each fined 2 shillings 3 pence.

Precedents for fines or prison had been set, but that did not stop others from "picking coal". In June, 1880 two women and a young boy were caught by P.C. Wood stealing coal from the East Cannock mound. Again they pleaded ignorance and only got off a heavy fine because the company did not appear at court to press charges. However, at the same session five women appeared having been apprehended by P.C. Grupie at West Cannock No. 2 Pit. Despite their pleas of ignorance, save for one woman who stated that she had been given permission to pick coal (she had not!), four of them were each fined while one was discharged on "account of poverty and illness".

And so it continued. In February, 1886 the *Cannock Advertiser* reported a case titled the "Three Mary Anne's". All teenage girls from High Town they had been caught by Benjamin Cooper, a coal inspector, on January 26th taking coal off one of the wagons (more serious than from mounds). They had run away when challenged, but later caught. Each was fined 7 shillings including costs.

But it was not only the women who picked coal. In November, 1881 an old man from Wimblebury had been watched carrying coal home on several occasions from the Cannock and Wimblebury Company. When P.C. Baldwin accosted him at the house he discovered a cellar "quite full of coal". The old man pleaded that he had paid for most of the cellar coal, but was still fined 23 shillings.

No matter how hard the companies tried to stamp out the theft they never stopped it completely as most people saw the mounds as waste which the companies had discarded. Court sessions continued to deal with "coal pickers" and even as late as the 1950's people could be seen scouring the pit mounds for coal.

108 Mary Bates alongside Superintendant Brookes in 1928.

Continuing cases which involved women there were those which sadly reflected the Victorian attitude to marriage. Although attitudes were changing and the wife was no longer considered to be the property of the husband some cases still reflected that old idea.

In 1887 a couple who had been married for fifty years appeared before the Petty Sessions. The wife complained that her husband beat her frequently and called her "vile names". On one occasion he had even locked her out of their home and when she did get back in the next morning he beat her again. His excuse to the court was that he was sure that his wife was unfaithful though he had no proof. Even when the daughter testified that her mother was innocent he still refused to believe it. Notice that he had no regrets, probably thinking it was his right to beat his wife. The court fined him the small sum of 11 shillings.

The reason for choosing that case is that in the same court session John Blewitt, a Pye Green farmer, was charged with "working his horse while it was in an unfit state". The Bench stated that "as the mare had been destroyed they should only fine him 14 shillings, but had it been otherwise it would have been a 40 shillings fine". Need I say more!

As late as 1913 attitudes had not altered a great deal. When a woman from Stafford Lane tried to summons her husband for desertion and wife beating during their thirty years of marriage his defence was that she deserved it as she had taken money from the home and constantly landed him in debt (the money was to feed their many children). She then told the court that money was always short owing to his gambling. Strangely the court did nothing about the assault and simply dismissed the case.

At the same session a couple from High Town appeared with the wife complaining of her husband's violence and bad gambling habit. He gave her little money to keep the home and often took back some which he had given. If she argued he beat her, once blacking her eyes and cutting her head open with a jam jar. She wanted the court to allow a separation which they granted and in their new enlightened thinking even ordered the husband to pay 10 shillings per week to his wife. Whether or not he paid the money could not be found, but with his

gambling habit it is doubtful.

A husband's gambling may have been a difficulty for the housewife, but illegal gambling was a serious problem for the police which they endeavoured to stamp out. One crime from Hednesford's past was that of cock fighting and Cockpit Hill, a slight dip in the land on Hednesford Hills just below today's raceway, obviously took its name from that notorious sport. Stories still abound about men almost being caught by the police, but evading capture because of the system of having young lads employed as lookouts.

How true those stories are cannot be verified as no one would ever knowingly admit to being involved. One notorious tale has it that at the turn of the twentieth century a gang of cockfighters had gathered in Splash Lane, but when they discovered that the police were in the vicinity they approached the landlord of the Cross Keys asking him if they might use the inn's long room for their sport. He informed them that the corpse of a miner was laid out there awaiting an inquest. On hearing that they asked if they might pay their last respects to the dead man and the landlord agreed. Once in the room they removed the body and set up their cock fighting ring. It must be stated that the landlord knew nothing of their exploit, but stories have it that when the Cross Keys was undergoing refurbishment in the 1920's/1930's a cock fighting pit was uncovered in the bar area.

Many other public houses had a reputation for allowing gambling and some were even caught in the act. On October 7th, 1890 P.C. Portrey from Willenhall and P.C. Dobson from New Cross, both dressed in plain clothes, had gone into the Trafalgar Inn at Rawnsley and witnessed a game of bar skittles and "The Devil Among the Tailors" played on a machine and for money. Three days later the same officers revisited the inn and again witnessed gambling. That second time they played the same games as well as a game of "Don" with cards. On both occasions the customers bet with ale or "smokes" as the winnings and the landlord was fully aware of what was happening as he held the stakes.

Incidentally for cover both officers had participated in the gambling so as not to give the game away, but they had not encouraged it. The court agreed their behaviour was correct and despite the landlord's protestations that he would loose his livelihood he was fined £5 with 15 shillings and 6 pence costs and his license was endorsed. The gamblers were also fined.

Besides using plain clothes police from other forces the police often used members of the public (snouts in today's language). In one case involving the landlord of the King's Arms, two such men were employed. They had been into the inn on August 8th and 10th, 1912 to try to discover if the illegal taking of bets was permitted by the landlord. On the first occasion a notorious "bookies runner" was observed to take no less than four bets in full view of the landlord; on the second visit the landlord became suspicious of the snout, threw him out and even assaulted him.

When the case came to court the landlord obviously denied all knowledge of the illegal betting, but the informer insisted that the landlord knew all about what was happening or if he did not "he would have to be very deaf" as bets took place right in front of him. Having heard all the evidence the Bench decided that the landlord was guilty and as they "were determined to try and stop this system of betting which did a considerable lot of mischief in the district" they fined him £20 and £11 and 2 shillings and 3 pence costs.

But if the police were determined to stop gambling in public houses they could do little to stop it happening in the streets, though they tried very hard. On November 23rd, 1883, a Sunday afternoon, five men were caught in Stafford Lane playing "Pitch and Toss", a game where you simply threw coins at a target and the nearest won all the money thrown. Such was the authorities' disapproval, the magistrate called it "disgraceful conduct", that they were each fined 20 shillings with 5 shillings two pence costs. On October, 1889 five more men were caught in Wood Lane "playing with coins" and fined, while five lads were caught on the Rugeley Road playing "Pitch and Toss" and fined 1 shilling each with 6 shillings and 3 pence costs at the same Petty Session.

Coin games were not the only offence. On February 18th, 1891 four men were caught in

109 "Bobby" George Bates on the steps of the Cross Keys. On the left is William Martin, the landlord, and on the right, Mr Chickley. C.1925.

Bradbury Lane playing "Bank" (a type of brag) with cards and coins. The ringleader was fined 10 shillings with 8 shillings and 3 pence costs while the remainder were fined 7 shillings and 6 pence with 5 shillings costs. These fines may seem small, but remember miners were being paid little more than a £1 a week wages in the 1890's and lads far less.

That case was only the tip of the iceberg. At the Cannock Police Court on Monday May 7th, 1900 almost fifty men were fined for gambling in the Hednesford area. No less than twenty eight men, most of them in their twenties, had been caught by P.Cs. Cook and Platt playing cards on the common near Rugeley Road. They were playing "bank" and when the officers intervened the men ran away, but left behind three packs of cards and 1 shilling and 8 pence. The officers had taken note of all their names and all, save one who had been wrongly identified, were fined. The next case involved ten men who had been caught playing cards and gambling by P.C. Jeffrey on the common in Hednesford. Lastly, ten men, all from the Green Heath area, were caught gambling at Green Heath by P.C. Cook on Sunday, April 29th. Again all were fined 3 shillings with 6 shillings and 3 pence costs. Incidentally some men were fined more than others because it was not the first time that they had been before the courts for illegal gambling.

There were other ways that the workers could be persuaded to part with their hard earned money. The Cross Keys had a reputation for allowing various sports to take place at the inn such as whippet racing which only became illegal if money parted hands. Whippets were a favourite amongst miners as they cost less to keep than greyhounds. Also prize fighters regularly used the inn as a training base, though they did not fight there. The public were encouraged to watch the training sessions. It must be stated that no court cases were brought against the landlords of the Cross Keys for any of theses events, unlike the landlord of the King's Arms (not the same one mentioned above). In March, 1888 he was taken to court for allowing fox terrier coursing at his inn.

Theft of animals or poaching was another regular crime which appeared before the Bench and some men were quite happy to travel miles to commit their crime. Strangely, although it undoubtedly did happen, deer poaching seemed to escape the attention of the police during the years studied. It seemed to mainly be fowl and rabbits.

In July, 1879 four men from Church Hill were taken before the court for fowl stealing from a Mr. Watwood of Bednall. Acting on information given the police had raided the home of one of the suspects and discovered one fowl in amongst some flock and another being carried "in a cooked state" into the front room. The men were committed to the Assizes, but the newspapers never recorded their sentence.

The June Session of 1881 was busy with poaching offences. Three men from Hednesford appeared before the Bench having been caught on Shoal Hill in pursuit of game. The gamekeeper, Mr. Williams, had found them in possession of three rabbits which were "quite warm". The men offered no resistance and in court were fined 20 shillings each with costs. In the next case four men had been caught on the same estate near the Mansty old tollgate house. They were beating the gorse, breaking the earth up with a rail and putting their arms up burrows. They were apprehended by the gamekeeper and P.C. North. They were each fined 12 shillings and 9 pence and 7 shillings and 3 pence costs (less than the others as they had not actually trapped anything). Finally the same Bench heard of fowl stealing in Hednesford from Mrs. Cliff (wife of the horse trainer at Stafford House). P.C. Grupie discovered the stolen fowl at one man's house and he was sentenced to three months hard labour.

Again in September, 1887 a Church Hill miner was caught on Hednesford Hills carrying a gun by John Murray, gamekeeper to Mr. Gardener. On being seen the man ran off, but was later discovered hiding under a hedge at Rawnsley. Although he had no dead animals on him he was still fined 7 shillings and 6 pence with 10 shillings costs, probably for carrying the gun.

The mention of guns leads to probably the worse case. On February 9th, 1900 Samuel Blewitt, a Pye Green farmer, intercepted two poachers on his farm. Determined not to be arrested one man fired at Mr. Blewitt and wounded him. Undeterred he still followed them and the same man even threatened to shoot him again. He eventually managed to reach Hednesford Police Station and the police later caught the two men. Two brothers, George and Thomas Jenkinson, were charged with grievous bodily harm.

At the Assizes at Stafford on March 8th George Jenkinson was found guilty and given a sentence of fifteen months while his younger brother, Thomas, was given one month as he had not fired the gun and had confessed to the police as soon as he was questioned. (More of this case will appear in a future book.)

The relative quiet of our area depended upon a vigilant police force and the constant pressure they applied. Most bobbies were highly respected members of their community, living as they did amongst the people, but occasionally they might be seen as overreacting to minor "crimes" which could lead to unpopularity. Unfortunately the police are only servants of the law and often find themselves having to act when discretion might be wiser. The following minor cases are all taken from 1881 and show the harshness of Victorian law and some might say its stupidity.

In January a young lad was fined 5 shillings including costs for "sliding on the footpath", obviously enjoying himself after a winter snowfall. In the same month another lad was charged with taking a wheelbarrow. He admitted the offence, but said that he had only borrowed it to take cinders home. Before he could return it the police had intercepted him. The court refused to believe his story and he was fined 15 shillings including costs.

In the April three men were each fined 5 shillings for trespassing on land at High Town and for picking manure off that land, while two others were charged with exactly the same offence and received 4 shillings 3 pence fine. So much for gardeners trying to fertilise their soil!

In July four lads were charged with entering the garden of Samuel Coope of Wimblebury on a Sunday and stealing apples, peas and beans (scrumping to you and me and just how many of us kids tried it at least once in our childhood?) Samuel did not press charges, but the court still fined the lads 7 shillings each.

In the summer of that year three men were charged for having their chimneys on fire and each fined 5 shillings including costs. I wonder just how many readers fired their chimneys when they had coal fires to clear the soot rather than spend money on a chimney sweep? It was common practise in Mount Street in the 1940's and 1950's.

Finally in September a scrap iron dealer was ordered to pay a 15 shillings fine for using his cart without having his name printed on the side.

And we think the law is harsh today!

REMNANTS OF OUR PAST

Unfortunately there is little remaining of our heritage – the mines have disappeared, the racing stables, save one, have long since vanished and many of our oldest buildings have been demolished. We could have lost even more had developers had their way in the late fifties and early sixties and destroyed the Cross Keys and Prospect House. It is hoped that this book may lead to the remaining history being preserved for future generations and perhaps our oldest buildings being given the status of listed buildings, as the Anglesey Hotel is.

The oldest building in Hednesford is probably the cottage now owned by Friel Homes, just opposite Splash Lane. It possibly dates from the sixteenth century and still has oak roof timbers and plaster work of lime and horse hair, mixed with farm dung (the old method of making plaster). Originally known as Cross Keys Farm, the building itself was originally timber framed, probably from trees felled from the Chase, though time has obviously meant that most of the timber has been replaced. There has, however, been little change to its original size, making it a prominent feature on the road from Birmingham. No doubt Wesley would have noticed it as he arrived in Hednesford in the early 1730's and may have even visited it.

Two rooms in the building possess elaborate coats of arms on their chimney breasts – the first appearing to be church heraldry, while the second appears to be the coat of arms of some noble family. Might that suggest possible links with the Bishops of Lichfield and even royalty? Certainly the heraldic designs on the one chimney represent lions and possibly the broom plant which might suggest links with the Plantagenet line of kings – the broom was their emblem. Could the first house have been associated with the Kings of England, a royal hunting lodge on the Chase known as a King's house?

Or might it have been a lodge for one of the king's representatives in the Chase area, namely his chief "forrester" or bailiff. If so it could have belonged to the Trumwyn family who held the title of Forrester in the area in the thirteenth century and who had close links with the Chase. The family certainly held the Bailiwick of Cheslyn Hay for some time in the thirteenth century and one part of the family had leased land from the Bishops of Lichfield close to Splash Lane.

110 The attic of Chase Farm Cottage. Notice the lime plaster and oak beams which have been whitewashed.

111 One of the heraldic designs above a chimney breast at Chase Farm Cottage. It would seem to suggest the Tudor Rose

Unfortunately little of that can be proved. The crest of the Trumwyn family who arrived in Hednesford was either not recorded or has been lost over time, unlike the crest of the Cannock branch of the family. As for the other connection, that with royalty, the College of Arms in London could find no connections with royalty. Its findings suggested that the coats of arms in the house were "clearly executed by a local vernacular artisan" who produced "an approximation of heraldry to provide the required atmosphere of gentility".

However, there is one strange anomaly left which might still suggest a very early noble history and that once lay in the grounds - the remains of what seemed to be a carp pool. It has now disappeared, due to development, but if it was there as local historian, Les Higgs, maintained then it would mean that there were royal or church connections as only those two institutions were allowed to keep or farm carp.

But what of the known history? It was certainly occupied in the seventeenth century and probably owned by Jone (Jane) Watson, a wealthy widow. She lived there with her daughter, Cassandra Evason, and her grandson, Robert. The Hearth Tax of 1666 shows her owning a house with three hearths, the same number as the cottage. When she died in 1669 it was left to her daughter who built up the farm behind the house. Cassandra had been married to Thomas Evason who probably kept the inn next door (see later) and so just moved in with her mother when he died in 1668.

Nothing is known of the house's history during the eighteenth century, but by the early 1800's Richard Spencer, who Cecil described as "one of the best country jockeys we had", was living there and training horses, although his training grounds were away from the house. When Spencer retired around 1835 Thomas Sanders moved into the house and the 1841 Census has him living there with his wife Elizabeth, three children, two trainers, one of whom was Florence O'Driscol, the other James Farrell, and eight stable lads. Also Mary Spencer lived at the house, a forty year-old who may have been Richard's daughter.

On the 1845 Land Title Map the house had been moved into by George Thackeray and was listed as "house, buildings and garden" with no reference to farm or stables. George had died by 1851 and his widow, Hannah, remained in the cottage being cared for by Ellen Spencer who had two small children, Thomas and Ann.

The last private owners were the Williams family and at the end of the nineteenth century the house was sold to the Cannock Chase Colliery Company who bought much of the property in the Old Hednesford area. By the 1960's the Williams family were still there as tenants. Finally the cottage was bought by Friel Homes and thankfully a great number of the old features have been preserved.

Just below the cottage lies the Cross Keys Inn built in 1746. It most likely stands on the site of a much earlier building, also an alehouse as it is the natural resting place for travellers before they began their climb up Hill Top and on to Stafford and beyond as far as Chester.

112 The Cross Keys photographed in 1997.

A study of various probate inventories of the seventeenth century give tantalising clues as to the possibility of such an inn on the site well before the Cross Keys. When Thomas Evason died in 1668 (the same man recorded in the Hearth Tax Returns as Thomas Yeavaston and probably Cassandra's husband mentioned before) his inventory recorded "in the chamber next to the brook two blankets, two bolsters, curtains about two beds, one cover of a table and one form, one chair and three cushions". The brook referred to, before it disappeared, ran alongside the Cross Keys and the Cross Keys was the only building in Old Hednesford which was near the brook. What is more interesting is that Thomas owned no less than eight beds and all their linen, far too much for an average home and most likely proving that he ran a rest house for travellers.

On his death the building seems to have been taken over by one Robert Berrisford and his inventory records him owning "one brewing tub, four barrels, one loom on which they stood and one tun dish" together with "three and twenty four noggins and dish". All those items are to do with brewing ale and obviously far more than a normal household would need. When he died in 1678 the building then seems to have been bought by John Stringer who, on his death in 1708, owned "five beer barrels" in the buttery. William Forrester was the next owner and at his death in 1730 that buttery contained "four barrels, three tubs and other things". Once again those items are more than a family's needs.

The construction of today's inn began in the 1740's and was completed by 1746. It was the practise in the eighteenth century for coaching or wagon companies to select known sites for inns to use as stopping stages for their customers. It is most likely then that the new inn in Hednesford was one of those sites. That would explain the T.W.C. above the date on the inn which could stand for Taylor's Wagon Company (Taylors was a very large coaching concern in the Midlands at the time).

The site might then have been purchased after William Forrester's death to be a great posting house, a place of call for road wagons, pack horses, post carriages and every other form of horse transport along Blake Street. Its main purpose would be to feed weary travellers and act as a post for exchanging horses. Horses would be changed every ten to fifteen miles and so the Cross Keys had to have stables large enough to cope with many horses. It had to have stables for horses coming north from Birmingham or Castle Bromwich, depending on the route taken, as well as those going south from Stone, those places being the next nearest stopping posts.

In the heyday of coaching life at the Cross Keys would have been hectic and money would have flowed freely (it cost a rider about three pence a mile to hire a horse), but with the coming of the railways and the decline of coaching, together with better routes north and south which missed out Hednesford trade in the nineteenth century gradually declined. It was around that time that the landlord of the inn

expanded his income by moving into farming and the stabling of race horses, though it is doubtful that the landlords ever trained horses themselves. It seems that they hired trainers like Charles Bemetzreider and Thomas Warren in the early 1840's and jockeys like Robert Denman.

Once again probate inventories give us a clue as to the inn's probable first owner. Thomas Johnson died in 1762 and he owned a building which contained a brewhouse and a cellar, not the sort of room for an ordinary home. The brewhouse contained "four barrels, one iron furnace and four bars, a mash tub and three pails" while in the cellar there were "two barrels, two tun dishes, two bowls and two throwls". In his parlour there were "one round table, six chairs and one leather bottom one and three maps". The reference to maps would suggest that travellers stopped there on their various journeys north or south.

White's Directory for Staffordshire in 1834 lists John Massey as the victualler and malster at the Cross Keys. He died in December, 1836 and his wife, Sarah, continued as the landlady. She was helped by a staff of six, including one Noah Cocking, an agricultural labourer, who probably took care of the farm at the rear. By 1851 the inn had changed hands and it was being kept by John Wilkins. It was during his time that the notorious Dr. Palmer frequented the inn and brought about the story of a ghost.

The story has it that Palmer had persuaded Wilkins to let out one of the stables for the prize-fighter, Bob Brettle, as a training room. The evening training sessions soon became general knowledge and people would flock to the inn to admire the fighter. However, as often happens men fancy their own chances against the experts and one night was no exception. Brettle and Palmer were in the tap room discussing tactics when it became clear that a drunken navvy, whom no one had seen before, was making jibes at them. He was also upsetting other locals by downing any ale left at the bar and offering to fight anyone who tried to stop him. He was obviously hoping that Brettle might challenge him.

Brettle was about to do so when Palmer stepped inn and persuaded the fighter to buy the lout a drink instead. Having got the ale Palmer took it to the navvy. Later rumours had it that

Palmer tipped some powder into the drink before giving it to the man. Not long after downing it the navvy collapsed at the bar and Palmer persuaded the landlord to allow the man to "sleep it off" in one of the stables. The following morning Brettle tried desperately to waken the navvy, but could not. He determined to fetch the police in the evening if the man had not recovered.

He made several visits to the stable during the day, but still could not revive the man. Determined to confront Palmer he waited for the doctor to arrive, but he never did. By that time Brettle was getting scared and so forced himself to make one last visit to the stable before summoning the police. When he got there the navvy had disappeared and despite him questioning locals no one could explain the disappearance.

It was only when Palmer was convicted of poisonings that Brettle's conscience weighed heavily. Had the doctor poisoned the navvy and got rid of the body? Nothing could be proved, but rumour has it that if a person dies in terrible circumstances their spirit never rests. Until some of the stables were demolished around the 1970's stories still abounded that a grey shadow often appeared in the corner of one sleeping soundly on the floor.

Brettle was not the last prize fighter to use the Cross Keys for training purposes. In 1890 S. Cooper trained there for his fight against W. Regan (by that time bare knuckle fighting had been outlawed). The actual fight took place at Calf Heath in the February and the police arrived and stopped it after seven rounds. Cooper got away, but Regan was arrested. The purse for the winner was £50, a huge amount in those days. The landlord of the Cross Keys, James Jones, was warned as to his future conduct.

As mentioned earlier landlords of the Cross Keys did involve themselves in dubious activities, but on a more pleasant note they did provide positive entertainment for the locals. There used to be a hall as part of the inn, standing close by the railway line to the Wimblebury Pit. William Martin, landlord from 1916 to 1928, organised many concerts there and money collected was often used to buy vouchers for hospital treatment for the needy. (Before the N.H.S. people had to buy tickets which would enable them to get hospital treatment.) Also during the miners' strike of 1926 he set up a soup kitchen in his scullery to feed the children from Littleworth and Splash Lane. Mondays and Wednesdays they got soup and on Fridays they were given a bag of bread and cakes.

Hednesford Football Team who have had strong links with the inn since 1904 had a goat as their mascot at the time, but unfortunately after many weeks of the strike it was killed and put into the pot for the soup. Mention of the football team rounds off the Cross Keys' history neatly as the present landlord, Christopher Brindley, has not only played for the team, but has managed it for two years.

The remaining eighteenth century building in Hednesford is Prospect Place, as it was originally called. It stands behind the Cottage and the Cross Keys, just at the end of Keys Close. Initially it was a small house with a stable, probably built around 1770, but not long after a much larger building was added, probably around 1790. Built in late-Georgian style its main purpose was to be a racing stables to accommodate the fast growing sport. The original owner is unknown, but by the 1820's Thomas Flintoff had moved in from Yorkshire with his wife, Anne. (St. Luke's Baptismal Records show that they had their first child, a daughter, Anne, baptised there in 1828.)

The 1841 Census shows that the stables were growing in size and popularity as there were no less than sixteen people living there. There were four female servants to look after the house and meals and eight stable lads who cared for and exercised the large string of horses. By 1851 Thomas was still there with four children (his

113 The Cross Keys c.1910

114 The old cottage section of Prospect Place and probably the oldest part of the building. The photograph shows the rear of the building and the stable block c.1957.

wife had died by then) together with three female servants (he had three daughters to help with the home) and a jockey, John Wells, and five stable lads. Flintoff was perhaps our most successful trainer, the only one to win one of the Classics.

115 Prospect House c.1950.

When he retired in the late 1850's Prospect Place was taken over by Thomas Cliff and remained a training stables. It was to remain in his hands until he unfortunately had an accident with a cart in 1874 which rendered him unconscious until his death in 1881. He left Prospect Place and moved to Stafford House (situated near the corner of Stafford Lane and Anglesey Street). By 1896 the stables were being run by Frederick Hassall who remained until the early twentieth century. After that it seems that they were run by A.Newey, both a jockey and trainer. He stayed there until well into the 1920's, after which the history of the building becomes rather vague. Like the Cross Keys it nearly fell under the developers' axe in the late 1960's, but

was saved and now is two separate homes – strangely what it was originally.

The last of the surviving old buildings is the Anglesey Hotel. It was built in 1831 by Edmund Peel, Esquire of Fazeley and brother to Robert Peel of the Police Force fame. Initially it was called Hednesford Lodge and was built to stable Edmund's race horses and accommodate him and his family when they wished to visit to ride out on Hednesford Hills in the summer months. He employed James Lord as his trainer and all went well until James died suddenly in July, 1832 and then a further mishap happened when a riding accident befell Edmund. Those two tragic events dented Peel's love for horses and by 1840 he had almost abandoned the lodge. William Dyott of Freeford, Lichfield, a close friend to Peel, wrote, *"I had not seen his training lodge, a remarkable snug-box on the border of Cannock Chase, where he had formerly trained all his studs, but now a great reduction made in his racers and I see he has changed to training black-faced sheep"*. (Peel and Dyott were the chief officials of the Lichfield Races.)

By the 1841 Census the Lodge was unoccupied save for four servants with William Fowler in charge who generally kept the place in order. The Peel family still owned the property, but there is no record of them ever returning to the Lodge again. By 1851 it was once again a thriving stables with George Taylor in charge, though he did not live at the Lodge but at Common Gate. There were, however, eleven stable lads and a groom working at the Lodge along with two female servants, but it was probably only used for stabling other trainers' horses.

By the early 1860's Henry Lister had moved into the house with his wife and four children. He was a trainer and so continued to use the Lodge as a stables for his horses. It was during the early 1860's that the Lodge took its first steps towards being a commercial hotel because of the opening of the railway line and its days as purely a racing stables were numbered. By 1867 the Marquis of Anglesey had acquired the building and it was transformed and renamed the Anglesey Commercial Hotel and run by Mrs. Margaret Eskrett. Her husband, Thomas, still a trainer, used the stables for his horses and Charles

116 Anglesey steps c.1910. Michael Glynn, a jockey, who worked for Rooney at Red House is standing second from the left. Who is the landlord?

117 Part of the stained glass window in St. Peter's Church dedicated to Thomas Eskrett.

Gooch worked there as the ostler. However, when Thomas died in 1875 the stables began to decline further.

Margaret Eskrett continued to run the hotel until the early 1880's when she finally moved into "The Limes", a house in what is now Eskrett Street. She died there in August, 1886. The Anglesey gradually became a public house along with the hotel side of the business while the stable block fell into disrepair. (The arrival of the motor car and other forms of transport meant that the era of the horse was doomed.) Finally the last remnants of the stable block were demolished some thirty years ago. What remains of the Lodge is now owned by Pritchard Plc.

LOCAL MYSTERIES

One of the most fascinating aspects of local history is that not every question arrives at an answer; there are always those little elements of doubt which keep the subject interesting. The following chapter explores some of those intriguing mysteries which, despite painstaking research, still have no definite answer.

The first baffling puzzle concerns the "Blue Pump" which was situated in Uxbridge Street, almost opposite the Centenary Hall of Our Lady of Lourdes Church, and stood where the Uxbridge Court buildings are today.

Until its demolition in the early 1930's it was one of the oldest houses in Hednesford. Popular legend had it that it was a public house and the infamous Dick Turpin once stayed there during his flight from London. Unfortunately so many inns have that same legend that it is difficult to believe any of them, unless his horse was petrol powered and he galloped around most of the Midlands staying in almost every available inn. Remember he was still only in his early thirties when he was finally caught and hanged.

Rumour also had it that there was a tunnel leading from the Blue Pump to Lichfield Cathedral, an escape tunnel for thieves and robbers. Just imagine the sheer distance of that supposed tunnel and the numerous obstacles faced by the tunnellers. What is more likely is that a stream once flowed near the house and a culvert had to be dug to stop possible flooding in the winter months. Ridings Brook does flow quite nearby.

So forgetting rumours what is actually known of the house's history? To make the task even more difficult the building does not appear on any of the early Census Reports by name. If it had been an inn it would clearly have been given its title, just as the Cross Keys was. In fact on the Tithe Map of the area for 1841 it is just labelled "House, building, garden and croft", while on the Land Title Map for 1845 it is known as exactly the same. The actual name of the "Blue Pump" only begins to appear after 1880 on the Ordnance Survey Maps.

However, what is very evident is that the property belonged to the Lord family who were race horse trainers. As stated before the first of the Lords to arrive in Hednesford was James around 1770 and he must have started his stables at the house. The Yates Map of 1775 has a building on the exact site, being the only building in the then Rugeley Road. He and his wife, Mary, had two sons, Samuel born in 1799 and James born in 1801. Both followed in their father's footsteps and became trainers with James taking over the stables at Hednesford Lodge while his older brother, Samuel, remained at the stables on Rugeley Road (now Uxbridge

118 The Blue Pump, Uxbridge Street.

Street). Both the Tithe Map and Land Title Map state that Samuel Lord was living at that house in the 1840's.

Further evidence to back that up occurs when John Craddock, born in 1843, was interviewed by the *Cannock Advertiser* in 1927. Even though a very old man his memory was excellent and he clearly stated that he remembered Samuel Lord as having the stables in Uxbridge Street (by 1927 it had changed name) when he was a lad. Strangely the map drawn up for the Cannock Chase Colliery Company around 1860 refers to the building as "Loads", but that was presumably merely a misprint for "Lords". Still there was no reference to a "Blue Pump". Almost at the same time as the colliery map Samuel died (his tombstone can be seen in St. Luke's Churchyard near to the south door, and is dated January 11th, 1857).

Having no children and therefore no one to leave the property to leaves us with a mystery. What happened to the building? It may very well have continued as stables under James

Dover who had been Samuel Lord's stableman in the 1850's, but he left Hednesford in the 1860's. Did it then become an alehouse? Later Census reports of the 1870's and 1880's have no mention of the name as would be expected if it had become an inn. However, the 1886 Ordnance Survey Map suddenly comes up with the name "Blue Pump" (the first mention of that title), but infuriatingly the 1891 Census never mentions it and neither does the 1901 Census.

However, some time after the turn of the century the building must have been an alehouse of sorts because, during a discussion of the infamous tunnel in the local papers in 1978, several people mention living there and describe it as a pub. Thomas Higgs stated that he lived at the pub until 1920 while Douglas Cowdle remembers his brother, Russ, courting the landlord's daughter in the 1930's. What is still a mystery is that the Staffordshire Directories from 1900 – 1936, which list all commercial buildings, have no mention of the Blue Pump at all. So the puzzle continues.

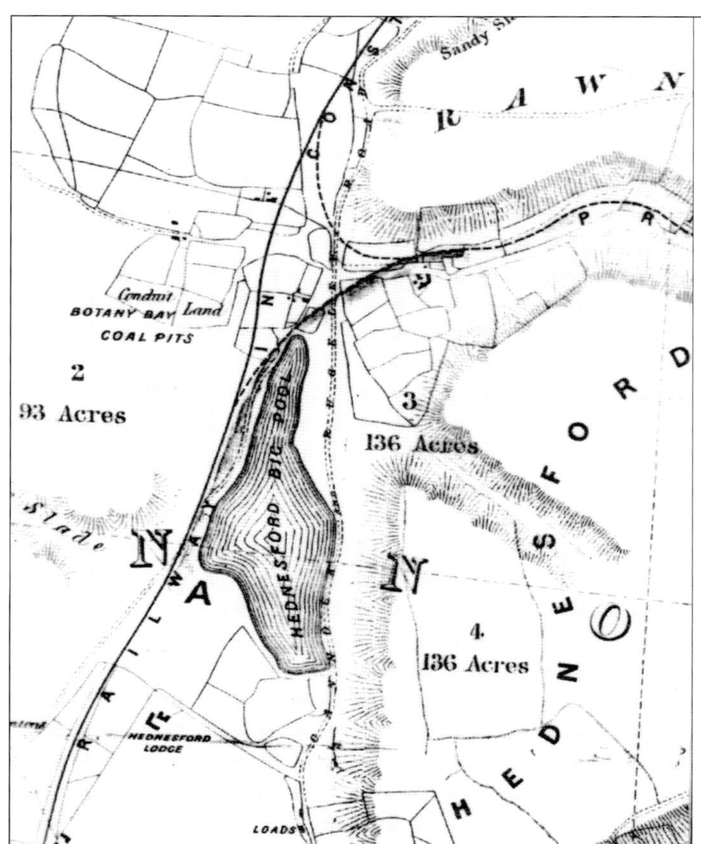

HEDNESFORD c.1856

1 Notice the Botany Bays Pits around Brindley Heath.

2 Railway is still under construction. It was finally opened in 1859.

3 There are no buildings in what is now Market Street save for the Hednesford Lodge.

4 Notice the curious spelling of "Loads", a misprint for Lords. Also there is no mention of the "Blue Pump".

(By kind permission of the Friends of the Museum)

Map XV

The next puzzles centre around names of various places in the area, the first of them being Tackeroo. No one seems to know exactly where the name came from or when. Four possibilities have been suggested though none can actually be proven beyond doubt.

The first suggestion is that the initial houses, built in one row, were constructed by and owned by a Mr. Thacker and so became known locally as Thacker's Row, which eventually, through local dialect, became Tackeroo. The second alternative is that there was some Australian connection with the area and people wishing to celebrate Cooke's discoveries named certain places after his epic voyages. That may seem preposterous, but there were gin pits in the locality which were called the Botany Bay Pits.

Another suggestion is that the village took its nickname from the "Tackeroo Express", a train which was used to transport men and supplies from Hednesford to the First World War Camps on the Chase which were under construction. That line was initially built for the West Cannock Colliery Company to service their new mine opened in 1914 (No. 5 Pit), but with the idea of the Camps on the Chase it was taken over to aid that construction.

The line and Camps were largely built by Irish labourers and one story has it that the local foreman, George Taylor, had so much trouble with his workforce that to gain their respect and keep them under control he actually fought their leader in a bare fist fight. Having beaten him it quelled the gangs' bad behaviour.

That was not the only difficulty faced. The original idea was to have the line going straight up the hill to the top of the Chase, but it proved so steep (men often had to get off and walk the final stretch) that in 1915 the route was altered and instead followed the Brindley Valley up to the White House. But still the engine had difficulties, as did the locals who regularly had to dampen fires caused by sparks from the engine. One rhyme tells of those hazards.

"A lot of jolly carpenters from many
another place,
Went up by special train one day to work
on Cannock Chase,
The gradient is very steep, of curves there
are a few,

And all the lively workers they entrain at
Tackeroo.

Chorus:- Our Tackeroo Express,
Our Tackeroo Express!
The scenery is wonderful, as you all confess,
Everything is splendid, especially the mess,
From the sparks which fly as we pass by,
On the Tackeroo Express.

You all know that the first stop is at
Platform Number One,
And then there is a scramble, and the sight is
awful fun,
The train then starts off with a jerk, and reaches
Number Two,
And after giving in our names, our work
we then pursue.

Chorus.

Of all the days we love best, that day is Saturday,
We rally round the office and there receive our
pay,
But if any of our money's short, we then look
rather blue,
And try to rectify it before going to Tackeroo.

Chorus.

In their book, *A Town for Four Winters*, the Whitehouses add the final suggestion for Tackeroo's name. They suggest that it could have been named by the labourers on the line with reference to "truckeroo", a builders' nickname for payday which originally derived from "truck" notes or tickets given to workers which actually replaced real money. Those truck notes could then only be used in local shops which were often owned by the employers. Although that practise had been outlawed by the government in the mid nineteenth century it was certainly still used in some mining areas in the late 1870's where the pits and the workforce were small. They were often referred to as "tommy notes".

However the nickname Tackeroo came about what is actually known about Brindley Heath, its real name, is more certain. The Brindley family can date their association with the area way back in history. In fact it is thought that the Brindley Heath area got its name from a Brindley who was the forest keeper for Thomas Paget in 1595.

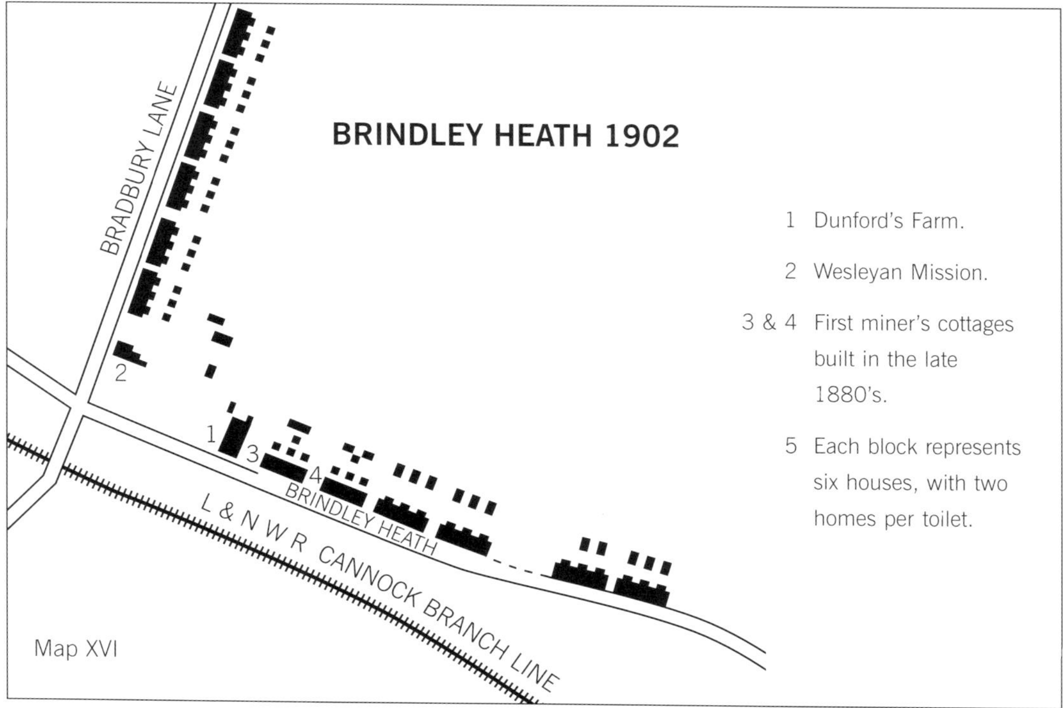

No doubt he had his cottage close by, hence Brindley Heath, Brindley Coppice or wood and Brindley Valley where a brook flowed into Ridings Brook. All these would signify the area that he controlled for his master, Lord Paget. These place names became a regular feature on maps around the second half of the nineteenth century.

As for the first housing, save for the occasional cottage dotted here or there, the first mention is in the 1891 Census Returns when ten miners' cottages have been constructed. They housed the following:-

John Barrett	Coal miner with his wife and 5 children, one being a miner.
Thomas Sherwood	Coal miner with a wife and one child.
George Tranter	Coal miner with wife and 6 children, one being a miner.
John Harding	Coal Miner with wife and 3 children.
John Richardson	Coal Engine Winder with a wife and one child.
John Holden	Coal miner and his wife.
James Evans	Coal miner with a wife and one child.
Elizabeth Duckhouse	Widow with one son a coal miner.
George Head	Wife and 2 children, plus William Evans a coal miner.
Joseph Jones	Coal miner with a wife and 3 children.

119 Bradbury Lane Wesleyan Chapel.

West Cannock Farm on the corner of Bradbury Lane and Brindley Heath was owned by Dennis Dunford with the newly constructed Wesleyan Mission and Temporary School just above.

By 1902 the village had grown to almost forty houses, most occupied by miners, and the opening of the West Cannock No. 5 Pit nearby encouraged further growth. Those miners' cottages were to remain until, like the rest of the area, they were finally demolished in the 1970's, the final stage of redevelopment in the area.

Perhaps the origin of the name "Skelly Bridge" is more obvious. When West Cannock Colliery Company opened up its No. 1 and No. 4 Pits between the Belt Road and Green Heath Road it had to transport its coal to the Canal Basin in East Cannock Road and so a railway line was constructed to connect them. It obviously followed the cheapest route, down Little Valley towards High Town. However, as you will see from a modern ordnance survey map that meant slicing the proposed road, Stanley Road, in two. Access, therefore, had to be made for the public and so a small wooden bridge was built as a temporary measure to go above the line.

Only wide enough for pedestrians, it could have been quickly dismantled and a more solid bridge constructed had the proposed road ever been completed. The bridge, perhaps a skeleton of the real bridge, soon became nicknamed the "Skelly" and stood there until the 1960's when the last remnants disappeared along with what remained of West Cannock's two pits. The ground was then levelled, but the name still lives on in local vocabulary. Older residents still talk of "going across the Skelly" from Green Heath Road to reach Belt Road and Stanley Road still appears on both sides of the valley.

If that puzzle is rather easy to solve then Pye Green's is more difficult. Where on earth did the name come from? In his *Encyclopaedia of Staffordshire* Tim Cockin suggests that with its original spelling of "pie" it could have derived from the Anglo-Saxon word which meant "gnats", hence "the green where gnats abound". Does that mean that today's version is down to a mere spelling mistake? Anything is possible in history.

Another local historian, Les Higgs, suggested that the name originated from James Pye, the last of the Forest Agisters on Cannock Chase. Unfortunately, unlike the Brindley name, Pye's name does not stay in the area as one might expect and Pye Green itself does not appear until the late 1870's. If that origin was correct, the

name being around since the 1400's, we might expect it to be on some maps as the name for an area of Cannock Chase.

Yet another suggestion is that the green or open woodland was a good place for the local hunt to stop and rest their mounts and have their lunch of meat pies. Names have come about for stranger reasons!

But what do we know of its actual history? The first record of it occurs in the 1881 Census when strangely it has two spellings, Pie and Pye. The difference between the two depended on exactly where the recorders were referring to. Pie Green seems to refer to all those properties north of West Chadsmoor, heading towards today's Pye Green hill, while Pye Green refers to just the very top of the hill and heading towards Bradbury Lane. However, it could just be that the recorder simply made a spelling mistake and wrote down "Pie" instead of "Pye" or there were two separate recorders, each with their own spelling.

By the late 1870's miners began to settle in the Pie Green area and the 1881 Census records no less than twenty miners and their families living in the area. However, Pye Green had only two cottages, known as Blewitt's Cottages, with James Blewitt living in one with his wife and two lodgers, Thomas Tomkinson, an agricultural labourer aged fifteen, and Thomas Minsper, a carpenter. Blewitt himself was a farmer. In the other cottage lived William Dewesbury, a coal miner, with his wife and three daughters.

By the 1891 Census there were thirty families living in the Pie Green area (though it was now spelt Pye Green), 34 of them coal miners and 4 agricultural labourers with one carpenter and a bricklayer. Thomas Duffield, who came from Uttoxeter, kept a small general store there known locally as the "Wood Shed". By that time twenty six year old Samson Blewitt had begun his farm on what is now Pye Green Road. His father, Enoch, had moved into the Hednesford area around 1868 and had set up a grocer and beer retailer business in the Green Heath area in the 1880's and the family were responsible for building houses in that district, hence Blewitt Street. The 1901 Census still has Enoch living in Blewitt Street where he ran a public house called the Hatherton Arms.

Samson, originally a carter, had moved to Pye

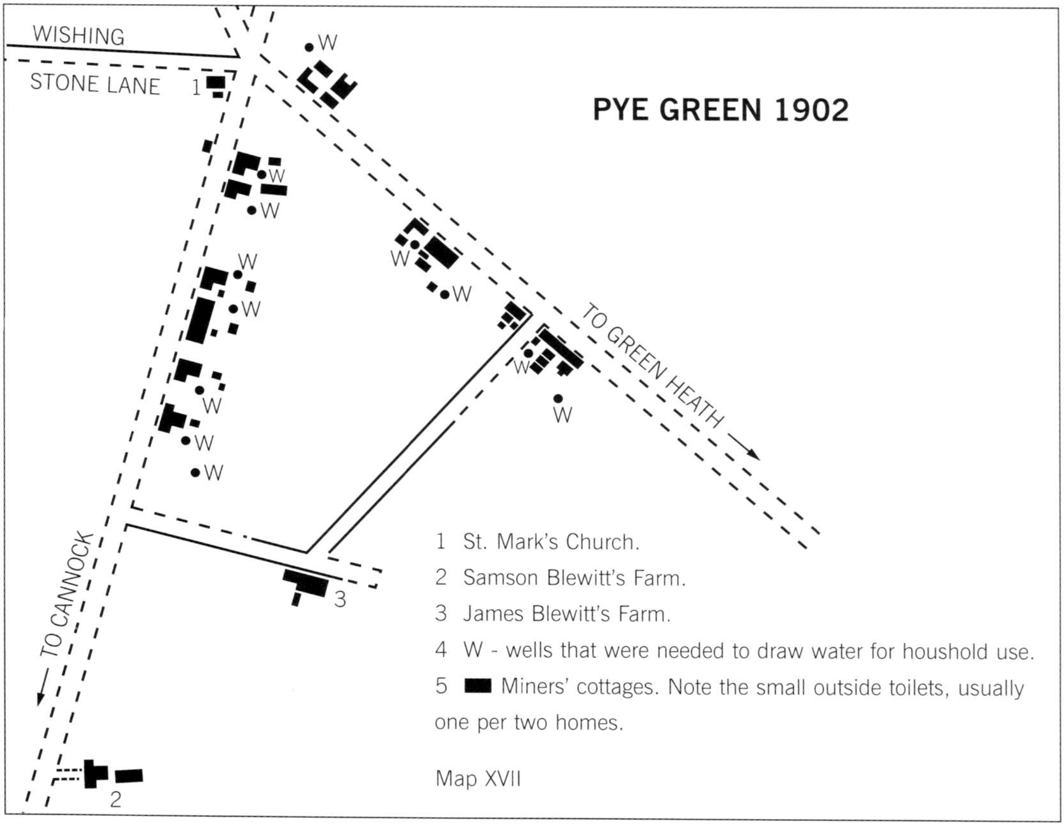

Green in 1886 and his farm prospered. He grew oats and potatoes as well as keeping sheep, pigs and a dairy herd. Ever the entrepreneur he was also a coal merchant and cut heather from the Chase to sell for the glass making industry in Stockport. During the First World War he also ran a taxi service for the soldiers at the Camps. His name still lives on in the public house built in the late 1980's which stands close by the original position of his farm.

*Strangely the two Blewitt families in Pye Green do not seem to be related even though the name only appears in our area in the 1870's with one Isaac Blewitt, a coal loader at the Canal Wharf. He also was not related to either of those families already mentioned, though they all came from the Black Country area originally and so they might have been distantly related.

By 1890 Pye Green itself still only had two cottages, one still occupied by James Blewitt and the other by Henry Elks with his wife and four children, but towards the end of the century some miners' cottages were being constructed along the road from Bradbury Lane and down the road heading towards Broadhurst Green. With the steady expansion of the area and growth in population a new church, St. Mark's, was built in 1894 on the corner of the junction, by the side of Wishing Stone Lane. Perhaps one of the smallest churches in England, its purpose was to serve the Green Heath and Pye Green area and in its early history had a thriving congregation. Unfortunately as numbers dwindled and the motor car gave easier access to larger churches it was eventually demolished.

120 St. Mark's, Pye Green 1933 Sunday School Anniversary Service

But what was stopping the real expansion of the village was the sewerage problems already described and the difficulty of piping fresh water up the hill to the housing. That was greatly improved with the building of a pumping station in Green Heath Road and the Tower at its summit in 1934. The area then grew considerably with the construction of the new estates in the 1940's and 1950's.

Another mystery, but perhaps the easiest to solve, concerns the disappearance of one of Hednesford's landmarks – the beehive which stood above the entrance to the shop. Local gossip had it that it was spirited away by the demolition crew, but exactly who? Other rumours suggested that it was stored at Shugborough Hall Museum. That proved not to be the case. The plea is then that should its present guardians read this history they might like to donate it to our museum, if it still survives, so that all can see it.

Finally, much in the news recently, there is the wall plaque above the chemist's in Market Street. The motto reads "Honi soit qui mal y pense" which translates into "Evil be to him who thinks evil". That is the motto of the Order of the Garter, probably founded by Edward III in 1348. The shield which it surrounds is the royal standard of Queen Victoria and would suggest

that the plaque was erected some time in the late 1800's (not as early as 1850 as previously suggested as there were no shops or dwellings in that part of Hednesford at that time).

Studying the frontage of the buildings which surround the plaque it would seem to suggest that it was put there at the same time, possibly to commemorate their construction which, according to the Census Reports, would place it around 1870. Another suggestion is that it commemorated Queen Victoria's Jubilee Year, but as has already been stated Hednesford did little in the way of celebrations that year and new building work would surely have been noted in the local papers. What can be safely stated is that it was definitely there in 1900, but like so many of our mysteries its definitive answer lies in our forgotten past.

121 Plaque above the chemist's in Hednesford.

TRACE YOUR ANCESTORS

For those who may be interested in tracing their own family history this chapter lists those residents known to have lived in the Hednesford area since the eighteenth century.

Taken from the Burial Registers and Marriage Registers from St. Luke's Church the following is only a snapshot of those inhabitants and does not claim to be a full list as only those registered are mentioned. Any people who were not of the Church of England faith could not be traced.

They appear in alphabetical order and not date of entry as in the church registers. Also very few females appear on the early lists unless it is known that that was their maiden name. They will appear on later lists under their married name. The Date of Birth may give an indication as to the relationship of various people with the same surname, but beware rushing to conclusions!

Finally be careful of the spelling of surnames. For example, Sanders and Saunders are probably the same family, as are the Jenkins and Jenkinsons, though it may not always be the case.

List A — Hednesford residents in 1725

Francis Benton
George Benton
Joshua Benton
Walter Benton
John Brockhouse (d. 1756)
John Clewley, Senior (d.1751)
Thomas Hickin
William Jenkins

Henry Sanders (d. 1753)
William Sanders
William Thomas (d. 1756)
Daniel Ward
Henry Wooton
John Wooton
Thomas Wooton

List B — Hednesford residents in 1750, but not necessarily still alive by 1775

★Those in List A are still alive plus the following:-

Joseph Arnot
Eleanor Benton (b. 1746 d. 1758)
Elizabeth Benton (b. 1747)
Frances Benton (b. 1746)
Job Benton
John Benton
Joseph Benton
Moses Benton
Robert Benton
Sarah Benton (dau. of Joshua b. 1748)
Sarah Benton (dau. of Walter b. 1749)
Walter Benton
Edward Bott
Eleanor Bott (b. 1750)
Thomas Bott

William Hickin
Elizabeth Jenkinson (d. 1759)
William Jenkins, Junior.
Thomas Johnson (d. 1752)
Elizabeth Sanders (b. 1745)
Hannah Sanders (b. 1749)
Henry Sanders
Rebecca Sanders (d. 1753 wife of William)
Thomas Sanders
Valentine Sanders (b. 1747)
William Shore
Richard Smith
John Steen
William Stringer
Katherine Thomas

<table>
<tr><td>Lydea Brockhouse (b. 1745)</td><td>Katherine Thomas, Junior (b. 1746)</td></tr>
<tr><td>Thomas Brockhouse</td><td>Henry Woolaston</td></tr>
<tr><td>Mary Clewley</td><td>David Wooton</td></tr>
<tr><td>Thomas Clewley</td><td>Elizabeth Wooton (b. 1747)</td></tr>
<tr><td>Isaac Cope</td><td>Henry Wooton, Junior</td></tr>
<tr><td>Ruth Forrester (d. 1752 wife of Simon)</td><td>Philip Wooton</td></tr>
<tr><td>Simon Forrester</td><td>Richard Wooton (d. 1754)</td></tr>
<tr><td>William Forrester</td><td>William Wooton</td></tr>
<tr><td>Mary Hickin</td><td></td></tr>
</table>

List C — Further Hednesford residents of 1750 and still alive by 1800 unless stated

Esther Adderley (m. 1760)	Isaac Craddock (m. 1773)
George Benton (b. 1743)	Joseph Craddock (m. 1761)
Job Benton (m. 1758)	Robert Craddock (m. 1769)
Moses Benton (m. 1760)	Samuel Craddock (m. 1764)
Robert Benton (m. 1757)	Thomas Craddock (m. 1755)
Walter Benton (d. 1779)	William Craddock (m. 1769)
John Bradbury (m. 1763)	John Ferguson (b. 1744, m. 1769)
Ann Brindley (m. 1758)	Thomas Johnson (d. 1762)★
Charles Brindley (m. 1770)	Jane Nevil (m. 1761)
James Brindley (m. 1761)	Mary Nevil (m. 1761)
Matthew Brindley (m. 1768)	William Preston (m. 1756)
Joseph Brockhouse (b. 1746)	Henry Sanders (b. 1746)
John Clewley (m. 1768)	William Sanders (m. 1760)
Thomas Clewley (m. 1760)	Thomas Wallbank (b. 1749)
William Clewley (m. 1758)	Josiah White (d. 1779)
Abraham Craddock (m. 1768)	

★Marriage Banns (1754-1773) include the following:-

William Clewley m. Ann Brindley Dec. 1758
William Sanders m. Esther Adderley Oct. 1760
James Brindley m. Mary Nevil Sept. 1761
Joseph Craddock m. Jane Nevil Nov. 1761
Matthew Brindley m. Elizabeth Benton Oct. 1768

★Elizabeth Benton appears in the 1775 list under her married name of Elizabeth Brindley. Thomas Johnson was probably the first landlord of the newly built Cross Keys, but where he was born is unknown.

List D — Hednesford residents in 1775 who were still alive in 1800

★Unless stated those in list C are still alive in 1775 along with the following:-

John Beard (b. 1765)	William Forrester (b. 1751)
Samuel Beard (b. Littleworth 1752)	Charles Hitchens (b. 1757)
Francis Benton (b. 1753)	John Jenkins (b. 1751)
John Benton (b. 1767)	Thomas Jenkins (b. 1750)
Robert Benton (b. 1753)	James Lord, Senior (b. ?)
William Bradbury (b. 1772)	Henry Sanders (b. 1767)
Elizabeth Brindley (b. 1751)	William Sanders (b. 1751)
Thomas Clewey (b. 1761)	Thomas Scott (b. 1753)
Eli Craddock (b. Hazel Slade 1752)	George Thackeray (b. 1773)

List E   Hednesford residents in 1800

★Unless stated those in Lists C and D are still alive along with the following:-

Samuel Adams (b. 1799)
Margaret Beard (b. 1769)
Mary Beard (b. Littleworth 1762)
Thomas Beard (b. 1796)
Anne Benton (b. 1785)
Elizabeth Benton (b. 1761)
Jane Benton (b. 1762)
John Benton (b. 1796)
Lewis Bird (b. 1790)
Charles Kent Blunt (b. 1789)
Richard Boulton (b. 1795)
Anne Bradbury (b. 1794)
Elizabeth Bradbury (b. 1797)
Sarah Bradbury (b. 1766)
Ruth Brindley (b. 1790)
Eleanor Brockhouse (b. 1763)
Anne Carter (b. 1723)
Anne Clewley (b. 1782)
David Clewley (b. 1794)
Dorothy Clewley (b. 1779)
Elizabeth Clewley (b. 1794)
Mary Clewley (b. 1751)
Elizabeth Cooke (b. 1790)
John Cooper (b. 1726)★
Anne Craddock (b. Hazel Slade 1754)
Hannah Craddock (b. Wimblebury 1786)
John Craddock (b. Rawnsley 1791)
Mary Craddock (b. 1757)
Mary Dean (b. 1793)
William Dean (b. 1783)
Robert Eaton (b. 1792)
Sarah Eaton (b. 1749)
Sarah Eaton, Junior (b. 1786)
Mary Edwards (b. 1783)
John Fellows (b. 1786)
Mary Fellows (b. 1775)
Anne Ferguson (b. 1762)
Mary Fletcher (b. 1735)
Mary Fletcher, Junior (b. 1752)
Mary Forester (b. 1776)
William Forester (b.1776)
Thomas Goodman (b. 1771)
John Green (b. 1781)
Mary Green (b. 1771)
Mary Greensill (b. 1788)
John Harvey (b. 1792)
Joseph Hawkins (b. 1791)
Sarah Haycock (b. 1745)

Elizabeth Hitchens (b. 1792)
Joseph Hitchens (b. 1793)
Joseph Holdcroft (b. 1788)
Elizabeth Jenkinson (b. 1777)
Elizabeth Jenkinson (b. 1780)
John Jenkinson (b. 1795)
Marie Jenkinson (b. 1784)
Mary Jenkinson (b. 1793)
Sarah Jenkinson (b. 1750)
Thomas Jenkinson (b. 1789)
William Jenkinson (b. 1776)
James Jukes (b. 1791)
Samuel Lawrence (b. 1790)
Joseph Littler (b. 1791)
James Lord (b. 1792)
Mary Lord (b. 1765)
Samuel Lord (b. 1799)
Edward Martin (b. 1780)
Elizabeth Martin (b. 1783)
John Massey (b. 1784)★
Ellen Oldcroft (b. 1796)
Jenny Oldcroft (b. 1764)
Mary Oldcroft (b. 1794)
Ruth Pickin (b. 1780)
Thomas Pickin (b. 1797)
John Preston (b. 1794)
Phoebe Rathbone (b Kingsbury, War. 1760)
Mary Richardson (b. 1800)
Sarah Rider (b. Hazel Slade 1787)
Alice Sanders (b. 1768)
Anne Sanders (b. 1719)
Anne Sanders (b. Littleworth 1744)
Elizabeth Sanders (b. 1785)
Samuel Sanders (b. 1794)
Sarah Sanders (b. 1795)
Job Saunders (b. 1776)
Sarah Saunders (b. 1781)
Thomas Saunders (b. 1796)
Dorothy Spencer (b. 1792)
Sidonia Thornley (b. 1798)
John Tuft (b. 1776)
John Turner (b. Hazel Slade 1779)
Mary Turner (b. Hazel Slade 1743)
Anne Wallbank (b. 1792)
John Wallbank (b. 1786)
Susannah Wallbank (b. 1757)
Thomas Wallbank (b. 1784)

*John Cooper was an innkeeper (probably the Cross Keys) and was born in 1726. When he arrived in Hednesford is not known. He died in 1812, aged 86. If Thomas Johnson was the first innkeeper at the Cross Keys then Cooper may have taken over from him.

John Massey eventually became the landlord of the Cross Keys.

The Beard family lived at Dugdales, a farm at the top of the hill leading from Wimblebury to Heath Hayes.

The Dean family owned Wimblebury Farm and the Clewleys the one at Heathy Leasows.

F. The 1841 Census

With the aid of the 1841 Census returns and the Land Title Map of 1845 it is just possible to trace the enumerator's ride through Hednesford as he gathered information. Information given to the enumerator included the person's name, occupation, whether born in the same county as they then lived and age. Exact ages were only required for those under 16; adult's ages were rounded down to the nearest 5 years. Thus a person stated to be 30 could be anywhere between 30 and 34. Omissions could include miners on shift or those at sea.

* Unfortunately Hednesford at the time was so small that there were no road names and so I have used the modern day equivalents. Perhaps you may spot some of your ancestors.

It was one of those pleasant summer evenings on 6th June 1841 when the enumerator turned into East Cannock Road from Cannock. His first call was at the small farm of George Gooch, close to today's Globe Inn. They had recently moved to Hednesford with their six children and had had one more girl, Sarah, since arriving. Next it was on to the racing stables owned by Thomas Walters, who with his wife and four children, had ten other workers living there.

Across the road and up a dirt track, now Lower Road, and across the meadow stood another racing stables, Prospect Place, occupied by Thomas Flintoff and family with a workforce of sixteen, including female servants and stable lads.

Retracing his steps he moved back into East Cannock Road and onwards towards Hill Top crossroads where he visited the Oldcrofts and Thomas Jenkinson who owned a nailer's business opposite the Plough and Harrow. From there he rode down Stafford Lane, having taken in the cottages of Thomas Wallbank, William Forrester and John Fellows, before he reached the farm owned by John Benton. It once stood almost opposite today's Bridge Inn and the railway.

Having completed that side of the village he then moved to the Hednesford Lodge which stood almost empty save for a few female servants whose task was to keep the place tidy and in running order should their masters, Edmund Peel's descendants, ever wish to visit.

That done he then rode to Hednesford Pool where several homesteads stood. (Strangely he appears to have missed the small cottage occupied by the Hitchens family which stood at the southerly end of the Pool, but they were still living there at the time. Joseph Hitchens had died a few years before the Census, but his wife and children were still there. St. Luke's Baptismal Register confirms that. Proof that even this Census was not entirely accurate). Instead he next visited the farms and cottages owned by the Clewleys, Wallbanks, Bradburys and Harveys which were to the north end of the Pool.

He then had to backtrack into Hednesford along the Rugeley Road (the only one with a name) and towards Hill Top again. In Uxbridge Street he encountered Samuel Lord's stables and then the blacksmith's shop at the top owned by George Benton (no relation to the other Bentons previously met). Next door he saw John Walters, Thomas's brother, who had a small racing stables at the top of the hill.

Having completed his census of the outlying homesteads and cottages he then rode down the hill towards the village proper (what we call Old Hednesford today). His first port of call would be at the Cross Keys Inn, run by Sarah Massey since her husband, John, had died some five years previously. She still dabbled in training racehorses which were stabled at the inn though most of the work was done by Thomas Warren, her boarder and trainer, together with Robert Denman, her jockey, who also lived at the inn.

Staying on the same side of the road the enumerator then went to the small cottage of Benjamin Witherton, Hednesford's one remaining shepherd who lived there with his wife and two small children. (A new bungalow stands there today). Next to it was the stables of Samuel Sanders who lived in today's Friel's Cottage with his wife and three children and three servants while the stables next door were managed by 11 stable hands, the most noteworthy being one Florence O'Driscol listed as a female trainer.

Crossing over the road where the bungalows stand today there lived Thomas and William Green, in two small cottages on land described as "a piece above the pit". Both men were registered as coal miners. Close by them in a much larger dwelling lived Robert Eaton, a farmer.

Moving back to the village and diagonally opposite the Cross Keys were a row of cottages on the corner of Splash Lane. Mainly occupied by agricultural labourers they included James Brindley, Thomas Craddock, James Sanders, Joseph Hawkins and James Jukes along with Charles Bemetzreider, a trainer and jockey, and Jacob Spencer, a butcher.

Still in the village, but moving into Littleworth Road near the flats of today there lived John Craddock, Richard Boulton, John Green, Thomas Goodman and Samuel Lawrence, all agricultural labourers save for Samuel Lawrence who was a shoemaker. On up that road he would have visited John Spencer, James Bradley, Samuel Beard and William Jenkinson who also owned a nailer's shop. Close by was a homestead with four stable lads who no doubt worked at the Littleworth stables, also run by Samuel Sanders.

Travelling further up the hill he visited John Harvey and Alice Foulk whose husband, Francis, had run the first brickworks in Hednesford and on to Job Sanders. Across the road from those three lived Sarah Jenkinson, Henry Sanders (Samuel's father possibly) and William Bradbury.

His final journey would take him on to Heathy Leasows (today's Rawnsley) where David Clewley farmed with his wife and three children and then across to Wimblebury Farm owned by William Dean who lived there with his wife and four children. His last port of call would have been Dugdales at the top of Cannel Mount, the home of seventy-five year old John Beard who farmed there with his wife and son, Thomas, his wife, and the Richards family.

★Another family, the Martins, who were definitely in the area, were also missed off the Census though I have not been able to trace exactly where they lived.

HEDNESFORD

I too can remember
The house where I was born
When rumbling bread cart woke me up
At six o'clock each morn.
Followed by the pot buzzers and
The noise of miners' clogs.
Knockers up and cockerels' call
And barking of the dogs.
I lived not in a village then
For Hednesford was a town
And anyone who didn't know
Was deemed to be a clown.
We had a town clock and Market Hall,
Town Station, Bridge and Yard,
Drill Hall, Rescue Station, Gasometer and all.
Life then was good, but hard
With Police and Fire Station
And pawn shops one or two,
A Billiard Hall, the best around,
There were lots of things to do.
No local walked to Cannock then
If he was on the dole
And strike-bound miners couldn't work
Down that dark, black hole.
We had a dole down Station Road,
Not me, I was just a lad,
But I was sometimes taken there
On the shoulders of my dad.
To register a birth or death,
Folks could do just that
Without a walk to Cannock Town –
They just crossed the welcome mat.

Written by Ken Baker (1924 – 2002)
who spent all his life in Hednesford.

INDEX OF VOCABULARY

Apsidal - a domed or semi-circular recess, especially at the west end of a church.

Bailiwick - district under a bailiff or magistrate, the chief officer of a Hundred.

Buffet - low stool or footstool or again a sideboard or side table.

Buttyman - companion at work.

Carucate - as much land as could be ploughed with 8 oxen in a year and kept maintained.

Cimnel/kimnel - tub used for brewing, kneading, salting meat or other purposes.

Chancel - part of a church containing the altar, sanctuary and choir.

Dataller - a man employed to do service work in the mine and usually paid by the day.

Frankpledge - the system by which every member of a tithing was answerable for the good conduct of, or damage done by, anyone of the other members.

Herbage - a liberty that a man had to feed his cattle in another man's grounds, such as a forest.

Hundred - a part of a County used for court purposes and taxation. Staffordshire had 5 Hundreds. Hednesford was in the Cuttlestone Hundred or more precisely the East Cuttlestone Hundred.

Husbandman - a man who tills or cultivates the soil, that is a farmer.

Messuage - the portion of land intended as the site of a dwelling house and all its appurtenances, for example, outhouses, etc.

Napery - table linen, towels or napkins.

Nave - the central aisle in the church, extending from the rear to the chancel.

Noggin - small drinking vessel, for example a mug or cup.

Pannage - feeding of swine, etc. in a forest or wood or the right to do so; or the payment to the owner for that right.

Prop - a support in the mine tunnels.

Stall - working area in a mine varying in length according to the thickness of the seam of coal. It could be from as little as a few feet to 80 yards or more.

Stall & room - working coal in compartments or in isolated chambers or pillars.

Throll - breathing hole.

Tithing - a tenth part of anything; originally a company of ten households in the system of frankpledge.

Transcept - the wing of a church at right angles to the nave, like the arm of a crucifix.

Tree - same as a prop.

Truckle bed - low bed running on castors, usually pushed beneath a higher bed when not in use.

Tun dish - wooden dish or a shallow vessel with a tube at the bottom fitting into the bung of a tun or cask, forming a kind of funnel used in brewing.

Victual - either food or the right in law to feed others for profit.

Virgate - a land measure which varied greatly throughout the country. In many cases it was about 30 acres.

Vill - a farm, country house or village. By law a territorial unit or division under the feudal system, consisting of a number of houses or buildings with their adjacent lands and having common organisation. It corresponds to the Anglo-Saxon tithing or modern township or civil parish.

Vivaries - Woods or woodland. Not forest as they would appear as chase or forest.

Yeoman - a man owning and cultivating a small estate; a freeholder under the rank of gentleman. In Late Middle England he was a farmer or countryman of respectable standing.

INDEX OF PLACE NAMES

Bold italic type denotes a photograph or map number, not the page number.

BIBLIOGRAPHY

Belcher, Sherry – *Cannock Chase Past.*
Cecil – *Sporting Magazine (1839), article XIX.*
Cocking, Tim – *The Staffordshire Encyclopaedia.*
Druigan, W.H. – *Notes on Staffordshire Place Names.*
Goodwin, Charles H. – *The Chase for Coal.*
Goodwin, Charles H. – *Twixt the Green and the Grime.*
Greenslade, M.W. – *History of Cannock.*
Hackwood, F.W. – *The Chronicles of Cannock Chase.*
Hunt, A. – *Our Lady of Lourdes Church.*
Kelly's Directory of Staffordshire for 1860 and 1880.
Langford, J.A. – *Staffordshire and Warwickshire, Past and Present (Vol. 1 Part 2).*
100 Years of Soccer History - Hednesford Town Football Club Book.
Pevsnor, N. – *The Buildings of England - Staffordshire.*
Pigot's Staffordshire Directory (1842).
Plot, R. – *History of Staffordshire.*
Roger, Francis J. – *History of Cannock Chase Colliery.*
St.John's Church Centenary Pamphlet (1873-1973).
Tildesley, J.C. – *The Rise and Progress of the Manufactures of Staffordshire.*
Victoria County History (Vol. 11).
Williams, A. & Mallet, W.H. – *Staffordshire Towns and Villages.*
William Salt Collection.
White's Directory of Staffordshire (1834).
Whitehouse C.J. & G.P. – *A Town for Four Winters.*
Wright, Mac. – *Hednesford War Memorial.*
Wright, M. – *The Best of Cannock Chase.*
Wright, M. – *The Friendship of Cannock Chase.*

Further information from:-
Census information from 1841 to 1901.

Newspapers – *Express and Star.*
The Cannock Advertiser.
The Hednesford Advertiser.
The Staffordshire Advertiser.

Probate Inventories of Cannock (1562-1791) transcribed by D.P. Adams and the 6th Form of Cannock Grammar School.

St. Luke's Baptism Records.
St. Luke's Burial Records.
St. Luke's Marriage Records.
Tithe Map of Hednesford (1841).
Land Title Map of Hednesford (1845).